Applied Text Analysis with Python

Enabling Language-Aware Data Products with Machine Learning

Benjamin Bengfort, Rebecca Bilbro, and Tony Ojeda

Beijing · Boston · Farnham · Sebastopol · Tokyo

Applied Text Analysis with Python

by Benjamin Bengfort, Rebecca Bilbro, and Tony Ojeda

Published by O'Reilly Media, Inc., 1005 Gravenstein Highway North, Sebastopol, CA 95472.

O'Reilly books may be purchased for educational, business, or sales promotional use. Online editions are also available for most titles (*http://oreilly.com/safari*). For more information, contact our corporate/institutional sales department: 800-998-9938 or *corporate@oreilly.com*.

Editor: Nicole Tache	**Indexer:** WordCo Indexing Services, Inc.
Production Editor: Nicholas Adams	**Interior Designer:** David Futato
Copyeditor: Jasmine Kwityn	**Cover Designer:** Karen Montgomery
Proofreader: Christina Edwards	**Illustrator:** Rebecca Demarest

June 2018:   First Edition

Revision History for the First Edition

2018-06-08:   First Release

See *http://oreilly.com/catalog/errata.csp?isbn=9781491963043* for release details.

978-1-491-96304-3

[LSI]

Table of Contents

Preface. ix

1. Language and Computation. 1
   The Data Science Paradigm   2
   Language-Aware Data Products   4
      The Data Product Pipeline   5
   Language as Data   8
      A Computational Model of Language   8
      Language Features   10
      Contextual Features   13
      Structural Features   15
   Conclusion   16

2. Building a Custom Corpus. 19
   What Is a Corpus?   19
      Domain-Specific Corpora   20
      The Baleen Ingestion Engine   21
   Corpus Data Management   22
      Corpus Disk Structure   24
   Corpus Readers   27
      Streaming Data Access with NLTK   28
      Reading an HTML Corpus   31
      Reading a Corpus from a Database   34
   Conclusion   36

3. Corpus Preprocessing and Wrangling. 37
   Breaking Down Documents   38
      Identifying and Extracting Core Content   38

Deconstructing Documents into Paragraphs   39
Segmentation: Breaking Out Sentences   42
Tokenization: Identifying Individual Tokens   43
Part-of-Speech Tagging   44
Intermediate Corpus Analytics   45
Corpus Transformation   47
Intermediate Preprocessing and Storage   48
Reading the Processed Corpus   51
Conclusion   53

4. Text Vectorization and Transformation Pipelines **55**
Words in Space   56
Frequency Vectors   57
One-Hot Encoding   59
Term Frequency–Inverse Document Frequency   62
Distributed Representation   65
The Scikit-Learn API   68
The BaseEstimator Interface   68
Extending TransformerMixin   70
Pipelines   74
Pipeline Basics   75
Grid Search for Hyperparameter Optimization   76
Enriching Feature Extraction with Feature Unions   77
Conclusion   79

5. Classification for Text Analysis **81**
Text Classification   82
Identifying Classification Problems   82
Classifier Models   84
Building a Text Classification Application   85
Cross-Validation   86
Model Construction   89
Model Evaluation   91
Model Operationalization   94
Conclusion   95

6. Clustering for Text Similarity **97**
Unsupervised Learning on Text   97
Clustering by Document Similarity   99
Distance Metrics   99
Partitive Clustering   102
Hierarchical Clustering   107

    Modeling Document Topics   111

Modeling Document Topics   111
Latent Dirichlet Allocation   111
Latent Semantic Analysis   119
Non-Negative Matrix Factorization   121
Conclusion   123

7. Context-Aware Text Analysis.   **125**
Grammar-Based Feature Extraction   126
Context-Free Grammars   126
Syntactic Parsers   127
Extracting Keyphrases   128
Extracting Entities   131
n-Gram Feature Extraction   132
An n-Gram-Aware CorpusReader   133
Choosing the Right n-Gram Window   135
Significant Collocations   136
n-Gram Language Models   139
Frequency and Conditional Frequency   140
Estimating Maximum Likelihood   143
Unknown Words: Back-off and Smoothing   145
Language Generation   147
Conclusion   149

8. Text Visualization.   **151**
Visualizing Feature Space   152
Visual Feature Analysis   152
Guided Feature Engineering   162
Model Diagnostics   170
Visualizing Clusters   170
Visualizing Classes   172
Diagnosing Classification Error   173
Visual Steering   177
Silhouette Scores and Elbow Curves   177
Conclusion   180

9. Graph Analysis of Text.   **183**
Graph Computation and Analysis   185
Creating a Graph-Based Thesaurus   185
Analyzing Graph Structure   186
Visual Analysis of Graphs   187
Extracting Graphs from Text   189
Creating a Social Graph   189

        Insights from the Social Graph   192
    Entity Resolution   200
        Entity Resolution on a Graph   201
        Blocking with Structure   202
        Fuzzy Blocking   202
    Conclusion   205

10. Chatbots. **207**
    Fundamentals of Conversation   208
        Dialog: A Brief Exchange   210
        Maintaining a Conversation   213
    Rules for Polite Conversation   215
        Greetings and Salutations   216
        Handling Miscommunication   220
    Entertaining Questions   222
        Dependency Parsing   223
        Constituency Parsing   225
        Question Detection   227
        From Tablespoons to Grams   229
    Learning to Help   233
        Being Neighborly   235
        Offering Recommendations   238
    Conclusion   240

11. Scaling Text Analytics with Multiprocessing and Spark. **241**
    Python Multiprocessing   242
        Running Tasks in Parallel   244
        Process Pools and Queues   249
        Parallel Corpus Preprocessing   251
    Cluster Computing with Spark   253
        Anatomy of a Spark Job   254
        Distributing the Corpus   255
        RDD Operations   257
        NLP with Spark   259
    Conclusion   270

12. Deep Learning and Beyond. **273**
    Applied Neural Networks   274
    Neural Language Models   274
        Artificial Neural Networks   275
        Deep Learning Architectures   280
    Sentiment Analysis   284

Deep Structure Analysis   286
The Future Is (Almost) Here   291

Glossary. **293**

Index. **303**

Preface

We live in a world increasingly filled with digital assistants that allow us to connect with other people as well as vast information resources. Part of the appeal of these smart devices is that they do not simply convey information; to a limited extent, they also *understand* it—facilitating human interaction at a high level by aggregating, filtering, and summarizing troves of data into an easily digestible form. Applications such as machine translation, question-and-answer systems, voice transcription, text summarization, and chatbots are becoming an integral part of our computing lives.

If you have picked up this book, it is likely that you are as excited as we are by the possibilities of including natural language understanding components into a wider array of applications and software. Language understanding components are built on a modern framework of text analysis: a toolkit of techniques and methods that combine string manipulation, lexical resources, computation linguistics, and machine learning algorithms that convert language data to a machine understandable form and back again. Before we get started discussing these methods and techniques, however, it is important to identify the challenges and opportunities of this framework and address the question of why this is happening now.

The typical American high school graduate has memorized around 60,000 words and thousands of grammatical concepts, enough to communicate in a professional context. While this may seem like a lot, consider how trivial it would be to write a short Python script to rapidly access the definition, etymology, and usage of any term from an online dictionary. In fact, the variety of linguistic concepts an average American uses in daily practice represents merely one-tenth the number captured in the Oxford dictionary, and only 5% of those currently recognized by Google.

And yet, instantaneous access to rules and definitions is clearly not sufficient for text analysis. If it were, Siri and Alexa would understand us perfectly, Google would return only a handful of search results, and we could instantly chat with anyone in the world in any language. Why is there such a disparity between computational versions of tasks humans can perform fluidly from a very early age—long before they've accumulated a fraction of the vocabulary they will possess as adults? Clearly, natural language requires more than mere rote memorization; as a result, deterministic computing techniques are not sufficient.

Computational Challenges of Natural Language

Rather than being defined by rules, natural languages are defined by *use* and must be reverse-engineered to be computed on. To a large degree, we are able to decide what the words we use mean, though this meaning-making is necessarily collaborative. Extending "crab" from a marine animal to a person with a sour disposition or a specific sidewise form of movement requires both the speaker/author and the listener/reader to agree on meaning for communication to occur. Language is therefore usually constrained by community and region—converging on meaning is often much easier with people who inhabit similar lived experiences to our own.

Unlike formal languages, which are necessarily domain specific, natural languages are general purpose and universal. We use the same word to order seafood for lunch, write a poem about a malcontent, and discuss astronomic nebulae. In order to capture the extent of expression across a variety of discourse, language must be redundant. Redundancy presents a challenge—since we cannot (and do not) specify a literal symbol for every association, every symbol is ambiguous by default. Lexical and structural ambiguity is the primary achievement of human language; not only does ambiguity give us the ability to create new ideas, it also allows people with diverse experiences to communicate, across borders and cultures, in spite of the near certainty of occasional misunderstandings.

Linguistic Data: Tokens and Words

In order to fully leverage the data encoded in language, we must retrain our minds to think of language not as intuitive and natural but as arbitrary and ambiguous. The unit of text analysis is the *token*, a string of encoded bytes that represent text. By contrast, *words* are symbols that are representative of meaning, and which map a textual or verbal construct to a sound and sight component. Tokens are not words (though it is hard for us to look at tokens and not see words). Consider the token `"crab"`, shown in Figure P-1. This token represents the word sense *crab-n1*—the first definition of the noun use of the token, a crustacean that can be food, lives near an ocean, and has claws that can pinch.

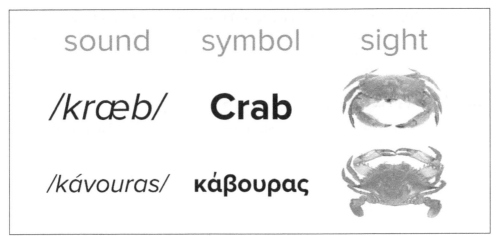

Figure P-1. Words map symbols to ideas

All of these other ideas are somehow attached to this symbol, and yet the symbol is entirely arbitrary; a similar mapping to a Greek reader will have slightly different connotations yet maintain the same meaning. This is because words do not have a fixed, universal meaning independent of contexts such as culture and language. Readers of English are used to adaptive word forms that can be prefixed and suffixed to change tense, gender, etc. Chinese readers, on the other hand, recognize many pictographic characters whose order decides meaning.

Redundancy, ambiguity, and perspective mean that natural languages are dynamic, quickly evolving to encompass current human experience. Today we don't bat an eye at the notion that there could be a linguistic study of emoticons sufficiently complete to translate Moby Dick![1] Even if we could systematically come up with a grammar that defines how emoticons work, by the time we finish, language will have moved on —even the language of emoticons! For example, since we started writing this book, the emoji symbol for a pistol (🔫) has evolved from a weapon to a toy (at least when rendered on a smartphone), reflecting a cultural shift in how we perceive the use of that symbol.

It's not just the inclusion of new symbols and structures that adapt language, but also the inclusion of new definitions, contexts, and usages. The token "battery" has shifted in meaning as a result of the electronic age to mean a repository for converting chemical energy to electricity. However, according to the Google Books Ngram Viewer[2] "battery" enjoyed far more usage, meaning also a connected array of machines or a fortified emplacement for heavy guns during the last part of the 19th century and

---

1 Fred Benenson, *Emoji Dick*, (2013) *http://bit.ly/2GKft1n*

2 Google, *Google Books Ngram Viewer*, (2013) *http://bit.ly/2GNlKtk*

beginning of the 20th. Language is understood in context, which goes beyond just the surrounding text to include also the time period. Clearly identifying and recognizing the meaning of words requires more computation than simply looking up an entry in a dictionary.

Enter Machine Learning

The same qualities that make natural language such a rich tool for human communication also make it difficult to parse using deterministic rules. The flexibility that humans employ in interpretation is why, with a meager 60,000 symbolic representations, we can far outperform computers when it comes to instant understanding of language. Therefore in a software environment, we need computing techniques that are just as fuzzy and flexible, and so the current state-of-the-art for text analysis is statistical machine learning techniques. While applications that perform natural language processing have been around for several decades, the addition of machine learning enables a degree of flexibility and responsiveness that would not otherwise be possible.

The goal of machine learning is to fit existing data to some model, creating a representation of the real world that is able to make decisions or generate predictions on new data based on discovered patterns. In practice, this is done by selecting a model family that determines the relationship between the target data and the input, specifying a form that includes parameters and features, then using some optimization procedure to minimize the error of the model on the training data. The fitted model can now be introduced to new data on which it will make a prediction—returning labels, probabilities, membership, or values based on the model form. The challenge is to strike a balance between being able to precisely learn the patterns in the known data and being able to generalize so the model performs well on examples it has never seen before.

Many language-aware software applications are comprised of not just a single machine-trained model but a rich tapestry of models that interact and influence each other. Models can also be retrained on new data, target new decision spaces, and even be customized per user so that they can continue to develop as they encounter new information and as different aspects of the application change over time. Under the hood of the application, competing models can be ranked, age, and eventually perish. This means that machine learning applications implement life cycles that can keep up with dynamism and regionality associated with language with a routine maintenance and monitoring workflow.

Tools for Text Analysis

Because text analysis techniques are primarily applied machine learning, a language that has rich scientific and numeric computing libraries is necessary. When it comes to tools for performing machine learning on text, Python has a powerhouse suite that includes Scikit-Learn, NLTK, Gensim, spaCy, NetworkX, and Yellowbrick.

- *Scikit-Learn* is an extension of SciPy (Scientific Python) that provides an API for generalized machine learning. Built on top of Cython to include high-performance C-libraries such as LAPACK, LibSVM, Boost, and others, Scikit-Learn combines high performance with ease of use to analyze small- to medium-sized datasets. Open source and commercially usable, it provides a single interface to many regression, classification, clustering, and dimensionality reduction models along with utilities for cross-validation and hyperparameter tuning.

- *NLTK*, the Natural Language Tool-Kit, is a "batteries included" resource for NLP written in Python by experts in academia. Originally a pedagogical tool for teaching NLP, it contains corpora, lexical resources, grammars, language processing algorithms, and pretrained models that allow Python programmers to quickly get started processing text data in a variety of languages.

- *Gensim* is a robust, efficient, and hassle-free library that focuses on unsupervised semantic modeling of text. Originally designed to find similarity between documents (generate similarity), it now exposes topic modeling methods for latent semantic techniques, and includes other unsupervised libraries such as word2vec.

- *spaCy* provides production-grade language processing by implementing the academic state-of-the-art into a simple and easy-to-use API. In particular, spaCy focuses on preprocessing text for deep learning or to build information extraction or natural language understanding systems on large volumes of text.

- *NetworkX* is a comprehensive graph analytics package for generating, serializing, analyzing, and manipulating complex networks. Although not specifically a machine learning or text analysis library, graph data structures are able to encode complex relationships that graph algorithms can traverse or find meaning in, and is therefore a critical part of the text analysis toolkit.

- *Yellowbrick* is a suite of visual diagnostic tools for the analysis and interpretation of machine learning workflows. By extending the Scikit-Learn API, Yellowbrick provides intuitive and understandable visualizations of feature selection, modeling, and hyperparameter tuning, steering the model selection process to find the most effective models of text data.

What to Expect from This Book

In this book, we focus on applied machine learning for text analysis using the Python libraries just described. The applied nature of the book means that we focus not on the academic nature of linguistics or statistical models, but instead on how to be effective at deploying models trained on text inside of a software application.

The model for text analysis we propose is directly related to the machine learning workflow—a search process to find a model composed of features, an algorithm, and hyperparameters that best operates on training data to produce estimations on unknown data. This workflow starts with the construction and management of a training dataset, called a corpus in text analysis. We will then explore feature extraction and preprocessing methodologies to compose text as numeric data that machine learning can understand. With some basic features in hand, we explore techniques for classification and clustering on text, concluding the first few chapters of the book.

The latter chapters focus on extending models with richer features to create text-aware applications. We begin by exploring how context can be embedded as features, then move on to a visual interpretation of text to steering the model selection process. Next, we examine how to analyze complex relationships extracted from text using graph analysis techniques. We then change focus to explore conversational agents and deepen our understanding of syntactic and semantic analysis of text. We conclude the book with a practical discussion of scaling text analysis with multiprocessing and Spark, and finally, we explore the next phase of text analytics: deep learning.

Who This Book Is For

This book is for Python programmers who are interested in applying natural language processing and machine learning to their software development toolkit. We don't assume any special academic background or mathematical knowledge from our readers, and instead focus on tools and techniques rather than lengthy explanations. We do primarily analyze the English language in this book, so basic grammatical knowledge such as how nouns, verbs, adverbs, and adjectives are related to each other is helpful. Readers who are completely new to machine learning and linguistics but have a solid understanding of Python programming will not feel overwhelmed by the concepts we present.

Code Examples and GitHub Repository

The code examples found in this book are meant to be descriptive of how to implement Python code to execute particular tasks. Because they are targeted toward readers, they are concise, often omitting key statements required during execution; for example, `import` statements from the standard library. Additionally they often build on code from other parts of the book or the chapter and occasionally pieces of code that must be modified slightly in order to work in the new context. For example, we may define a class as follows:

```
class Thing(object):

    def __init__(self, arg):
        self.property = arg
```

This class definition serves to describe the basic properties of the class and sets up the structure of a larger conversation about implementation details. Later we may add methods to the class as follows:

```
...

    def method(self, *args, **kwargs):
        return self.property
```

Note the ellipsis at the top of the snippet, indicating that this is a continuation from the class definition in the previous snippet. This means that simply copying and pasting example snippets may not work. Importantly, the code also is designed to operate on data that must be stored on disk in a location readable by the executing Python program. We have attempted to be as general as possible, but cannot account for all operating systems or data sources.

In order to support our readers who may want to run the examples found in this book, we have implemented complete, executable examples on our GitHub repository (*https://github.com/foxbook/atap*). These examples may vary slightly from the text but should be easily runnable with Python 3 on any system. Also note that the repository is kept up-to-date; check the *README* to find any changes that have occurred. You can of course fork the repository and modify the code for execution in your own environment—which we strongly encourage you to do!

Conventions Used in This Book

The following typographical conventions are used in this book:

Italic
> Indicates new terms, URLs, email addresses, filenames, and file extensions.

`Constant width`
> Used for program listings, as well as within paragraphs to refer to program elements such as variable or function names, databases, data types, environment variables, statements, and keywords.

`Constant width bold`
> Shows commands or other text that should be typed literally by the user.

`Constant width italic`
> Shows text that should be replaced with user-supplied values or by values determined by context.

This element signifies a tip or suggestion.

 This element signifies a general note.

 This element indicates a warning or caution.

Using Code Examples

Supplemental material (code examples, exercises, etc.) is available for download at *https://github.com/foxbook/atap*.

This book is here to help you get your job done. In general, if example code is offered with this book, you may use it in your programs and documentation. You do not need to contact us for permission unless you're reproducing a significant portion of the code. For example, writing a program that uses several chunks of code from this book does not require permission. Selling or distributing a CD-ROM of examples from O'Reilly books does require permission. Answering a question by citing this book and quoting example code does not require permission. Incorporating a significant amount of example code from this book into your product's documentation does require permission.

We appreciate, but do not require, attribution. An attribution usually includes the title, author, publisher, and ISBN. For example: "*Applied Text Analysis with Python* by Benjamin Bengfort, Rebecca Bilbro, and Tony Ojeda (O'Reilly). 978-1-491-96304-3."

The BibTex for this book is as follows:

```
@book{
    title = {Applied {{Text Analysis}} with {{Python}}},
    subtitle = {Enabling Language Aware {{Data Products}}},
    shorttitle = {Applied {{Text Analysis}} with {{Python}}},
    publisher = {{O'Reilly Media, Inc.}},
    author = {Bengfort, Benjamin and Bilbro, Rebecca and Ojeda, Tony},
    month = jun,
    year = {2018}
}
```

If you feel your use of code examples falls outside fair use or the permission given above, feel free to contact us at *permissions@oreilly.com*.

O'Reilly Safari

 *Safari* (formerly Safari Books Online) is a membership-based training and reference platform for enterprise, government, educators, and individuals.

Members have access to thousands of books, training videos, Learning Paths, interactive tutorials, and curated playlists from over 250 publishers, including O'Reilly Media, Harvard Business Review, Prentice Hall Professional, Addison-Wesley Professional, Microsoft Press, Sams, Que, Peachpit Press, Adobe, Focal Press, Cisco Press, John Wiley & Sons, Syngress, Morgan Kaufmann, IBM Redbooks, Packt, Adobe Press, FT Press, Apress, Manning, New Riders, McGraw-Hill, Jones & Bartlett, and Course Technology, among others.

For more information, please visit *http://oreilly.com/safari*.

How to Contact Us

Please address comments and questions concerning this book to the publisher:

O'Reilly Media, Inc.
1005 Gravenstein Highway North
Sebastopol, CA 95472
800-998-9938 (in the United States or Canada)
707-829-0515 (international or local)
707-829-0104 (fax)

We have a web page for this book, where we list errata, examples, and any additional information. You can access this page at *http://bit.ly/applied-text-analysis-with-python*.

To comment or ask technical questions about this book, send email to *bookquestions@oreilly.com*.

For more information about our books, courses, conferences, and news, see our website at *http://www.oreilly.com*.

Find us on Facebook: *http://facebook.com/oreilly*

Follow us on Twitter: *http://twitter.com/oreillymedia*

Watch us on YouTube: *http://www.youtube.com/oreillymedia*

Acknowledgments

We would like to thank our technical reviewers for the time and commitment they spent on our first drafts and for the feedback they provided, which dramatically shaped the book. Dan Chudnov and Darren Cook provided excellent technical feedback that helped us stay on track, and Nicole Donnelly provided a perspective that allowed us to tailor our content to our readers. We would also like to thank Lev Konstantinovskiy and Kostas Xirogiannopoulos who provided academic feedback to ensure that our discussion was the state-of-the-art.

To our ever-smiling and unfailingly encouraging editor, Nicole Tache, we can't say enough nice things. She shepherded this project from the very beginning and believed in us even as the finish line seemed to get further away. Her commitment to us and our writing process, her invaluable feedback and advice, and her timely suggestions are the reasons this book exists.

To our friends and families, we could not do our work without your support and encouragement. To our parents, Randy and Lily, Carla and Griff, and Tony and Teresa; you have instilled in us the creative minds, work ethic, technical ability, and love of learning that made this book possible. To our spouses, Jacquelyn, Jeff, and Nikki; your steadfast resolve even in the face of missed deadlines and late nights and weekends writing means the world to us. And finally, to our children, Irena, Henry, Oscar, and Baby Ojeda, we hope that you will someday find this book and think "Wow, our parents wrote books about when computers couldn't talk like a normal person…how old are they?"

## CHAPTER 1

Language and Computation

Applications that leverage natural language processing to understand text and audio data are becoming fixtures of our lives. On our behalf, they curate the myriad of human-generated information on the web, offering new and personalized mechanisms of human-computer interaction. These applications are so prevalent that we have grown accustomed to a wide variety of behind-the-scenes applications, from spam filters that groom our email traffic, to search engines that take us right where we want to go, to virtual assistants who are always listening and ready to respond.

Language-aware features are data products built at the intersection of experimentation, research, and practical software development. The application of text and speech analysis is directly experienced by users whose response provides feedback that tailors both the application and the analysis. This virtuous cycle often starts somewhat naively, but over time can grow into a deep system with rewarding outcomes.

Ironically, while the potential for integrating language-based features into applications continues to multiply, a disproportionate number are being rolled out by the "big guys." So why aren't more people doing it? Perhaps it is in part because as these features become increasingly prevalent, they also become increasingly invisible, masking the complexity required to implement them. But it's also because the rising tide of data science hasn't yet permeated the prevailing culture of software development.

We believe applications that rely on natural language interfaces are only going to become more common, replacing much of what is currently done with forms and clicks. To develop these future applications, software development must embrace hypothesis-driven data science techniques. To ensure that language-aware data products become more robust, data scientists must employ software engineering practices that create production-grade code. These efforts are integrated by a newly evolving paradigm of data science, which leads to the creation of *language-aware data products*, the primary focus of this book.

The Data Science Paradigm

Thanks to innovations in machine learning and scalable data processing, the past decade has seen "data science" and "data product" rapidly become household terms. It has also led to a new job description, *data scientist*—one part statistician, one part computer scientist, and one part domain expert. Data scientists are the pivotal value creators of the information age, and so this new role has become one of the most significant, even sexy, jobs of the 21st century, but also one of the most misunderstood.

Data scientists bridge work traditionally done in an academic context, research and experimentation, to the workflow of a commercial product. This is in part because many data scientists have previously spent time in postgraduate studies (giving them the jack-of-all-trades and creative skills required for data science), but is primarily because the process of data product development is necessarily experimental.

The challenge, which prominent voices in the field have begun to signal, is that the data science workflow is not always compatible with software development practices. Data can be unpredictable, and signal is not always guaranteed. As Hilary Mason says of data product development, data science isn't always particularly agile.[1]

Or, said another way:

> There is a fundamental difference between delivering production software and actionable insights as artifacts of an agile process. The need for insights to be actionable creates an element of uncertainty around the artifacts of data science—they might be "complete" in a software sense, and yet lack any value because they don't yield real, actionable insights….agile software methodologies don't handle this uncertainty well.
>
> —Russell Jurney, *Agile Data Science 2.0*

As a result, data scientists and data science departments often operate autonomously from the development team in a work paradigm described in Figure 1-1. In this context, data science work produces business analytics for senior management, who communicate changes to the technology or product leadership; those changes are eventually passed on to the development team for implementation.

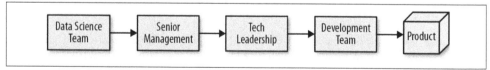

Figure 1-1. The current data science paradigm

---

1 Hillary Mason, *The Next Generation of Data Products*, (2017) *http://bit.ly/2GOF894*

While this structure may be sufficient for some organizations, it is not particularly efficient. If data scientists were integrated with the development team from the start as in Figure 1-2, improvements to the product would be much more immediate and the company much more competitive. There aren't many companies that can afford to build things twice! More importantly, the efforts of data science practice are directed toward users, requiring an in-the-loop approach alongside frontend development.

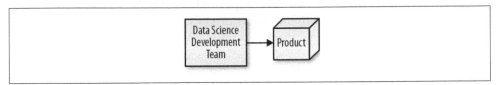

Figure 1-2. Toward a better paradigm for data science development

One of the impediments to a more integrated data science development paradigm is the lack of applications-focused data science content. Most of the published resources on machine learning and natural language processing are written in ways that support research, but do not scale well to application development. For instance, while there are a number of excellent tools for machine learning on text, the available resources, documentation, tutorials, and blog posts tend to lean heavily on toy datasets, data exploration tools, and research code. Few resources exist to explain, for example, how to build a sufficiently large corpus to support an application, how to manage its size and structure as it grows over time, or how to transform raw documents into usable data. In practice, this is unquestionably the majority of the work involved in building scalable language-based data products.

This book is intended to bridge that gap by empowering a development-oriented approach to text analytics. In it, we will demonstrate how to leverage the available open source technologies to create data products that are modular, testable, tunable, and scalable. Together with these tools, we hope the applied techniques presented in this book will enable data scientists to build the next generation of data products.

This chapter serves as the foundation to the more practical, programming-focused chapters of the rest of the book. It begins by framing what we mean by language-aware data products and talking about how to begin spotting them in the wild. Next, we'll discuss architectural design patterns that are well suited to text analytics applications. Finally, we'll consider the features of language that can be used to model it computationally.

Language-Aware Data Products

Data scientists build data products. Data products are applications that derive their value from data and generate new data in return.[2] In our view, the goal of applied text analytics is to enable the creation of "language-aware data products"—user-facing applications that are not only responsive to human input and can adapt to change but also are impressively accurate and relatively simple to design. At their core, these applications accept text data as input, parse it into composite parts, compute upon those composites, and recombine them in a way that delivers a meaningful and tailored result.

One of our favorite examples of this is "Yelpy Insights," a review filtering application that leverages a combination of sentiment analysis, significant collocations (words that tend to appear together), and search techniques to determine if a restaurant is suitable for your tastes and dietary restrictions. This application uses a rich, domain-specific corpus and presents results to users in an intuitive way that helps them decide whether to patronize a particular restaurant. Because of the application's automatic identification of significant sentences in reviews and term highlighting, it allows potential restaurant-goers to digest a large amount of text quickly and make dining decisions more easily. Although language analysis is not Yelp's core business, the impact this feature has on the experience of their users is undeniable. Since introducing "Yelpy Insights" in 2012, Yelp has steadily rolled out new language-based features, and during that same period, has seen annual revenue rise by a factor of 6.5.[3]

Another simple example of bolt-on language analysis with oversized effects is the "suggested tag" feature incorporated into the data products of companies like Stack Overflow, Netflix, Amazon, YouTube, and others. Tags are meta information about a piece of content that are essential for search and recommendations, and they play a significant role in determining what content is viewed by specific users. Tags identify properties of the content they describe, which can be used to group similar items together and propose descriptive topic names for a group.

There are many, many more. Reverb offers a personalized news reader trained on the Wordnik lexicon. The Slack chatbot provides contextual automatic interaction. Google Smart Reply can suggest responses based on the text of the email you're replying to. Textra, iMessage, and other instant messaging tools try to predict what you'll type next based on the text you just entered, and autocorrect tries to fix our spelling mistakes for us. There are also a host of new voice-activated virtual assistants—Alexa, Siri, Google Assistant, and Cortana—trained on audio data, that are able to parse speech and provide (usually) appropriate responses.

---

2 Mike Loukides, *What is data science?*, (2010) *https://oreil.ly/2GJBEoj*

3 Market Watch, (2018) *https://on.mktw.net/2suTk24*

So what about speech data? While this book is focused on text rather than on audio or speech analysis, audio data is typically transcribed into text and then applied to the analytics described in this book. Transcription itself is a machine learning process, one that is also becoming more common!

Features like these highlight the basic methodology of language-aware applications: clustering similar text into meaningful groups or classifying text with specific labels, or said another way—unsupervised and supervised machine learning.

In the next section, we'll explore some architectural design patterns that support the machine learning model lifecycle.

The Data Product Pipeline

The standard data product pipeline, shown in Figure 1-3, is an iterative process consisting of two phases—build and deploy—which mirror the machine learning pipeline.[4] During the build phase, data is ingested and wrangled into a form that allows models to be fit and experimented on. During the deploy phase, models are selected and then used to make estimations or predictions that directly engage a user.

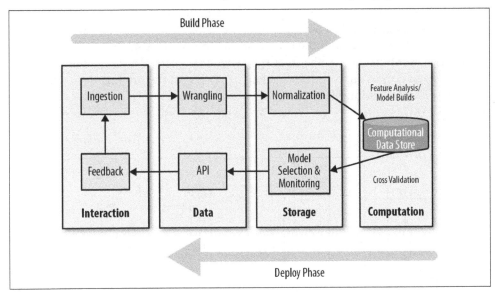

Figure 1-3. A data product pipeline

---

4 Benjamin Bengfort, *The Age of the Data Product*, (2015) *http://bit.ly/2GJBEEP*

Users respond to the output of models, creating feedback, which is in turn reingested and used to adapt models. The four stages—interaction, data, storage, and computation—describe the architectural components required for each phase. For example, during interaction the build phase requires a scraper or utility to ingest data while the user requires some application frontend. The data stage usually refers to internal components that act as glue to the storage stage, which is usually a database. Computation can take many forms from simple SQL queries, Jupyter notebooks, or even cluster computing using Spark.

The deploy phase, other than requiring the selection and use of a fitted model, does not significantly differ from more straightforward software development. Often data science work products end at the API, which is consumed by other APIs or a user frontend. The build phase for a data product, however, does require more attention—and even more so in the case of text analytics. When we build language-aware data products, we create additional lexical resources and artifacts (such as dictionaries, translators, regular expressions, etc.) on which our deployed application will depend.

A more detailed view of the build phase is shown in Figure 1-4, a pipeline that supports robust, language-aware machine learning applications. The process of moving from raw data to deployed model is essentially a series of incremental data transformations. First, we transform the data from its original state into an ingested corpus, stored and managed inside a persistent data store. Next, the ingested data is aggregated, cleaned, normalized, and then transformed into vectors so that we can perform meaningful computation. In the final transformation, a model or models are fit on the vectorized corpus and produce a generalized view of the original data, which can be employed from within the application.

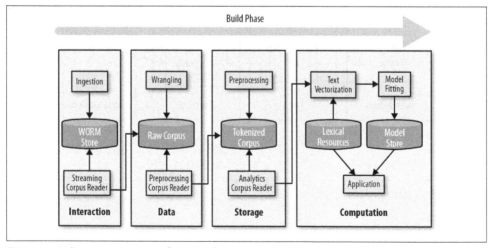

Figure 1-4. Language-aware data products

The model selection triple

What differentiates the construction of machine learning products is that the architecture must support and streamline these data transformations so that they are efficiently testable and tunable. As data products have become more successful, there has been increasing interest in generally defining a machine learning workflow for more rapid—or even automated—model building. Unfortunately, because the search space is large, automatic techniques for optimization are not sufficient.

Instead, the process of selecting an optimal model is complex and iterative, involving repeated cycling through feature engineering, model selection, and hyperparameter tuning. Results are evaluated after each iteration in order to arrive at the best combination of features, model, and parameters that will solve the problem at hand. We refer to this as the *model selection triple*[5] workflow. This workflow, shown in Figure 1-5, aims to treat iteration as central to the science of machine learning, something to be facilitated rather than limited.

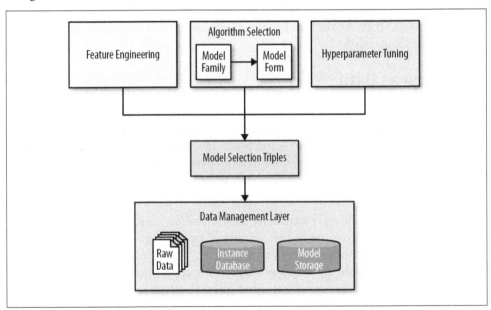

Figure 1-5. The model selection triple workflow

In a 2015 article, Wickham et al.[6] neatly disambiguate the overloaded term "model" by describing its three principal uses in statistical machine learning: model family,

5 Arun Kumar, Robert McCann, Jeffrey Naughton, and Jignesh M. Patel, *Model Selection Management Systems: The Next Frontier of Advanced Analytics*, (2015) *http://bit.ly/2GOFa0G*

6 Hadley Wickham, Dianne Cook, and Heike Hofmann, *Visualizing Statistical Models: Removing the Blindfold*, (2015) *http://bit.ly/2JHq92J*

model form, and fitted model. The model family loosely describes the relationships of variables to the target of interest (e.g., a "linear model" or a "recurrent tensor neural network"). The model form is a specific instantiation of the model selection triple: a set of features, an algorithm, and specific hyperparameters. Finally, the fitted model is a model form that has been fit to a specific set of training data and is available to make predictions. Data products are composed of many fitted models, constructed through the model selection workflow, which creates and evaluates model forms.

Because we are not accustomed to thinking of language as data, the primary challenge of text analysis is interpreting what is happening during each of these transformations. With each successive transformation, the text becomes less and less directly meaningful to us because it becomes less and less like language. In order to be effective in our construction of language-aware data products, we must shift the way we think about language.

Throughout the rest of this chapter, we will frame how to think about language as data that can be computed upon. Along the way, we will build a small vocabulary that will enable us to articulate the kinds of transformations we will be performing on text data in subsequent chapters.

Language as Data

Language is *unstructured* data that has been produced by people to be understood by other people. By contrast, *structured* or *semistructured* data includes fields or markup that enable it to be easily parsed by a computer. However, while it does not feature an easily machine-readable structure, unstructured data is not random. On the contrary, it is governed by linguistic properties that make it very understandable to other people.

Machine learning techniques, particularly supervised learning, are currently the most well-studied and promising means of computing upon languages. Machine learning allows us to train (and retrain) statistical models on language as it changes. By building models of language on context-specific corpora, applications can leverage narrow windows of meaning to be accurate without interpretation. For example, building an automatic prescription application that reads medical charts requires a very different model than an application that summarizes and personalizes news.

A Computational Model of Language

As data scientists building language-aware data products, our primary task is to create a model that describes language and can make inferences based on that description.

The formal definition of a language model attempts to take as input an incomplete phrase and infer the subsequent words most likely to complete the utterance. This type of language model is hugely influential to text analytics because it demonstrates the basic mechanism of a language application—the use of context to guess meaning. Language models also reveal the basic hypothesis behind applied machine learning on text: *text is predictable*. In fact, the mechanism used to score language models in an academic context, *perplexity*, is a measure of how predictable the text is by evaluating the *entropy* (the level of uncertainty or surprial) of the language model's probability distribution.

Consider the following partial phrases: "man's best…" or "the witch flew on a…". These low entropy phrases mean that language models would guess "friend" and "broomstick," respectively, with a high likelihood (and in fact, English speakers would be surprised if the phrase wasn't completed that way). On the other hand, high entropy phrases like "I'm going out to dinner tonight with my…" lend themselves to a lot of possibilities ("friend," "mother," and "work colleagues" could all be equally likely). Human listeners can use experience, imagination, and memory as well as situational context to fill in the blank. Computational models do not necessarily have the same context and as a result must be more constrained.

Language models demonstrate an ability to infer or define relationships between tokens, the UTF-8 encoded strings of data the model observes that human listeners and readers identify as words with meaning. In the formal definition, the model is taking advantage of context, defining a narrow decision space in which only a few possibilities exist.

This insight gives us the ability to generalize the formal model to other models of language that operate in applications such as machine translation or sentiment analysis. To take advantage of the predictability of text, we need to define a constrained, numeric decision space on which the model can compute. By doing this, we can leverage statistical machine learning techniques, both supervised and unsupervised, to build models of language that expose meaning from data.

The first step in machine learning is the identification of the features of data that predict our target. Text data provides many opportunities to extract features either at a shallow level by simply using string splitting, to deeper levels that parse text to extract morphological, syntactic, and even semantic representations from the data.

In the following sections we'll explore some simple ways that language data can expose complex features for modeling purposes. First, we'll explore how the linguistic properties of a specific language (e.g., gender in English) can give us the quick ability to perform statistical computation on text. We'll then take a deeper look at how context modifies interpretation, and how this is usually used to create the traditional "bag-of-words" model. Finally we'll explore richer features that are parsed using morphologic, syntactic, and semantic natural language processing.

Language Features

Consider a simple model that uses linguistic features to identify the predominant gender in a piece of text. In 2013 Neal Caren, an assistant professor of Sociology at the University of North Carolina Chapel Hill, wrote a blog post[7] that investigated the role of gender in news to determine if men and women come up in different contexts. He applied a gender-based analysis of text to *New York Times* articles and determined that in fact male and female words appeared in starkly different contexts, potentially reinforcing gender biases.

What was particularly interesting about this analysis was the use of gendered words to create a frequency-based score of maleness or femaleness. In order to implement a similar analysis in Python, we can begin by building sets of words that differentiate sentences about men and about women. For simplicity, we'll say that a sentence can have one of four states—it can be about men, about women, about both men and women, or *unknown* (since sentences can be about neither men nor women, and also because our MALE_WORDS and FEMALE_WORDS sets are not exhaustive):

```python
MALE = 'male'
FEMALE = 'female'
UNKNOWN = 'unknown'
BOTH = 'both'

MALE_WORDS = set([
    'guy','spokesman','chairman',"men's",'men','him',"he's",'his',
    'boy','boyfriend','boyfriends','boys','brother','brothers','dad',
    'dads','dude','father','fathers','fiance','gentleman','gentlemen',
    'god','grandfather','grandpa','grandson','groom','he','himself',
    'husband','husbands','king','male','man','mr','nephew','nephews',
    'priest','prince','son','sons','uncle','uncles','waiter','widower',
    'widowers'
])

FEMALE_WORDS = set([
    'heroine','spokeswoman','chairwoman',"women's",'actress','women',
    "she's",'her','aunt','aunts','bride','daughter','daughters','female',
    'fiancee','girl','girlfriend','girlfriends','girls','goddess',
    'granddaughter','grandma','grandmother','herself','ladies','lady',
    'lady','mom','moms','mother','mothers','mrs','ms','niece','nieces',
    'priestess','princess','queens','she','sister','sisters','waitress',
    'widow','widows','wife','wives','woman'
])
```

Now that we have gender word sets, we need a method for assigning gender to a sentence; we'll create a genderize function that examines the numbers of words from a sentence that appear in our MALE_WORDS list and in our FEMALE_WORDS list. If a

---

7 Neal Caren, *Using Python to see how the Times writes about men and women*, (2013) *http://bit.ly/2GJBGfV*

sentence has only MALE_WORDS, we'll call it a *male* sentence, and if it has only FEMALE_WORDS, we'll call it a *female* sentence. If a sentence has nonzero counts for both male and female words, we'll call it *both*; and if it has zero male and zero female words, we'll call it *unknown*:

```python
def genderize(words):

    mwlen = len(MALE_WORDS.intersection(words))
    fwlen = len(FEMALE_WORDS.intersection(words))

    if mwlen > 0 and fwlen == 0:
        return MALE
    elif mwlen == 0 and fwlen > 0:
        return FEMALE
    elif mwlen > 0 and fwlen > 0:
        return BOTH
    else:
        return UNKNOWN
```

We need a method for counting the frequency of gendered words and sentences within the complete text of an article, which we can do with the collections.Counters class, a built-in Python class. The count_gender function takes a list of sentences and applies the genderize function to evaluate the total number of gendered words and gendered sentences. Each sentence's gender is counted and all words in the sentence are also considered as belonging to that gender:

```python
from collections import Counter

def count_gender(sentences):

    sents = Counter()
    words = Counter()

    for sentence in sentences:
        gender = genderize(sentence)
        sents[gender] += 1
        words[gender] += len(sentence)

    return sents, words
```

Finally, in order to engage our gender counters, we require some mechanism for parsing the raw text of the articles into component sentences and words, and for this we will use the NLTK library (which we'll discuss further later in this chapter and in the next) to break our paragraphs into sentences. With the sentences isolated, we can then tokenize them to identify individual words and punctuation and pass the tokenized text to our gender counters to print a document's percent *male, female, both,* or *unknown*:

```
import nltk

def parse_gender(text):

    sentences = [
        [word.lower() for word in nltk.word_tokenize(sentence)]
        for sentence in nltk.sent_tokenize(text)
    ]

    sents, words = count_gender(sentences)
    total = sum(words.values())

    for gender, count in words.items():
        pcent = (count / total) * 100
        nsents = sents[gender]

        print(
            "{0.3f}% {} ({} sentences)".format(pcent, gender, nsents)
        )
```

Running our `parse_gender` function on an article from the *New York Times* entitled "Rehearse, Ice Feet, Repeat: The Life of a New York City Ballet Corps Dancer" yields the following, unsurprising results:

```
50.288% female (37 sentences)
42.016% unknown (49 sentences)
4.403% both (2 sentences)
3.292% male (3 sentences)
```

The scoring function here takes into account the length of the sentence in terms of the number of words it contains. Therefore even though there are fewer total female sentences, over 50% of the article is female. Extensions of this technique can analyze words that are in female sentences versus in male sentences to see if there are any auxiliary terms that are by default associated with male and female genders. We can see that this analysis is relatively easy to implement in Python, and Caren found his results very striking:

> If your knowledge of men's and women's roles in society came just from reading last week's *New York Times*, you would think that men play sports and run the government. Women do feminine and domestic things. To be honest, I was a little shocked at how stereotypical the words used in the women subject sentences were.
>
> —Neal Caren

So what exactly is happening here? This mechanism, while deterministic, is a very good example of how words contribute to predictability in context (stereotypical though it may be). However, this mechanism works specifically because gender is a feature that is encoded directly into language. In other languages (like French, for example), gender is even more pronounced: ideas, inanimate objects, and even body parts can have genders (even if at times they are counter-intuitive). Language features do not necessarily convey definitional meaning, but often convey other information; for example, plurality and tense are other features we can extract from a language—we could potentially apply a similar analysis to detect past, present, or future language. However, language features are only part of the equation when it comes to predicting meaning in text.

Contextual Features

Sentiment analysis, which we will discuss in greater depth in Chapter 12, is an extremely popular text classification technique because the tone of text can convey a lot of information about the subject's perspective and lead to aggregate analyses of reviews, message polarity, or reactions. One might assume that sentiment analysis can be conducted with a technique similar to the gender analysis of the previous section: gather lists of positive words ("awesome," "good," "stupendous") and negative words ("horrible," "tasteless," "bland") and compute the relative frequencies of these tokens in their context. Unfortunately, this technique is naive and often produces highly inaccurate results.

Sentiment analysis is fundamentally different from gender classification because sentiment is not a language feature, but instead dependent on *word sense*; for example, "that kick flip was sick" is positive whereas "the chowder made me sick" is negative, and "I have a sick pet iguana" is somewhat ambiguous—the definition of the word "sick" in these examples is changing. Moreover, sentiment is dependent on context even when definitions remain constant; "bland" may be negative when talking about hot peppers, but can be a positive term when describing cough syrup. Finally, unlike gender or tense, sentiment can be negated: "not good" means bad. Negation can flip the meaning of large amounts of positive text; "I had high hopes and great expectations for the movie dubbed wonderful and exhilarating by critics, but was hugely disappointed." Here, though words typically indicating positive sentiment such as "high hopes," "great," "wonderful and exhilarating," and even "hugely" outnumber the sole negative sentiment of "disappointed," the positive words not only do not *lessen* the negative sentiment, they actually enhance it.

However, all of these examples are predictable; a positive or negative sentiment is clearly communicated, and it seems that a machine learning model should be able to detect sentiment and perhaps even highlight noisy or ambiguous utterances. An *a priori* deterministic or structural approach loses the flexibility of context and sense—so instead, most language models take into account the localization of words in their context, utilizing machine learning methods to create predictions.

Figure 1-6 shows the primary method of developing simple language models, often called the "bag-of-words" model. This model evaluates the frequency with which words co-occur with themselves and other words in a specific, limited context. Co-occurrences show which words are likely to proceed and succeed each other and by making inferences on limited pieces of text, large amounts of meaning can be captured. We can then use statistical inference methods to make predictions about word ordering.

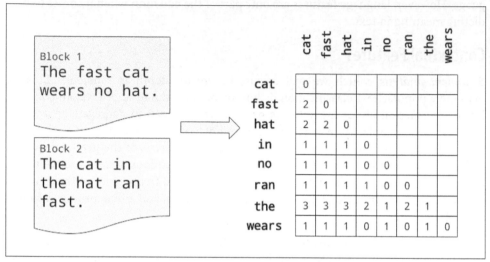

	cat	fast	hat	in	no	ran	the	wears
cat	0							
fast	2	0						
hat	2	2	0					
in	1	1	1	0				
no	1	1	1	0	0			
ran	1	1	1	1	0	0		
the	3	3	3	2	1	2	1	
wears	1	1	1	0	1	0	1	0

Block 1
The fast cat wears no hat.

Block 2
The cat in the hat ran fast.

Figure 1-6. A word co-occurrence matrix

Extensions of the "bag-of-words" model consider not only single word co-occurrences, but also phrases that are highly correlated to indicate meaning. If "withdraw money at the bank" contributes a lot of information to the sense of "bank," so does "fishing by the river bank." This is called *n-gram analysis*, where *n* specifies a ordered sequence of either characters or words to scan on (e.g., a 3-gram is ('withdraw', 'money', 'at') as opposed to the 5-gram ('withdraw', 'money', 'at', 'the', 'bank')). *n*-grams introduce an interesting opportunity because the vast majority of possible *n*-grams are nonsensical (e.g., ('bucket', 'jumps', 'fireworks')), though the evolving nature of language means that even that 3-gram could eventually become sensical! Language models that take advantage of context in this way therefore require some ability to learn the relationship of text to some target variable.

Both language features and contextual ones contribute to the overall predictability of language for analytical purposes. But identifications of these features require the ability to parse and define language according to units. In the next section we will discuss the coordination of both language features and context into meaning from the linguistic perspective.

Structural Features

Finally, language models and text analytics have benefited from advances in computational linguistics. Whether we are building models with contextual or linguistic features (or both), it is necessary to consider the high-level units of language used by linguists, which will give us a vocabulary for the operations we'll perform on our text corpus in subsequent chapters. Different units of language are used to compute at a variety of levels, and understanding the linguistic context is essential to understanding the language processing techniques used in machine learning.

Semantics refer to meaning; they are deeply encoded in language and difficult to extract. If we think of an utterance (a simple phrase instead of a whole paragraph, such as "She borrowed a book from the library.") in the abstract, we can see there is a template: a subject, the head verb, an object, and an instrument that relates back to the object (`subject - predicate - object`). Using such templates, *ontologies* can be constructed that specifically define the relationships between entities, but such work requires significant knowledge of the context and domain, and does not tend to scale well. Nonetheless, there is promising recent work on extracting ontologies from sources such as Wikipedia or DBPedia (e.g., DBPedia's entry on libraries begins "A library is a collection of sources of information and similar resources, made accessible to a defined community for reference or borrowing.").

Semantic analysis is not simply about understanding the meaning of text, but about generating data structures to which logical reasoning can be applied. Text meaning representations (or thematic meaning representations, TMRs) can be used to encode sentences as predicate structures to which first-order logic or *lambda calculus* can be applied. Other structures such as networks can be used to encode predicate interactions of interesting features in the text. Traversal can then be used to analyze the centrality of terms or subjects and reason about the relationships between items. Although not necessarily a complete semantic analysis, *graph analysis* can produce important insights.

Syntax refers to sentence formation rules usually defined by grammar. Sentences are what we use to build meaning and encode much more information than words, and for this reason we will treat them as the smallest logical unit of language. Syntactic analysis is designed to show the meaningful relationship of words, usually by carving the sentence into chunks or showing the relationship of tokens in a tree structure (similar to the sentence diagramming you probably did in grammar school). Syntax is a necessary prerequisite to reasoning on discourse or semantics because it is a vital tool to understanding how words modify each other in the formation of *phrases*. For example, syntactic analysis should identify the prepositional phrase "from the library" and the noun phrase "a book from the library" as being subcomponents of the verb phrase "borrowed a book from the library."

Morphology refers to the form of things, and in text analysis, the form of individual words or tokens. The structure of words can help us to identify plurality (*wife* versus *wives*), gender (*fiancé* versus *fiancée*), tense (*ran* versus *run*), conjugation (*to run* versus *he runs*), etc. Morphology is challenging because most languages have many exceptions and special cases. English punctuation, for instance, has both orthographic rules, which merely adjust the ending of a word (*puppy - puppies*), as well as morphological rules that are complete translations (*goose - geese*). English is an affixal language, which means that we simply add characters to the beginning or end of a word to modify it. Other languages have different morphologic modes: Hebrew uses templates of consonants that are filled in with vowels to create meaning, whereas Chinese uses pictographic symbols that are not necessarily modified directly.

The primary goal of morphology is to understand the parts of words so that we can assign them to classes, often called part-of-speech tags. For example, we want to know if a word is a singular noun, a plural noun, or a proper noun. We might also want to know if a verb is infinitive, past tense, or a gerund. These parts of speech are then used to build up larger structures such as chunks or phrases, or even complete trees, that can then in turn be used to build up semantic reasoning data structures.

Semantics, syntax, and morphology allow us to add data to simple text strings with linguistic meaning. In Chapter 3 we will explore how to carve up text into units of reason, using tokenization and segmentation to break up text into their units of logic and meaning, as well as assign part-of-speech tags. In Chapter 4 we will apply vectorization to these structures to create numeric feature spaces—for example, normalizing text with stemming and lemmatization to reduce the number of features. Finally, in Chapter 7, we will directly use the structures to encode information into our machine learning protocols to improve performance and target more specific types of analytics.

Conclusion

Natural language is one of the most untapped forms of data available today. It has the ability to make data products even more useful and integral to our lives than they already are. Data scientists are uniquely poised to build these types of language-aware data products, and by combining text data with machine learning, they have the potential to build powerful applications in a world where information often equates to value and a competitive advantage. From email to maps to search, our modern life is powered by natural language data sources, and language-aware data products are what make their value accessible.

In the next few chapters, we will discuss the necessary precursors to machine learning on text, namely corpus management (in Chapter 2), preprocessing (in Chapter 3), and vectorization (in Chapter 4). We will then experiment with formulating machine learning problems to those of classification (in Chapter 5) and clustering (Chapter 6).

In Chapter 7 we'll implement feature extraction to maximize the effectiveness of our models, and in Chapter 8 we'll see how to employ text visualization to surface results and diagnose modeling errors. In Chapter 9, we will explore a different approach to modeling language, using the graph data structure to represent words and their relationships. We'll then explore more specialized methods of retrieval, extraction, and generation for chatbots in Chapter 10. Finally, in Chapters 11 and 12 we will investigate techniques for scaling processing power with Spark and scaling model complexity with artificial neural networks.

As we will see in the next chapter, in order to perform scalable analytics and machine learning on text, we will first need both domain knowledge and a domain-specific corpus. For example, if you are working in the financial domain, your application should be able to recognize stock symbols, financial terms, and company names, which means that the documents in the corpus you construct need to contain these entities. In other words, developing a language-aware data product begins with acquiring the right kind of text data and building a custom corpus that contains the structural and contextual features from the domain in which you are working.

## CHAPTER 2

Building a Custom Corpus

As with any machine learning application, the primary challenge is to determine if and where the signal is hiding within the noise. This is done through the process of *feature analysis*—determining which features, properties, or dimensions about our text best encode its meaning and underlying structure. In the previous chapter, we began to see that, in spite of the complexity and flexibility of natural language, it is possible to model if we can extract its structural and contextual features.

The bulk of our work in the subsequent chapters will be in "feature extraction" and "knowledge engineering"—where we'll be concerned with the identification of unique vocabulary words, sets of synonyms, interrelationships between entities, and semantic contexts. As we will see throughout the book, the representation of the underlying linguistic structure we use largely determines how successful we will be. Determining a representation requires us to define the units of language—the things that we count, measure, analyze, or learn from.

At some level, text analysis is the act of breaking up larger bodies of work into their constituent components—unique vocabulary words, common phrases, syntactical patterns—then applying statistical mechanisms to them. By learning on these components we can produce models of language that allow us to augment applications with a predictive capability. We will soon see that there are many levels to which we can apply our analysis, all of which revolve around a central text dataset: the *corpus*.

What Is a Corpus?

Corpora are collections of related documents that contain natural language. A corpus can be large or small, though generally they consist of dozens or even hundreds of gigabytes of data inside of thousands of documents. For instance, considering that the average email inbox is 2 GB (for reference, the full version of the Enron corpus, now roughly 15 years old, includes 1 M emails between 118 users and is 160 GB in size[1]), a moderately sized company of 200 employees would have around a half-terabyte email corpus. Corpora can be *annotated*, meaning that the text or documents are labeled with the correct responses for supervised learning algorithms (e.g., to build a filter to detect spam email), or *unannotated*, making them candidates for topic modeling and document clustering (e.g., to explore shifts in latent themes within messages over time).

A corpus can be broken down into categories of documents or individual documents. Documents contained by a corpus can vary in size, from tweets to books, but they contain text (and sometimes metadata) and a set of related ideas. Documents can in turn be broken into paragraphs, units of *discourse* that generally each express a single idea. Paragraphs can be further broken down into sentences, which are units of *syntax*; a complete sentence is structurally sound as a specific expression. Sentences are made up of words and punctuation, the *lexical* units that indicate general meaning but are far more useful in combination. Finally, words themselves are made up of syllables, phonemes, affixes, and characters, units that are only meaningful when combined into words.

Domain-Specific Corpora

It is very common to begin testing out a natural language model with a generic corpus. There are, for instance, many examples and research papers that leverage readily available datasets such as the Brown corpus, Wikipedia corpus, or Cornell movie dialogue corpus. However, the best language models are often highly constrained and application-specific.

Why is it that models trained in a specific field or domain of the language would perform better than ones trained on general language? Different domains use different language (vocabulary, acronyms, common phrases, etc.), so a corpus that is relatively pure in domain will be able to be analyzed and modeled better than one that contains documents from several different domains.

Consider that the term "bank" is very likely to be an institution that produces fiscal and monetary tools in an economics, financial, or political domain, whereas in an aviation or vehicular domain it is more likely to be a form of motion that results in the change of direction of a vehicle or aircraft. By fitting models in a narrower context, the prediction space is smaller and more specific, and therefore better able to handle the flexible aspects of language.

Acquiring a domain-specific corpus will be essential to producing a language-aware data product that performs well. Naturally the next question should then be "How do

---

1 Federal Energy Regulatory Committee, FERC Enron Dataset. *http://bit.ly/2JJTOIv*

we construct a dataset with which to build a language model?" Whether it is done via scraping, RSS ingestion, or an API, ingesting a raw text corpus in a form that will support the construction of a data product is no trivial task.

Often data scientists start by collecting a single, static set of documents and then applying routine analyses. However, without considering routine and programmatic data ingestion, analytics will be static and unable to respond to new feedback or to the dynamic nature of language.

In this chapter, our primary focus will be not on how the data is acquired, but on how it should be structured and managed in a way that will support machine learning. However, in the next section, we will briefly present a framework for an ingestion engine called Baleen, which is particularly well-suited to the construction of domain-specific corpora for applied text analysis.

The Baleen Ingestion Engine

Baleen[2] is an open source tool for building custom corpora. It works by ingesting natural language data from the discourse of professional and amateur writers, like bloggers and news outlets, in a categorized fashion.

Given an OPML file of RSS feeds (a common export format for news readers), Baleen downloads all the posts from those feeds, saves them to MongoDB storage, then exports a text corpus that can be used for analytics. While this task seems like it could be easily completed with a single function, the actual implementation of ingestion can become complex; APIs and RSS feeds can and often do change. Significant forethought is required to determine how best to put together an application that will conduct not only robust, autonomous ingestion, but also secure data management.

The complexity of routine text ingestion via RSS is shown in Figure 2-1. The fixture that specifies what feeds to ingest and how they're categorized is an OPML file that must be read from disk. Connecting and inserting posts, feeds, and other information to the MongoDB store requires an object document mapping (ODM), and tools are needed to define a single ingestion job that synchronizes entire feeds and then fetches and wrangles individual posts or articles.

With these mechanisms in place, Baleen exposes utilities to run the ingestion job on a routine basis (e.g., hourly), though some configuration is required to specify database connection parameters and how often to run. Since this will be a long-running process, Baleen also provides a console to assist with scheduling, logging, and monitoring for errors. Finally, Baleen's `export` tool exports the corpus out of the database.

---

2 District Data Labs, *Baleen: An automated ingestion service for blogs to construct a corpus for NLP research*, (2014) *http://bit.ly/2GOFaxI*

As currently implemented, the Baleen ingestion engine collects RSS feeds from 12 categories, including sports, gaming, politics, cooking, and news. As such, Baleen produces not one but 12 domain-specific corpora, a sample of which are available via our GitHub repository for the book: *https://github.com/foxbook/atap/*.

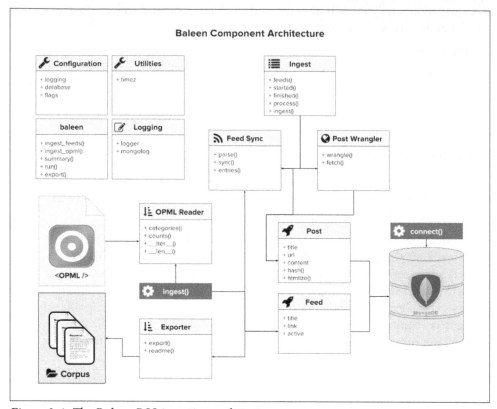

Figure 2-1. The Baleen RSS ingestion architecture

Whether documents are routinely ingested or part of a fixed collection, some thought must go into how to manage the data and prepare it for analytical processing and model computation. In the next section, we will discuss how to monitor corpora as our ingestion routines continue and the data change and grow.

Corpus Data Management

The first assumption we should make is that the corpora we will be dealing with will be nontrivial in size—that is, they will contain thousands or tens of thousands of documents comprising gigabytes of data. The second assumption is that the language data will come from a source that will need to be cleaned and processed into data structures that we can perform analytics on. The former assumption requires a computing methodology that can scale (which we'll explore more fully in Chapter 11), and the latter implies that we will be performing irreversible transformations on the data (as we'll see in Chapter 3).

Data products often employ write-once, read-many (WORM) storage as an intermediate data management layer between ingestion and preprocessing as shown in Figure 2-2. WORM stores (sometimes referred to as data lakes) provide streaming read accesses to raw data in a repeatable and scalable fashion, addressing the requirement for performance computing. Moreover, by keeping data in a WORM store, preprocessed data can be reanalyzed without reingestion, allowing new hypotheses to be easily explored on the raw data format.

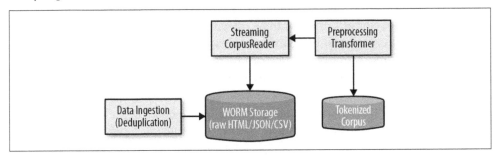

Figure 2-2. WORM storage supports an intermediate wrangling step

The addition of the WORM store to our data ingestion workflow means that we need to store data in two places—the raw corpus as well as the preprocessed corpus—which leads to the question: Where should that data be stored? When we think of data management, we usually think of databases first. Databases are certainly valuable tools in building language-aware data products, and many provide full-text search functionality and other types of indexing. However, most databases are constructed to retrieve or update only a couple of rows per transaction. In contrast, computational access to a text corpus will be a complete read of every single document, and will cause no in-place updates to the document, nor search or select individual documents. As such, databases tend to add overhead to computation without real benefit.

 Relational database management systems are great for transactions that operate on a small collection of rows at a time, particularly when those rows are updated frequently. Machine learning on a text corpus has a different computational profile: many sequential reads of the entire dataset. As a result, storing corpora on disk (or in a document database) is often preferred.

For text data management, the best choice is often to store data in a NoSQL document storage database that allows streaming reads of the documents with minimal overhead, or to simply write each document to disk. While a NoSQL application might be worthwhile in large applications, consider the benefits of using a file-based approach: compression techniques on directories are well suited to text information and the use of a file synchronization service provides automatic replication. The construction of a corpus in a database is beyond the scope of this book, though we will briefly explore a Sqlite corpus later in this chapter. Instead, we proceed by structuring our data on disk in a meaningful way that will support systematic access to our corpus.

Corpus Disk Structure

The simplest and most common method of organizing and managing a text-based corpus is to store individual documents in a file system on disk. By organizing the corpus into subdirectories, corpora can be categorized or meaningfully partitioned by meta information, like dates. By maintaining each document as its own file, corpus readers can seek quickly to different subsets of documents and processing can be parallelized, with each process taking a different subset of documents.

 NLTK `CorpusReader` objects, which we'll explore in the next section, can read from either a path to a directory or a path to a Zip file.

Text is also the most compressible format, making Zip files, which leverage directory structures on disk, an ideal distribution and storage format. Finally, corpora stored on disk are generally static and treated as a whole, fulfilling the requirement for WORM storage presented in the previous section.

Storing a single document per file could lead to some challenges, however. Smaller documents like emails or tweets don't make sense to store as individual files. Alternatively, email is typically stored in an MBox format—a plain-text format that uses separators to delimit multipart mime messages containing text, HTML, images, and attachments. These can typically be organized by the categories contained within the email service (Inbox, Starred, Archive, etc.). Tweets are generally small JSON data structures that include not just the text of the tweet but other metadata like user or location. The typical way to store multiple tweets is in newline-delimited JSON, sometimes called the JSON lines format. This format makes it easy to read one tweet at a time by parsing only a single line at a time, but also to seek to different tweets in the file. A single file of tweets can be large, so organizing tweets in files by user, location, or day can reduce overall file sizes and create a meaningful disk structure of multiple files.

An alternative technique to storing the data in some logical structure is simply to write files with a maximum size limit. For example, we can keep writing data to a file, respecting document boundaries, until it reaches some size limit (e.g., 128 MB) and then open a new file and continue writing there.

 A corpus on disk will necessarily contain many files that represent one or more documents in the corpus—sometimes partitioned into subdirectories that represent meaningful splits like category. Corpus and document meta information must also be stored along with its documents. As a result a standard structure for corpora on disk is vital to ensuring that data can be meaningfully read by Python programs.

Whether documents are aggregated into multidocument files or each stored as its own file, a corpus represents many files that need to be organized. If corpus ingestion occurs over time, a meaningful organization may be subdirectories for year, month, and day with documents placed into each folder, respectively. If the documents are categorized by sentiment, as positive or negative, each type of document can be grouped together into their own category subdirectory. If there are multiple users in a system that generate their own subcorpora of user-specific writing, such as reviews or tweets, then each user can have their own subdirectory. All subdirectories need to be stored alongside each other in a single corpus root directory. Importantly, corpus meta information such as a license, manifest, README, or citation must also be stored along with documents such that the corpus can be treated as an individual whole.

The Baleen disk structure

The choice of organization on disk has a large impact on how documents are read by CorpusReader objects, which we'll explore in the next section. The Baleen corpus ingestion engine writes an HTML corpus to disk as follows:

```
corpus
├── citation.bib
├── feeds.json
├── LICENSE.md
├── manifest.json
├── README.md
└── books
│   ├── 56d629e7c1808113ffb87eaf.html
│   ├── 56d629e7c1808113ffb87eb3.html
│   └── 56d629ebc1808113ffb87ed0.html
└── business
│   ├── 56d625d5c1808113ffb87730.html
│   ├── 56d625d6c1808113ffb87736.html
│   └── 56d625ddc1808113ffb87752.html
```

```
└─ cinema
│   ├─ 56d629b5c1808113ffb87d8f.html
│   ├─ 56d629b5c1808113ffb87d93.html
│   └─ 56d629b6c1808113ffb87d9a.html
└─ cooking
    ├─ 56d62af2c1808113ffb880ec.html
    ├─ 56d62af2c1808113ffb880ee.html
    └─ 56d62af2c1808113ffb880fa.html
```

There are a few important things to note here. First, all documents are stored as HTML files, named according to their MD5 hash (to prevent duplication), and each stored in its own category subdirectory. It is simple to identify which files are documents and which files are meta both by the directory structure and the name of each file. In terms of meta information, a *citation.bib* file provides attribution for the corpus and the *LICENSE.md* file specifies the rights others have to use this corpus. While these two pieces of information are usually reserved for public corpora, it is helpful to include them so that it is clear how the corpus can be used—for the same reason that you would add this type of information to a private software repository. The *feeds.json* and *manifest.json* files are two corpus-specific files, that serve to identify information about the categories and each specific file, respectively. Finally, the *README.md* file is a human-readable description of the corpus.

Of these files, *citation.bib*, *LICENSE.md*, and *README.md* are special files because they can be automatically read from an NLTK `CorpusReader` object with the `citation()`, `license()`, and `readme()` methods.

A structured approach to corpus management and storage means that applied text analytics follows a scientific process of reproducibility, a method that encourages the interpretability of analytics as well as confidence in their results. Moreover, structuring a corpus as above enables us to use `CorpusReader` objects, which will be explained in detail in the next section.

Modifying these methods to deal with Markdown or to read corpus-specific files like the manifest is fairly simple:

```python
import json

# In a custom corpus reader class
def manifest(self):
    """
    Reads and parses the manifest.json file in our corpus if it exists.
    """
    return json.load(self.open("README.md"))
```

These methods are specifically exposed programmatically to allow corpora to remain compressed, but still readable, minimizing the amount of storage required on disk. Consider that the *README.md* file is essential to communicating about the composition of the corpus, not just to other users or developers of the corpus, but also to "future you," who may not remember specifics, and to be able to identify which models were trained on which corpora and what information those models have.

Corpus Readers

Once a corpus has been structured and organized on disk, two opportunities present themselves: a systematic approach to accessing the corpus in a programming context, and the ability to monitor and manage change in the corpus. We will discuss the latter at the end of the chapter, but for now we will tackle the subject of how to load documents for use in analytics.

Most nontrivial corpora contain thousands of documents with potentially gigabytes of text data. The raw text strings loaded from the documents then need to be preprocessed and parsed into a representation suitable for analysis, an additive process whose methods may generate or duplicate data, increasing the amount of required working memory. From a computational standpoint, this is an important consideration, because without some method to stream and select documents from disk, text analytics would quickly be bound to the performance of a single machine, limiting our ability to generate interesting models. Luckily, tools for streaming accesses of a corpus from disk have been well thought out by the NLTK library, which exposes corpora in Python via `CorpusReader` objects.

 Distributed computing frameworks such as Hadoop were created in response to the amount of text generated by web crawlers to produce search engines (Hadoop, inspired by two Google papers, was a follow-on project to the Nutch search engine). We will discuss cluster computing techniques to scaling with Spark, Hadoop's distributed computing successor, in Chapter 11.

A `CorpusReader` is a programmatic interface to read, seek, stream, and filter documents, and furthermore to expose data wrangling techniques like encoding and preprocessing for code that requires access to data within a corpus. A `CorpusReader` is instantiated by passing a `root` path to the directory that contains the corpus files, a signature for discovering document names, as well as a file encoding (by default, UTF-8).

Because a corpus contains files beyond the documents meant for analysis (e.g., the README, citation, license, etc.) some mechanism must be provided to the reader to identify exactly what documents are part of the corpus. This mechanism is a parameter that can be specified explicitly as a list of names or implicitly as a regular expression that will be matched upon all documents under the `root` (e.g., `\w+\.txt`), which matches one or more characters or digits in the filename preceding the file extension, *.txt*. For instance, in the following directory, this regex pattern will match the three speeches and the transcript, but not the license, README, or metadata files:

```
corpus
├── LICENSE.md
├── README.md
├── citation.bib
├── transcript.txt
└── speeches
    ├── 04102008.txt
    ├── 10142009.txt
    ├── 09012014.txt
    └── metadata.json
```

These three simple parameters then give the `CorpusReader` the ability to list the absolute paths of all documents in the corpus, to open each document with the correct encoding, and to allow programmers to access metadata separately.

 By default, NLTK `CorpusReader` objects can even access corpora that are compressed as Zip files, and simple extensions allow the reading of Gzip or Bzip compression as well.

By itself, the concept of a `CorpusReader` may not seem particularly spectacular, but when dealing with a myriad of documents, the interface allows programmers to read one or more documents into memory, to seek forward and backward to particular places in the corpus without opening or reading unnecessary documents, to stream data to an analytical process holding only one document in memory at a time, and to filter or select only specific documents from the corpus at a time. These techniques are what make in-memory text analytics possible for nontrivial corpora because they apply work to only a few documents in-memory at a time.

Therefore, in order to analyze your own text corpus in a specific domain that targets exactly the models you are attempting to build, you will need an application-specific corpus reader. This is so critical to enabling applied text analytics that we have devoted most of the remainder of this chapter to the subject! In this section we will discuss the corpus readers that come with NLTK and the possibility of structuring your corpus so that you can simply use one of them out of the box. We will then move forward into a discussion of how to define a custom corpus reader that does application-specific work, namely dealing with HTML files collected during the ingestion process.

Streaming Data Access with NLTK

NLTK comes with a variety of corpus readers (66 at the time of this writing) that are specifically designed to access the text corpora and lexical resources that can be

---

downloaded with NLTK. It also comes with slightly more generic utility `Corpus Reader` objects, which are fairly rigid in the corpus structure in that they expect but provide the opportunity to quickly create corpora and associate them with readers. They also give hints as to how to customize a `CorpusReader` for application-specific purposes. To name a few notable utility readers:

`PlaintextCorpusReader`
A reader for corpora that consist of plain-text documents, where paragraphs are assumed to be split using blank lines.

`TaggedCorpusReader`
A reader for simple part-of-speech tagged corpora, where sentences are on their own line and tokens are delimited with their tag.

`BracketParseCorpusReader`
A reader for corpora that consist of parenthesis-delineated parse trees.

`ChunkedCorpusReader`
A reader for chunked (and optionally tagged) corpora formatted with parentheses.

`TwitterCorpusReader`
A reader for corpora that consist of tweets that have been serialized into line-delimited JSON.

`WordListCorpusReader`
List of words, one per line. Blank lines are ignored.

`XMLCorpusReader`
A reader for corpora whose documents are XML files.

`CategorizedCorpusReader`
A mixin for corpus readers whose documents are organized by category.

The tagged, bracket parse, and chunked corpus readers are *annotated* corpus readers; if you're going to be doing domain-specific hand annotation in advance of machine learning, then the formats exposed by these readers are important to understand. The Twitter, XML, and plain-text corpus readers all give hints about how to deal with data on disk that has different parseable formats, allowing for extensions related to CSV corpora, JSON, or even from a database. If your corpus is already in one of these formats, then you have little work to do. For example, consider a corpus of the plain-text scripts of the *Star Wars* and *Star Trek* movies organized as follows:

```
corpus
├── LICENSE
├── README
└── Star Trek
```

```
|       ├── Star Trek - Balance of Terror.txt
|       ├── Star Trek - First Contact.txt
|       ├── Star Trek - Generations.txt
|       ├── Star Trek - Nemesis.txt
|       ├── Star Trek - The Motion Picture.txt
|       ├── Star Trek 2 - The Wrath of Khan.txt
|       └── Star Trek.txt
└── Star Wars
|       ├── Star Wars Episode 1.txt
|       ├── Star Wars Episode 2.txt
|       ├── Star Wars Episode 3.txt
|       ├── Star Wars Episode 4.txt
|       ├── Star Wars Episode 5.txt
|       ├── Star Wars Episode 6.txt
|       └── Star Wars Episode 7.txt
└── citation.bib
```

The `CategorizedPlaintextCorpusReader` is perfect for accessing data from the movie scripts since the documents are *.txt* files and there are two categories, namely "Star Wars" and "Star Trek." In order to use the `CategorizedPlaintextCorpus Reader`, we need to specify a regular expression that allows the reader to automatically determine both the `fileids` and `categories`:

```
from nltk.corpus.reader.plaintext import CategorizedPlaintextCorpusReader

DOC_PATTERN = r'(?!\.)[\w_\s]+/[\w\s\d\-]+\.txt'
CAT_PATTERN = r'([\w_\s]+)/.*'

corpus = CategorizedPlaintextCorpusReader(
    '/path/to/corpus/root', DOC_PATTERN, cat_pattern=CAT_PATTERN
)
```

The document pattern regular expression specifies documents as having paths under the corpus root such that there is one or more letters, digits, spaces, or underscores, followed by the / character, then one or more letters, digits, spaces, or hyphens followed by .txt. This will match documents such as *Star Wars/Star Wars Episode 1.txt* but not documents such as *episode.txt*. The `categories` pattern regular expression truncates the original regular expression with a capture group that indicates that a category is any directory name (e.g., *Star Wars/anything.txt* will capture `Star Wars` as the category). You can start to access the data on disk by inspecting how these names are captured:

```
corpus.categories()
# ['Star Trek', 'Star Wars']

corpus.fileids()
# ['Star Trek/Star Trek - Balance of Terror.txt',
#  'Star Trek/Star Trek - First Contact.txt', ...]
```

Although regular expressions can be difficult, they do provide a powerful mechanism for specifying exactly what should be loaded by the corpus reader, and how. Alternatively, you could explicitly pass a list of categories and `fileids`, but that would make the corpus reader a lot less flexible. By using regular expressions you could add new categories by simply creating a directory in your corpus, and add new documents by moving them to the correct directory.

Now that we have access to the `CorpusReader` objects that come with NLTK, we will explore a methodology to stream the HTML data we have ingested.

Reading an HTML Corpus

Assuming we are ingesting data from the internet, it is a safe bet that the data we're ingesting is formatted as HTML. One option for creating a streaming corpus reader is to simply strip all the tags from the HTML, writing it as plain text and using the `CategorizedPlaintextCorpusReader`. However, if we do that, we will lose the benefits of HTML—namely computer parseable, *structured* text, which we can take advantage of when preprocessing. Therefore, in this section we will begin to design a custom `HTMLCorpusReader` that we will extend in the next chapter:

```python
from nltk.corpus.reader.api import CorpusReader
from nltk.corpus.reader.api import CategorizedCorpusReader

CAT_PATTERN = r'([a-z_\s]+)/.*'
DOC_PATTERN = r'(?!\.)[a-z_\s]+/[a-f0-9]+\.json'
TAGS = ['h1', 'h2', 'h3', 'h4', 'h5', 'h6', 'h7', 'p', 'li']

class HTMLCorpusReader(CategorizedCorpusReader, CorpusReader):
    """
    A corpus reader for raw HTML documents to enable preprocessing.
    """

    def __init__(self, root, fileids=DOC_PATTERN, encoding='utf8',
                 tags=TAGS, **kwargs):
        """
        Initialize the corpus reader.  Categorization arguments
        (``cat_pattern``, ``cat_map``, and ``cat_file``) are passed to
        the ``CategorizedCorpusReader`` constructor.  The remaining
        arguments are passed to the ``CorpusReader`` constructor.
        """
        # Add the default category pattern if not passed into the class.
        if not any(key.startswith('cat_') for key in kwargs.keys()):
            kwargs['cat_pattern'] = CAT_PATTERN

        # Initialize the NLTK corpus reader objects
        CategorizedCorpusReader.__init__(self, kwargs)
        CorpusReader.__init__(self, root, fileids, encoding)
```

```
# Save the tags that we specifically want to extract.
self.tags = tags
```

Our `HTMLCorpusReader` class extends both the `CategorizedCorpusReader` and the `CorpusReader`, similarly to how the `CategorizedPlaintextCorpusReader` uses the categorization mixin. *Multiple inheritance* can by tricky, so the bulk of the code in the `__init__` function simply figures out which arguments to pass to which class. In particular, the `CategorizedCorpusReader` takes in generic keyword arguments, and the `CorpusReader` will be initialized with the root directory of the corpus, as well as the `fileids` and the HTML encoding scheme. However, we have also added our own customization, allowing the user to specify which HTML tags should be treated as independent paragraphs.

The next step is to augment the `HTMLCorpusReader` with a method that will allow us to *filter* how we read text data from disk, either by specifying a list of categories, or a list of filenames:

```
def resolve(self, fileids, categories):
    """
    Returns a list of fileids or categories depending on what is passed
    to each internal corpus reader function. Implemented similarly to
    the NLTK ``CategorizedPlaintextCorpusReader``.
    """
    if fileids is not None and categories is not None:
        raise ValueError("Specify fileids or categories, not both")

    if categories is not None:
        return self.fileids(categories)
    return fileids
```

This method returns a list of `fileids` whether or not they have been categorized. In this sense, it both adds flexibility and exposes the method signature that we will use for pretty much every other method on the reader. In our `resolve` method, if both `categories` and `fileids` are specified, it will complain. If they are not specified, the method will use a `CorpusReader` method to compute the `fileids` associated with the specific categories. Note that `categories` can either be a single category or a list of categories. Otherwise, we will simply return the `fileids`—if this is None, the `Corpus Reader` will automatically read every single document in the corpus without filtering.

 Note that the ability to read only part of a corpus will become essential as we move toward machine learning, particularly for doing cross-validation where we will have to create training and testing splits of the corpus.

At the moment, our `HTMLCorpusReader` doesn't have a method for reading a stream of complete documents, one document at a time. Instead, it will expose the entire text of every single document in the corpus in a streaming fashion to our methods. However, we will want to parse one HTML document at a time, so the following method gives us access to the text on a document-by-document basis:

```
import codecs

def docs(self, fileids=None, categories=None):
    """
    Returns the complete text of an HTML document, closing the document
    after we are done reading it and yielding it in a memory safe fashion.
    """
    # Resolve the fileids and the categories
    fileids = self.resolve(fileids, categories)

    # Create a generator, loading one document into memory at a time.
    for path, encoding in self.abspaths(fileids, include_encoding=True):
        with codecs.open(path, 'r', encoding=encoding) as f:
            yield f.read()
```

Our custom corpus reader now knows how to deal with individual documents in the corpus, one document at a time, allowing us to filter and seek to different places in the corpus. It can handle fileids and categories, and has all the tools imported from NLTK to make disk access easier.

Corpus monitoring

As we have established so far in this chapter, applied text analytics requires substantial data management and preprocessing. The methods described for data ingestion, management, and preprocessing are laborious and time-intensive, but also critical precursors to machine learning. Given the requisite time, energy, and disk storage commitments, it is good practice to include with the rest of the data some meta information about the details of how the corpus was built.

In this section, we will describe how to create a monitoring system for ingestion and preprocessing. To begin, we should consider what specific kinds of information we would like to monitor, such as the dates and sources of ingestion. Given the massive size of the corpora with which we will be working, we should at the very least, keep track of the size of each file on disk.

```
def sizes(self, fileids=None, categories=None):
    """
    Returns a list of tuples, the fileid and size on disk of the file.
    This function is used to detect oddly large files in the corpus.
    """
    # Resolve the fileids and the categories
    fileids = self.resolve(fileids, categories)

    # Create a generator, getting every path and computing filesize
    for path in self.abspaths(fileids):
        yield os.path.getsize(path)
```

One of our observations in working with RSS HTML corpora in practice is that in addition to text, a significant number of the ingested files came with embedded images, audio tracks, and video. These embedded media files quickly ate up memory during ingestion and were disruptive to preprocessing. The above `sizes` method is in part a reaction to these kinds of experiences with real-world corpora, and will help us to perform diagnostics and identify individual files within the corpus that are much larger than expected (e.g., images and video that have been encoded as text). This method will enable us to compute the complete size of the corpus, to track over time, and see how it is growing and changing.

Reading a Corpus from a Database

No two corpora are exactly alike, and just as every novel application will require a novel and domain-specific corpus, each corpus will require an application-specific corpus reader. In Chapter 12 we will explore a sentiment analysis application that uses a corpus of about 18,000 album reviews from the website Pitchfork.com. The extracted dataset is stored in a Sqlite database with the schema shown in Figure 2-3.

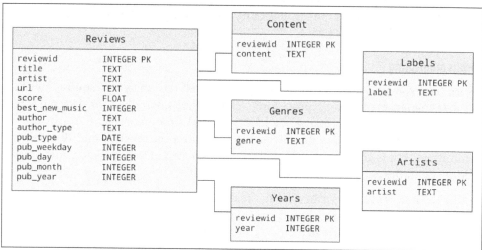

Figure 2-3. Schema for the album review corpus stored in a Sqlite database

To interact with this corpus, we will create a custom `SqliteCorpusReader` class to access its different components, mimicking the behavior of an NLTK `CorpusReader`, but not inheriting from it.

We want our `SqliteCorpusReader` to be able to fetch results from the database in a memory safe fashion; as with the `HTMLCorpusReader` from the previous section, we need to be able access one record at a time to perform wrangling, normalization, and transformation (which will be discussed in Chapter 3) in an efficient and streamlined way. For this reason, using the SQL-like `fetchall()` command is not advisable, and might keep us waiting for a long time for the results to come back before our iteration can begin. Instead, our `ids()`, `scores()`, and `texts()` methods each make use of `fetchone()`, a good alternative in this case, though with a larger database, batch-wise fetching (e.g., with `fetchmany()`) would be more performant.

```python
import sqlite3

class SqliteCorpusReader(object):

    def __init__(self, path):
        self._cur = sqlite3.connect(path).cursor()

    def ids(self):
        """
        Returns the review ids, which enable joins to other
        review metadata
        """
        self._cur.execute("SELECT reviewid FROM content")
        for idx in iter(self._cur.fetchone, None):
            yield idx

    def scores(self):
        """
        Returns the review score, to be used as the target
        for later supervised learning problems
        """
        self._cur.execute("SELECT score FROM reviews")
        for score in iter(self._cur.fetchone, None):
            yield score

    def texts(self):
        """
        Returns the full review texts, to be preprocessed and
        vectorized for supervised learning
        """
        self._cur.execute("SELECT content FROM content")
        for text in iter(self._cur.fetchone, None):
            yield text
```

As we can see from the `HTMLCorpusReader` and `SqliteCorpusReader` examples, we should be prepared to write a new corpus reader for each new dataset. However, we hope that these examples demonstrate not only their utility but their similarities. In the next chapter, we will extend our `HTMLCorpusReader` so that we can use it to access more granular components of our text, which will be useful for preprocessing and feature engineering.

Conclusion

In this chapter, we have learned that text analytics requires a large, robust, domain-specific corpus. Since these will be very large, often unpredictable datasets, we discussed methods for structuring and managing these corpora over time. We learned how corpus readers can leverage this structure and also reduce memory pressure through streaming data loading. Finally, we started to build some custom corpus readers—one for a corpus of HTML documents stored on disk and one for a documents stored in a Sqlite database.

In the next chapter, we will learn how to preprocess our data and extend the work we have done in this chapter with methods to preprocess the raw HTML as it is streamed in a memory safe fashion and achieve our final text data structure in advance of machine learning—a list of documents, composed of lists of paragraphs, which are lists of sentences, where a sentence is a list of tuples containing a token and its part-of-speech tag.

## CHAPTER 3

Corpus Preprocessing and Wrangling

In the previous chapter, we learned how to build and structure a custom, domain-specific corpus. Unfortunately, any real corpus in its raw form is completely unusable for analytics without significant preprocessing and compression. In fact, a key motivation for writing this book is the immense challenge we ourselves have encountered in our efforts to build and wrangle corpora large and rich enough to power meaningfully literate data products. Given how much of our own routine time and effort is dedicated to text preprocessing and wrangling, it is surprising how few resources exist to support (or even acknowledge!) these phases.

In this chapter, we propose a multipurpose preprocessing framework that can be used to systematically transform our raw ingested text into a form that is ready for computation and modeling. Our framework includes the five key stages shown in Figure 3-1: content extraction, paragraph blocking, sentence segmentation, word tokenization, and part-of-speech tagging. For each of these stages, we will provide functions conceived as methods under the `HTMLCorpusReader` class defined in the previous chapter.

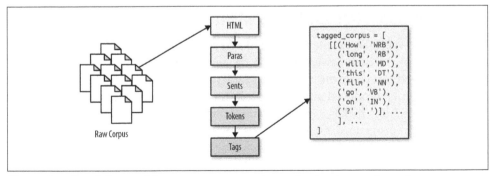

Figure 3-1. Breakdown of document segmentation, tokenization, and tagging

Breaking Down Documents

In the previous chapter, we began constructing a custom `HTMLCorpusReader`, providing it with methods for filtering, accessing, and counting our documents (`resolve()`, `docs()`, and `sizes()`). Because it inherits from NLTK's `CorpusReader` object, our custom corpus reader also implements a standard preprocessing API that also exposes the following methods:

`raw()`
    Provides access to the raw text without preprocessing

`sents()`
    A generator of individual sentences in the text

`words()`
    Tokenizes the text into individual words

In order to fit models using machine learning techniques on our text, we will need to include these methods as part of the feature extraction process. Throughout the rest of this chapter, we will discuss the details of preprocessing and show how to leverage and modify these methods to access content and explore features within our documents.

 While our focus here will be on language processing methods for a corpus reader designed to process HTML documents collected from the web, other methods may be more convenient depending on the form of your corpus. It is worth noting that NLTK `Corpus Reader` objects already expose many other methods for different use cases; for example, automatically tagging or parsing sentences, converting annotated text into meaningful data structures like `Tree` objects, or providing format-specific utilities like individual XML elements.

Identifying and Extracting Core Content

Although the web is an excellent source of text with which to build novel and useful corpora, it is also a fairly lawless place in the sense that the underlying structures of web pages need not conform to any set standard. As a result, HTML content, while structured, can be produced and rendered in numerous and sometimes erratic ways. This unpredictability makes it very difficult to extract data from raw HTML text in a methodical and programmatic way.

The readability-lxml library is an excellent resource for grappling with the high degree of variability in documents collected from the web. Readability-lxml is a Python wrapper for the JavaScript Readability experiment by Arc90. Just as browsers like Safari and Chrome offer a reading mode, Readability removes distractions from the content of the page, leaving just the text.

Given an HTML document, Readability employs a series of regular expressions to remove navigation bars, advertisements, page script tags, and CSS, then builds a new Document Object Model (DOM) tree, extracts the text from the original tree, and reconstructs the text within the newly restructured tree. In the following example, which extends our `HTMLCorpusReader`, we import two readability modules, `Unparseable` and `Document`, which we can use to extract and clean the raw HTML text for the first phase of our preprocessing workflow.

The `html` method iterates over each file and uses the `summary` method from the `readability.Document` class to remove any nontext content as well as script and stylistic tags. It also corrects any of the most commonly misused tags (e.g., `<div>` and `<br>`), only throwing an exception if the original HTML is found to be unparseable. The most likely reason for such an exception is if the function is passed an empty document, which has nothing to parse:

```
from readability.readability import Unparseable
from readability.readability import Document as Paper


    def html(self, fileids=None, categories=None):
        """
        Returns the HTML content of each document, cleaning it using
        the readability-lxml library.
        """
        for doc in self.docs(fileids, categories):
            try:
                yield Paper(doc).summary()
            except Unparseable as e:
                print("Could not parse HTML: {}".format(e))
                continue
```

Note that the above method may generate warnings about the `readability` logger; you can adjust the level of verbosity according to your taste by adding:

```
import logging
log = logging.getLogger("readability.readability")
log.setLevel('WARNING')
```

The result of our new `html()` method is clean and well-structured HTML text. In the next few sections, we will create additional methods to incrementally decompose this text into paragraphs, sentences, and tokens.

Deconstructing Documents into Paragraphs

Now that we are able to filter the raw HTML text that we ingested in the previous chapter, we will move toward building a preprocessed corpus that is structured in a way that will facilitate machine learning. In Figure 3-2 we see how meaning is distributed across the elements of a *New York Times* news article.[1] As we can see, the granularity with which we inspect this document may dramatically impact whether we classify it as a "popular sports" article or instead one about "personal health" (or both!).

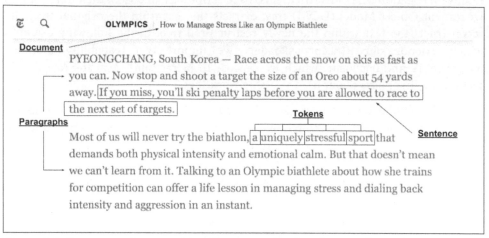

Figure 3-2. Document decomposition illustrating the distribution of meaning across paragraphs, sentences, and individual tokens

This example illustrates why the vectorization, feature extraction, and machine learning tasks we will perform in subsequent chapters will rely so much on our ability to effectively break our documents down into their component pieces while also preserving their original structure.

The precision and sensitivity of our models will rely on how effectively we are able to link tokens with the textual contexts in which they appear.

Paragraphs encapsulate complete ideas, functioning as the unit of document structure, and our first step will be to isolate the paragraphs that appear within the text. Some NLTK corpus readers, such as the `PlaintextCorpusReader`, implement a `paras()` method, which is a generator of paragraphs defined as blocks of text delimited with double newlines.

Our text, however, is not plain text, so we will need to create a method that extracts the paragraphs from HTML. Fortunately, our `html()` method retains the structure of

---

1 Tara Parker-Pope, *How to Manage Stress Like a Biathlete*, (2018) *https://nyti.ms/2GJBGwr*

our HTML documents. This means we can isolate content that appears within paragraphs by searching for <p> tags, the element that formally defines an HTML paragraph. Because content can also appear in other ways (e.g., embedded inside other structures within the document like headings and lists), we will search broadly through the text using BeautifulSoup.

 Recall that in Chapter 2 we defined our `HTMLCorpusReader` class so that reader objects will have the HTML document tags as a class attribute. This tag set can be expanded, abbreviated, or otherwise modified according to your context.

We will define a `paras()` method to iterate through each `fileid` and pass each HTML document to the BeautifulSoup constructor, specifying that the HTML should be parsed using the lxml HTML parser. The resulting `soup` is a nested tree structure that we can navigate using the original HTML tags and elements. For each of our document soups, we then iterate through each of the tags from our predefined set and yield the text from within that tag. We can then call BeautifulSoup's `decompose` method to destroy the tree when we're done working with each file to free up memory.

```
import bs4

# Tags to extract as paragraphs from the HTML text
tags = [
    'h1', 'h2', 'h3', 'h4', 'h5', 'h6', 'h7', 'p', 'li'
]

    def paras(self, fileids=None, categories=None):
        """
        Uses BeautifulSoup to parse the paragraphs from the HTML.
        """
        for html in self.html(fileids, categories):
            soup = bs4.BeautifulSoup(html, 'lxml')
            for element in soup.find_all(tags):
                yield element.text
            soup.decompose()
```

The result of our `paras()` method is a generator with the raw text paragraphs from every document, from first to last, with no document boundaries. If passed a specific `fileid`, `paras` will return the paragraphs from that file only.

It's worth noting that the `paras()` methods for many of the NLTK corpus readers, such as `PlaintextCorpusReader`, function differently, frequently doing segmentation and tokenization in addition to isolating the paragraphs. This is because NLTK methods tend to expect a corpus that has already been annotated, and are thus not concerned with reconstructing paragraphs. By contrast, our methods are designed to work on raw, unannotated corpora and will need to support corpus reconstruction.

Segmentation: Breaking Out Sentences

If we can think of paragraphs as the units of document structure, it is useful to see sentences as the units of discourse. Just as a paragraph within a document comprises a single idea, a sentence contains a complete language structure, one that we want to be able to identify and encode.

In this section, we'll perform *segmentation* to parse our text into sentences, which will facilitate the part-of-speech tagging methods we will use a bit later in this chapter (which rely on an internally consistent morphology). To get to our sentences, we'll write a new method, `sents()`, that wraps `paras()` and returns a generator (an iterator) yielding each sentence from every paragraph.

Syntactic segmentation is not necessarily a prerequisite for part-of-speech tagging. Depending on your use case, tagging can be used to break text into sentences, as with spoken or transcribed speech data, where sentence boundaries are less clear. In written text, performing segmentation first facilitates part-of-speech tagging. SpaCy's tools often work better with speech data, while NLTK's work better with written language.

Our `sents()` method iterates through each of the paragraphs isolated with our `paras` method, using the built-in NLTK `sent_tokenize` method to conduct segmentation. Under the hood, `sent_tokenize` employs the `PunktSentenceTokenizer`, a pretrained model that has learned transformation rules (essentially a series of regular expressions) for the kinds of words and punctuation (e.g., periods, question marks, exclamation points, capitalization, etc.) that signal the beginnings and ends of sentences. The model can be applied to a paragraph to produce a generator of sentences:

```
from nltk import sent_tokenize

def sents(self, fileids=None, categories=None):
    """
    Uses the built in sentence tokenizer to extract sentences from the
    paragraphs. Note that this method uses BeautifulSoup to parse HTML.
    """
```

```
    for paragraph in self.paras(fileids, categories):
        for sentence in sent_tokenize(paragraph):
            yield sentence
```

NLTK's `PunktSentenceTokenizer` is trained on English text, and it works well for most European languages. It performs well when provided standard paragraphs:

```
['Beautiful is better than ugly.', 'Explicit is better than implicit.',
 'Simple is better than complex.', 'Complex is better than complicated.',
 'Flat is better than nested.', 'Sparse is better than dense.',
 'Readability counts.', "Special cases aren't special enough to break the
rules.", 'Although practicality beats purity.', 'Errors should never pass
silently.', 'Unless explicitly silenced.', 'In the face of ambiguity, refuse
the temptation to guess.', 'There should be one-- and preferably only one --
obvious way to do it.', "Although that way may not be obvious at first unless
you're Dutch.", 'Now is better than never.', 'Although never is often better
than *right* now.', "If the implementation is hard to explain, it's a bad
idea.", 'If the implementation is easy to explain, it may be a good idea.',
 "Namespaces are one honking great idea -- let's do more of those!"]
```

However, punctuation marks can be ambiguous; while periods frequently signal the end of a sentence, they can also appear in floats, abbreviations, and ellipses. In other words, identifying the boundaries between sentences can be tricky. As a result, you may find that using `PunktSentenceTokenizer` on nonstandard text will not always produce usable results:

```
['Baa, baa, black sheep,\nHave you any wool?', 'Yes, sir, yes, sir,\nThree
bags full;\nOne for the master,\nAnd one for the dame,\nAnd one for the little
boy\nWho lives down the lane.']
```

NLTK does provide alternative sentences tokenizers (e.g., for tweets), which are worth exploring. Nonetheless, if your domain space has special peculiarities in the way that sentences are demarcated, it's advisable to train your own tokenizer using domain-specific content.

Tokenization: Identifying Individual Tokens

We've defined sentences as the units of discourse and paragraphs as the units of document structure. In this section, we will isolate *tokens*, the syntactic units of language that encode semantic information within sequences of characters.

Tokenization is the process by which we'll arrive at those tokens, and we'll use `Word PunctTokenizer`, a regular expression–based tokenizer that splits text on both whitespace and punctuation and returns a list of alphabetic and nonalphabetic characters:

```
from nltk import wordpunct_tokenize

def words(self, fileids=None, categories=None):
    """
    Uses the built-in word tokenizer to extract tokens from sentences.
    Note that this method uses BeautifulSoup to parse HTML content.
```

```
"""
for sentence in self.sents(fileids, categories):
    for token in wordpunct_tokenize(sentence):
        yield token
```

As with sentence demarcation, tokenization is not always straightforward. We must consider things like: do we want to remove punctuation from tokens, and if so, should we make punctuation marks tokens themselves? Should we preserve hyphenated words as compound elements or break them apart? Should we approach contractions as one token or two, and if they are two tokens, where should they be split?

We can select different tokenizers depending on our responses to these questions. Of the many word tokenizers available in NLTK (e.g., `TreebankWordTokenizer`, `Word PunctTokenize`, `PunktWordTokenizer`, etc.), a common choice for tokenization is `word_tokenize`, which invokes the Treebank tokenizer and uses regular expressions to tokenize text as in Penn Treebank. This includes splitting standard contractions (e.g., "wouldn't" becomes "would" and "n't") and treating punctuation marks (like commas, single quotes, and periods followed by whitespace) as separate tokens. By contrast, `WordPunctTokenizer` is based on the `RegexpTokenizer` class, which splits strings using the regular expression `\w+|[^\w\s]+`, matching either tokens or separators between tokens and resulting in a sequence of alphabetic and nonalphabetic characters. You can also use the `RegexpTokenizer` class to create your own custom tokenizer.

Part-of-Speech Tagging

Now that we can access the tokens within the sentences of our document paragraphs, we will proceed to tag each token with its *part of speech*. Parts of speech (e.g., verbs, nouns, prepositions, adjectives) indicate how a word is functioning within the context of a sentence. In English, as in many other languages, a single word can function in multiple ways, and we would like to be able to distinguish those uses (e.g., "building" can be either a noun or a verb). Part-of-speech tagging entails labeling each token with the appropriate tag, which will encode information both about the word's definition and its use in context.

We'll use the off-the-shelf NLTK tagger, `pos_tag`, which at the time of this writing uses the `PerceptronTagger()` and the Penn Treebank tagset. The Penn Treebank tagset consists of 36 parts of speech, structural tags, and indicators of tense (NN for singular nouns, NNS for plural nouns, JJ for adjectives, RB for adverbs, VB for verbs, PRP for personal pronouns, etc.).

The `tokenize` method returns a generator that can give us a list of lists containing paragraphs, which are lists of sentences, which in turn are lists of part-of-speech tagged tokens. The tagged tokens are represented as (`tag`, `token`) tuples, where the tag is a case-sensitive string that specifies how the token is functioning in context:

```
from nltk import pos_tag, sent_tokenize, wordpunct_tokenize

def tokenize(self, fileids=None, categories=None):
    """
    Segments, tokenizes, and tags a document in the corpus.
    """
    for paragraph in self.paras(fileids=fileids):
        yield [
            pos_tag(wordpunct_tokenize(sent))
            for sent in sent_tokenize(paragraph)
        ]
```

Consider the paragraph "The old building is scheduled for demolition. The contractors will begin building a new structure next month." The pos_tag method will differentiate how word "building" is used in context, first as a singular noun and then as the present participle of the verb "to build":

```
[[('The', 'DT'), ('old', 'JJ'), ('building', 'NN'), ('is', 'VBZ'),
('scheduled', 'VBN'), ('for', 'IN'), ('demolition', 'NN'), ('.', '.')],
[('The', 'DT'), ('contractors', 'NNS'), ('will', 'MD'), ('begin', 'VB'),
('building', 'VBG'), ('a', 'DT'), ('new', 'JJ'), ('structure', 'NN'),
('next', 'JJ'), ('month', 'NN'), ('.', '.')]]
```

 Here's the rule of thumb for deciphering part-of-speech tags: nouns start with an *N*, verbs with a *V*, adjectives with a *J*, adverbs with an *R*. Anything else is likely to be some kind of a structural element. A full list of tags can be found here: *http://bit.ly/2JfUOrq*.

NLTK provides several options for part-of-speech taggers (e.g., DefaultTagger, RegexpTagger, UnigramTagger, BrillTagger). Taggers can also be used in combination, such as the BrillTagger, which uses Brill transformational rules to improve initial tags.

Intermediate Corpus Analytics

Our HTMLCorpusReader now has all of the methods necessary to perform the document decompositions that will be needed in later chapters. In Chapter 2, we provided our reader with a sizes() method that enabled us to get a rough sense of how the corpus was changing over time. We can now add a new method, describe(), which will allow us to perform intermediate corpus analytics on its changing categories, vocabulary, and complexity.

First, describe() will start the clock and initialize two frequency distributions: the first, counts, to hold counts of the document substructures, and the second, tokens, to contain the vocabulary. Note that we'll discuss and leverage frequency distributions in much greater detail in Chapter 7. We'll keep a count of each paragraph, sentence, and word, and we'll also store each unique token in our vocabulary. We then compute the number of files and categories in our corpus, and return a dictionary with a statistical summary of our corpus—its total number of files and categories; the total number of paragraph, sentences, and words; the number of unique terms; the lexical diversity, which is the ratio of unique terms to total words; the average number of paragraphs per document; the average number of sentences per paragraph; and the total processing time:

```python
import time

    def describe(self, fileids=None, categories=None):
        """
        Performs a single pass of the corpus and
        returns a dictionary with a variety of metrics
        concerning the state of the corpus.
        """
        started = time.time()

        # Structures to perform counting.
        counts = nltk.FreqDist()
        tokens = nltk.FreqDist()

        # Perform single pass over paragraphs, tokenize and count
        for para in self.paras(fileids, categories):
            counts['paras'] += 1

            for sent in para:
                counts['sents'] += 1

                for word, tag in sent:
                    counts['words'] += 1
                    tokens[word] += 1

        # Compute the number of files and categories in the corpus
        n_fileids = len(self.resolve(fileids, categories) or self.fileids())
        n_topics  = len(self.categories(self.resolve(fileids, categories)))

        # Return data structure with information
        return {
            'files':  n_fileids,
            'topics': n_topics,
            'paras':  counts['paras'],
            'sents':  counts['sents'],
            'words':  counts['words'],
            'vocab':  len(tokens),
            'lexdiv': float(counts['words']) / float(len(tokens)),
            'ppdoc':  float(counts['paras']) / float(n_fileids),
            'sppar':  float(counts['sents']) / float(counts['paras']),
            'secs':   time.time() - started,
        }
```

As our corpus grows through ingestion, preprocessing, and compression, `describe()` allows us to recompute these metrics to see how they change over time. This can become a critical monitoring technique to help diagnose problems in the application; machine learning models will expect certain features of the data such as the lexical diversity and number of paragraphs per document to remain consistent, and if the corpus changes, it is very likely to impact performance. As such, the `describe()` method can be used to monitor for changes in the corpus that are sufficiently big to trigger a rebuild of any downstream vectorization and modeling.

Corpus Transformation

Our reader can now stream raw documents from the corpus through the stages of content extraction, paragraph blocking, sentence segmentation, word tokenization, and part-of-speech tagging, and send the resulting processed documents to our machine learning models, as shown in Figure 3-3.

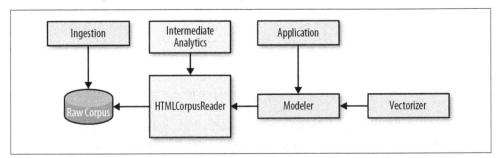

Figure 3-3. The pipeline from raw corpus to preprocessed corpus

Unfortunately, this preprocessing isn't cheap. For smaller corpora, or in cases where many virtual machines can be allotted to preprocessing, a raw corpus reader such as `HTMLCorpusReader` may be enough. But on a corpus of roughly 300,000 HTML news articles, these preprocessing steps took over 12 hours. This is not something we will want to have to do every time we run our models or test out a new set of hyperparameters.

In practice, we address this by adding two additional classes, a `Preprocessor` class that wraps our `HTMLCorpusReader` to wrangle the raw corpus to store an intermediate transformed corpus artifact, and a `PickledCorpusReader` that can stream the transformed documents from disk in a standardized fashion for downstream vectorization and analysis, as shown in Figure 3-4.

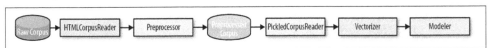

Figure 3-4. A pipeline with intermediate storage of preprocessed corpus

Intermediate Preprocessing and Storage

In this section we'll write a `Preprocessor` that takes our `HTMLCorpusReader`, executes the preprocessing steps, and writes out a new text corpus to disk, as shown in Figure 3-5. This new corpus is the one on which we will perform our text analytics.

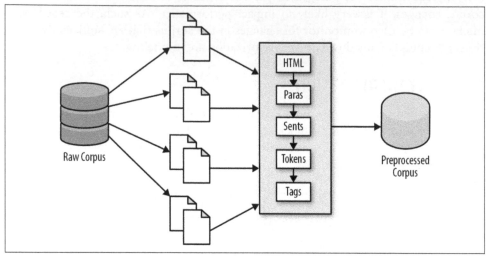

Figure 3-5. An intermediate preprocessing stage to produce a transformed corpus artifact

We begin by defining a new class, `Preprocessor`, which will wrap our corpus reader and manage the stateful tokenization and part-of-speech tagging of our documents. The objects will be initialized with a `corpus`, the path to the raw corpus, and `target`, the path to the directory where we want to store the postprocessed corpus. The `fileids()` method will provide convenient access to the `fileids` of the `HTMLCorpus Reader` object, and `abspath()` will returns the absolute path to the target `fileid` for each raw corpus `fileid`:

```python
import os

class Preprocessor(object):
    """
    The preprocessor wraps an `HTMLCorpusReader` and performs tokenization
    and part-of-speech tagging.
    """
    def __init__(self, corpus, target=None, **kwargs):
        self.corpus = corpus
        self.target = target

    def fileids(self, fileids=None, categories=None):
        fileids = self.corpus.resolve(fileids, categories)
        if fileids:
            return fileids
        return self.corpus.fileids()
```

```python
    def abspath(self, fileid):
        # Find the directory, relative to the corpus root.
        parent = os.path.relpath(
            os.path.dirname(self.corpus.abspath(fileid)), self.corpus.root
        )

        # Compute the name parts to reconstruct
        basename  = os.path.basename(fileid)
        name, ext = os.path.splitext(basename)

        # Create the pickle file extension
        basename  = name + '.pickle'

        # Return the path to the file relative to the target.
        return os.path.normpath(os.path.join(self.target, parent, basename))
```

Next, we add a `tokenize()` method to our `Preprocessor`, which, given a raw document, will perform segmentation, tokenization, and part-of-speech tagging using the NLTK methods we explored in the previous section. This method will return a generator of paragraphs for each document that contains a list of sentences, which are in turn lists of part-of-speech tagged tokens:

```python
from nltk import pos_tag, sent_tokenize, wordpunct_tokenize

...

    def tokenize(self, fileid):
        for paragraph in self.corpus.paras(fileids=fileid):
            yield [
                pos_tag(wordpunct_tokenize(sent))
                for sent in sent_tokenize(paragraph)
            ]
```

 As we gradually build up the text data structure we need (a list of documents, composed of lists of paragraphs, which are lists of sentences, where a sentence is a list of token, tag tuples), we are adding much more content to the original text than we are removing. For this reason, we should be prepared to apply a compression method to keep disk storage under control.

Writing to pickle

There are several options for transforming and saving a preprocessed corpus, but our preferred method is using `pickle`. With this approach we write an iterator that loads one document into memory at a time, converts it into the target data structure, and dumps a string representation of that structure to a small file on disk. While the resulting string representation is not human readable, it is compressed, easier to load, serialize and deserialize, and thus fairly efficient.

To save the transformed documents, we'll add a preprocess() method. Once we have established a place on disk to retrieve the original files and to store their processed, pickled, compressed counterparts, we create a temporary document variable that creates our list of lists of lists of tuples data structure. Then, after we serialize the document and write it to disk using the highest compression option, we delete it before moving on to the next file to ensure that we are not holding extraneous content in memory:

```python
import pickle
...

    def process(self, fileid):
        """
        For a single file, checks the location on disk to ensure no errors,
        uses +tokenize()+ to perform the preprocessing, and writes transformed
        document as a pickle to target location.
        """
        # Compute the outpath to write the file to.
        target = self.abspath(fileid)
        parent = os.path.dirname(target)

        # Make sure the directory exists
        if not os.path.exists(parent):
            os.makedirs(parent)

        # Make sure that the parent is a directory and not a file
        if not os.path.isdir(parent):
            raise ValueError(
                "Please supply a directory to write preprocessed data to."
            )

        # Create a data structure for the pickle
        document = list(self.tokenize(fileid))

        # Open and serialize the pickle to disk
        with open(target, 'wb') as f:
            pickle.dump(document, f, pickle.HIGHEST_PROTOCOL)

        # Clean up the document
        del document

        # Return the target fileid
        return target
```

Our preprocess() method will be called multiple times by the following trans form() runner:

```
    ...

        def transform(self, fileids=None, categories=None):
            # Make the target directory if it doesn't already exist
            if not os.path.exists(self.target):
                os.makedirs(self.target)

            # Resolve the fileids to start processing
            for fileid in self.fileids(fileids, categories):
                yield self.process(fileid)
```

In Chapter 11, we will explore methods for parallelizing this `transform()` method, which will enable rapid preprocessing and intermediate storage.

Reading the Processed Corpus

Once we have a compressed, preprocessed, pickled corpus, we can quickly access our corpus data without having to reapply tokenization methods or any string parsing—instead directly loading Python data structures and thus saving a significant amount of time and effort.

To read our corpus, we require a `PickledCorpusReader` class that uses `pickle.load()` to quickly retrieve the Python structures from one document at a time. This reader contains all the functionality of the `HTMLCorpusReader` (since it extends it), but since it isn't working with raw text under the hood, it will be many times faster. Here, we override the `HTMLCorpusReader` `docs()` method with one that knows to load documents from pickles:

```
import pickle

PKL_PATTERN = r'(?!\.)[a-z_\s]+/[a-f0-9]+\.pickle'

class PickledCorpusReader(HTMLCorpusReader):

    def __init__(self, root, fileids=PKL_PATTERN, **kwargs):
        if not any(key.startswith('cat_') for key in kwargs.keys()):
            kwargs['cat_pattern'] = CAT_PATTERN
        CategorizedCorpusReader.__init__(self, kwargs)
        CorpusReader.__init__(self, root, fileids)

    def docs(self, fileids=None, categories=None):
        fileids = self.resolve(fileids, categories)
        # Load one pickled document into memory at a time.
        for path in self.abspaths(fileids):
            with open(path, 'rb') as f:
                yield pickle.load(f)
```

Because each document is represented as a Python list of paragraphs, we can implement a `paras()` method as follows:

```
    ...
        def paras(self, fileids=None, categories=None):
            for doc in self.docs(fileids, categories):
                for para in doc:
                    yield para
```

Each paragraph is also a list of sentences, so we can implement the `sents()` method similarly to return all sentences from the requested documents. Note that in this method like in the `docs()` and `paras()` method, the `fileids` and `categories` arguments allow you to specify exactly which documents to fetch information from; if both these arguments are `None` then the entire corpus is returned. A single document can be retrieved by passing its relative path to the corpus root to the `fileids` argument.

```
    ...
        def sents(self, fileids=None, categories=None):
            for para in self.paras(fileids, categories):
                for sent in para:
                    yield sent
```

Sentences are lists of (`token`, `tag`) tuples, so we need two methods to access the ordered set of words that make up a document or documents. The first `tagged()` method returns the token and tag together, the second `words()` method returns only the token in question.

```
    ...
        def tagged(self, fileids=None, categories=None):
            for sent in self.sents(fileids, categories):
                for tagged_token in sent:
                    yield tagged_token

        def words(self, fileids=None, categories=None):
            for tagged in self.tagged(fileids, categories):
                yield tagged[0]
```

When dealing with large corpora, the `PickledCorpusReader` makes things immensely easier. Although preprocessing and accessing data can be parallelized using the `multiprocessing` Python library (which we'll see in Chapter 11), once the corpus is used to build models, a single sequential scan of all the documents before vectorization is required. Though this process can also be parallelized, it is not common to do so because of the experimental nature of exploratory modeling. Utilizing the pickle serialization speeds up the modeling and exploration process significantly!

Conclusion

In this chapter, we learned how to preprocess a corpus by performing segmentation, tokenization, and part-of-speech tagging in preparation for machine learning. In the next chapter, we will establish a common vocabulary for machine learning and discuss the ways in which machine learning on text differs from the kind of statistical programming we have done for previous applications.

First, we will consider how to frame learning problems now that our input data is text, meaning we are working in a very high-dimensional space where our instances are complete documents, and our features can include word-level attributes like vocabulary and token frequency, but also metadata like author, date, and source. Our next step will be to prepare our preprocessed text data for machine learning by encoding it as vectors. We'll weigh several techniques for vector encoding, and discuss how to wrap that encoding process in a pipeline to allow for systematic loading, normalization, and feature extraction. Finally, we'll discuss how to reunite the extracted features to allow for more complex analysis and more sophisticated modeling. These steps will leave us poised to extract meaningful patterns from our corpus and to use those patterns to make predictions about new, as-yet unseen data.

## CHAPTER 4

Text Vectorization and Transformation Pipelines

Machine learning algorithms operate on a numeric feature space, expecting input as a two-dimensional array where rows are instances and columns are features. In order to perform machine learning on text, we need to transform our documents into vector representations such that we can apply numeric machine learning. This process is called *feature extraction* or more simply, *vectorization*, and is an essential first step toward language-aware analysis.

Representing documents numerically gives us the ability to perform meaningful analytics and also creates the *instances* on which machine learning algorithms operate. In text analysis, instances are entire documents or utterances, which can vary in length from quotes or tweets to entire books, but whose vectors are always of a uniform length. Each property of the vector representation is a *feature*. For text, features represent attributes and properties of documents—including its content as well as meta attributes, such as document length, author, source, and publication date. When considered together, the features of a document describe a multidimensional feature space on which machine learning methods can be applied.

For this reason, we must now make a critical shift in how we think about language—from a sequence of words to points that occupy a high-dimensional semantic *space*. Points in space can be close together or far apart, tightly clustered or evenly distributed. Semantic space is therefore mapped in such a way where documents with similar meanings are closer together and those that are different are farther apart. By encoding similarity as distance, we can begin to derive the primary components of documents and draw decision boundaries in our semantic space.

The simplest encoding of semantic space is the *bag-of-words* model, whose primary insight is that meaning and similarity are encoded in vocabulary. For example, the

Wikipedia articles about baseball and Babe Ruth are probably very similar. Not only will many of the same words appear in both, they will not share many words in common with articles about casseroles or quantitative easing. This model, while simple, is extremely effective and forms the starting point for the more complex models we will explore.

In this chapter, we will demonstrate how to use the vectorization process to combine linguistic techniques from NLTK with machine learning techniques in Scikit-Learn and Gensim, creating custom *transformers* that can be used inside repeatable and reusable *pipelines*. By the end of this chapter, we will be ready to engage our preprocessed corpus, transforming documents to model space so that we can begin making predictions.

Words in Space

To vectorize a corpus with a bag-of-words (BOW) approach, we represent every document from the corpus as a vector whose length is equal to the vocabulary of the corpus. We can simplify the computation by sorting token positions of the vector into alphabetical order, as shown in Figure 4-1. Alternatively, we can keep a dictionary that maps tokens to vector positions. Either way, we arrive at a vector mapping of the corpus that enables us to uniquely represent every document.

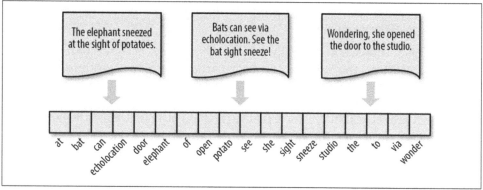

Figure 4-1. Encoding documents as vectors

What should each element in the document vector be? In the next few sections, we will explore several choices, each of which extends or modifies the base bag-of-words model to describe semantic space. We will look at four types of vector encoding—frequency, one-hot, TF–IDF, and distributed representations—and discuss their implementations in Scikit-Learn, Gensim, and NLTK. We'll operate on a small corpus of the three sentences in the example figures.

To set this up, let's create a list of our documents and tokenize them for the proceeding vectorization examples. The tokenize method performs some lightweight normalization, stripping punctuation using the `string.punctuation` character set and setting the text to lowercase. This function also performs some feature reduction using the `SnowballStemmer` to remove affixes such as plurality ("bats" and "bat" are the same token). The examples in the next section will utilize this example corpus and some will use the tokenization method.

```
import nltk
import string

def tokenize(text):
    stem = nltk.stem.SnowballStemmer('english')
    text = text.lower()

    for token in nltk.word_tokenize(text):
        if token in string.punctuation: continue
        yield stem.stem(token)

corpus = [
    "The elephant sneezed at the sight of potatoes.",
    "Bats can see via echolocation. See the bat sight sneeze!",
    "Wondering, she opened the door to the studio.",
]
```

The choice of a specific vectorization technique will be largely driven by the problem space. Similarly, our choice of implementation—whether NLTK, Scikit-Learn, or Gensim—should be dictated by the requirements of the application. For instance, NLTK offers many methods that are especially well-suited to text data, but is a big dependency. Scikit-Learn was not designed with text in mind, but does offer a robust API and many other conveniences (which we'll explore later in this chapter) particularly useful in an applied context. Gensim can serialize dictionaries and references in matrix market format, making it more flexible for multiple platforms. However, unlike Scikit-Learn, Gensim doesn't do any work on behalf of your documents for tokenization or stemming.

For this reason, as we walk through each of the four approaches to encoding, we'll show a few options for implementation—"With NLTK," "In Scikit-Learn," and "The Gensim Way."

Frequency Vectors

The simplest vector encoding model is to simply fill in the vector with the frequency of each word as it appears in the document. In this encoding scheme, each document is represented as the multiset of the tokens that compose it and the value for each word position in the vector is its count. This representation can either be a straight count (integer) encoding as shown in Figure 4-2 or a normalized encoding where each word is weighted by the total number of words in the document.

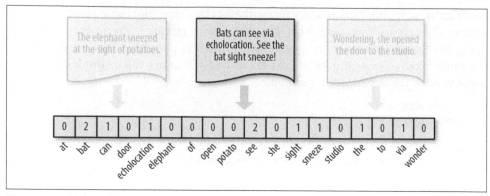

Figure 4-2. Token frequency as vector encoding

With NLTK

NLTK expects features as a `dict` object whose keys are the names of the features and whose values are boolean or numeric. To encode our documents in this way, we'll create a `vectorize` function that creates a dictionary whose keys are the tokens in the document and whose values are the number of times that token appears in the document.

The `defaultdict` object allows us to specify what the dictionary will return for a key that hasn't been assigned to it yet. By setting `defaultdict(int)` we are specifying that a 0 should be returned, thus creating a simple counting dictionary. We can `map` this function to every item in the corpus using the last line of code, creating an iterable of vectorized documents.

```
from collections import defaultdict

def vectorize(doc):
    features = defaultdict(int)
    for token in tokenize(doc):
        features[token] += 1
    return features

vectors = map(vectorize, corpus)
```

In Scikit-Learn

The `CountVectorizer` transformer from the `sklearn.feature_extraction` model has its own internal tokenization and normalization methods. The `fit` method of the vectorizer expects an iterable or list of strings or file objects, and creates a dictionary of the vocabulary on the corpus. When `transform` is called, each individual document is transformed into a sparse array whose index tuple is the row (the document ID) and the token ID from the dictionary, and whose value is the count:

```
from sklearn.feature_extraction.text import CountVectorizer

vectorizer = CountVectorizer()
vectors = vectorizer.fit_transform(corpus)
```

Vectors can become extremely sparse, particularly as vocabularies get larger, which can have a significant impact on the speed and performance of machine learning models. For very large corpora, it is recommended to use the Scikit-Learn `HashingVectorizer`, which uses a hashing trick to find the token string name to feature index mapping. This means it uses very low memory and scales to large datasets as it does not need to store the entire vocabulary and it is faster to pickle and fit since there is no state. However, there is no inverse transform (from vector to text), there can be collisions, and there is no inverse document frequency weighting.

The Gensim way

Gensim's frequency encoder is called doc2bow. To use doc2bow, we first create a Gensim `Dictionary` that maps tokens to indices based on observed order (eliminating the overhead of lexicographic sorting). The dictionary object can be loaded or saved to disk, and implements a doc2bow library that accepts a *pretokenized document* and returns a sparse matrix of (id, count) tuples where the id is the token's id in the dictionary. Because the doc2bow method only takes a single document instance, we use the list comprehension to restore the entire corpus, loading the tokenized documents into memory so we don't exhaust our generator:

```
import gensim

corpus  = [tokenize(doc) for doc in corpus]
id2word = gensim.corpora.Dictionary(corpus)
vectors = [
    id2word.doc2bow(doc) for doc in corpus
]
```

One-Hot Encoding

Because they disregard grammar and the relative position of words in documents, frequency-based encoding methods suffer from the *long tail*, or Zipfian distribution, that characterizes natural language. As a result, tokens that occur very frequently are orders of magnitude more "significant" than other, less frequent ones. This can have a significant impact on some models (e.g., generalized linear models) that expect normally distributed features.

A solution to this problem is *one-hot encoding*, a boolean vector encoding method that marks a particular vector index with a value of true (1) if the token exists in the document and false (0) if it does not. In other words, each element of a one-hot encoded vector reflects either the presence or absence of the token in the described text as shown in Figure 4-3.

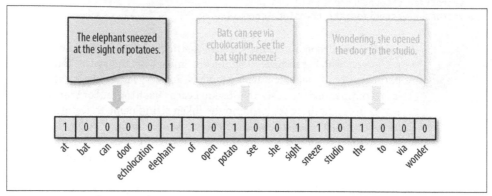

Figure 4-3. One-hot encoding

One-hot encoding reduces the imbalance issue of the distribution of tokens, simplifying a document to its constituent components. This reduction is most effective for very small documents (sentences, tweets) that don't contain very many repeated elements, and is usually applied to models that have very good smoothing properties. One-hot encoding is also commonly used in artificial neural networks, whose activation functions require input to be in the discrete range of [0,1] or [-1,1].

With NLTK

The NLTK implementation of one-hot encoding is a dictionary whose keys are tokens and whose value is True:

```
def vectorize(doc):
    return {
        token: True
        for token in doc
    }

vectors = map(vectorize, corpus)
```

Dictionaries act as simple sparse matrices in the NLTK case because it is not necessary to mark every absent word False. In addition to the boolean dictionary values, it is also acceptable to use an integer value; 1 for present and 0 for absent.

In Scikit-Learn

In Scikit-Learn, one-hot encoding is implemented with the Binarizer transformer in the preprocessing module. The Binarizer takes only numeric data, so the text data must be transformed into a numeric space using the CountVectorizer ahead of one-hot encoding. The Binarizer class uses a threshold value (0 by default) such that all values of the vector that are less than or equal to the threshold are set to zero, while those that are greater than the threshold are set to 1. Therefore, by default, the Binarizer converts all frequency values to 1 while maintaining the zero-valued frequencies.

```
from sklearn.preprocessing import Binarizer

freq   = CountVectorizer()
corpus = freq.fit_transform(corpus)

onehot = Binarizer()
corpus = onehot.fit_transform(corpus.toarray())
```

The corpus.toarray() method is optional; it converts the sparse matrix representation to a dense one. In corpora with large vocabularies, the sparse matrix representation is much better. Note that we could also use CountVectorizer(binary=True) to achieve one-hot encoding in the above, obviating the Binarizer.

 In spite of its name, the OneHotEncoder transformer in the sklearn.preprocessing module is not exactly the right fit for this task. The OneHotEncoder treats each vector component (column) as an independent categorical variable, expanding the dimensionality of the vector for each observed value in each column. In this case, the component (sight, 0) and (sight, 1) would be treated as two categorical dimensions rather than as a single binary encoded vector component.

The Gensim way

While Gensim does not have a specific one-hot encoder, its doc2bow method returns a list of tuples that we can manage on the fly. Extending the code from the Gensim frequency vectorization example in the previous section, we can one-hot encode our vectors with our id2word dictionary. To get our vectors, an inner list comprehension converts the list of tuples returned from the doc2bow method into a list of (token_id, 1) tuples and the outer comprehension applies that converter to all documents in the corpus:

```
corpus  = [tokenize(doc) for doc in corpus]
id2word = gensim.corpora.Dictionary(corpus)
vectors = [
    [(token[0], 1) for token in id2word.doc2bow(doc)]
    for doc in corpus
]
```

One-hot encoding represents similarity and difference at the *document* level, but because all words are rendered equidistant, it is not able to encode per-word similarity. Moreover, because all words are equally distant, *word form* becomes incredibly important; the tokens "trying" and "try" will be equally distant from unrelated tokens like "red" or "bicycle"! Normalizing tokens to a single word class, either through *stemming* or *lemmatization*, which we'll explore later in this chapter, ensures that different forms of tokens that embed plurality, case, gender, cardinality, tense, etc., are treated as single vector components, reducing the feature space and making models more performant.

Term Frequency–Inverse Document Frequency

The bag-of-words representations that we have explored so far only describe a document in a standalone fashion, not taking into account the context of the corpus. A better approach would be to consider the relative frequency or rareness of tokens in the document against their frequency in other documents. The central insight is that meaning is most likely encoded in the more rare terms from a document. For example, in a corpus of sports text, tokens such as "umpire," "base," and "dugout" appear more frequently in documents that discuss baseball, while other tokens that appear frequently throughout the corpus, like "run," "score," and "play," are less important.

TF–IDF, *term frequency–inverse document frequency*, encoding normalizes the frequency of tokens in a document with respect to the rest of the corpus. This encoding approach accentuates terms that are very relevant to a specific instance, as shown in Figure 4-4, where the token studio has a higher relevance to this document since it only appears there.

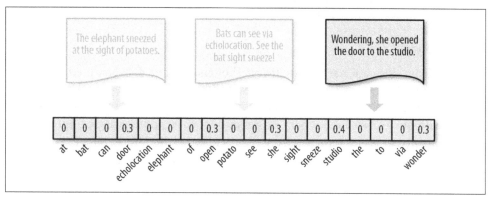

Figure 4-4. TF–IDF encoding

TF–IDF is computed on a per-term basis, such that the relevance of a token to a document is measured by the scaled frequency of the appearance of the term in the document, normalized by the inverse of the scaled frequency of the term in the entire corpus.

Computing TF–IDF

The term frequency of a term given a document, $tf(t, d)$, can be the boolean frequency (as in one-hot encoding, 1 if t occurs in d 0 otherwise), or the count. However, generally both the term frequency and inverse document frequency are scaled logarithmically to prevent bias of longer documents or terms that appear much more frequently relative to other terms: $tf(t, d) = 1 + \log f_{t, d}$.

Similarly, the inverse document frequency of a term given the set of documents can be logarithmically scaled as follows: $idf(t, D) = \log 1 + \frac{N}{n_t}$, where N is the number of documents and n_t is the number of occurrences of the term t in all documents. TF–IDF is then computed completely as $tfidf(t, d, D) = tf(t, d) \cdot idf(t, D)$.

Because the ratio of the idf log function is greater or equal to 1, the TF–IDF score is always greater than or equal to zero. We interpret the score to mean that the closer the TF–IDF score of a term is to 1, the more informative that term is to that document. The closer the score is to zero, the less informative that term is.

With NLTK

To vectorize text in this way with NLTK, we use the `TextCollection` class, a wrapper for a list of texts or a corpus consisting of one or more texts. This class provides support for counting, concordancing, collocation discovery, and more importantly, computing `tf_idf`.

Because TF–IDF requires the entire corpus, our new version of `vectorize` does not accept a single document, but rather all documents. After applying our tokenization function and creating the text collection, the function goes through each document in the corpus and yields a dictionary whose keys are the terms and whose values are the TF–IDF score for the term in that particular document.

```
from nltk.text import TextCollection

def vectorize(corpus):
    corpus = [tokenize(doc) for doc in corpus]
    texts  = TextCollection(corpus)

    for doc in corpus:
        yield {
            term: texts.tf_idf(term, doc)
            for term in doc
        }
```

In Scikit-Learn

Scikit-Learn provides a transformer called the `TfidfVectorizer` in the module called `feature_extraction.text` for vectorizing documents with TF–IDF scores. Under the hood, the `TfidfVectorizer` uses the `CountVectorizer` estimator we used to produce the bag-of-words encoding to count occurrences of tokens, followed by a `Tfidf Transformer`, which normalizes these occurrence counts by the inverse document frequency.

The input for a `TfidfVectorizer` is expected to be a sequence of filenames, file-like objects, or strings that contain a collection of raw documents, similar to that of the `CountVectorizer`. As a result, a default tokenization and preprocessing method is applied unless other functions are specified. The vectorizer returns a sparse matrix representation in the form of `((doc, term), tfidf)` where each key is a document and term pair and the value is the TF–IDF score.

```
from sklearn.feature_extraction.text import TfidfVectorizer

tfidf  = TfidfVectorizer()
corpus = tfidf.fit_transform(corpus)
```

The Gensim way

In Gensim, the `TfidfModel` data structure is similar to the `Dictionary` object in that it stores a mapping of terms and their vector positions in the order they are observed, but additionally stores the corpus frequency of those terms so it can vectorize documents on demand. As before, Gensim allows us to apply our own tokenization method, expecting a corpus that is a list of lists of tokens. We first construct the lexicon and use it to instantiate the `TfidfModel`, which computes the normalized inverse document frequency. We can then fetch the TF–IDF representation for each vector using a `getitem`, dictionary-like syntax, after applying the `doc2bow` method to each document using the lexicon.

```
corpus  = [tokenize(doc) for doc in corpus]
lexicon = gensim.corpora.Dictionary(corpus)
tfidf   = gensim.models.TfidfModel(dictionary=lexicon, normalize=True)
vectors = [tfidf[lexicon.doc2bow(doc)] for doc in corpus]
```

Gensim provides helper functionality to write dictionaries and models to disk in a compact format, meaning you can conveniently save both the TF–IDF model and the lexicon to disk in order to load them later to vectorize new documents. It is possible (though slightly more work) to achieve the same result by using the `pickle` module in combination with Scikit-Learn. To save a Gensim model to disk:

```
lexicon.save_as_text('lexicon.txt', sort_by_word=True)
tfidf.save('tfidf.pkl')
```

This will save the lexicon as a text-delimited text file, sorted lexicographically, and the TF–IDF model as a pickled sparse matrix. Note that the `Dictionary` object can also be saved more compactly in a binary format using its `save` method, but `save_as_text` allows easy inspection of the dictionary for later work. To load the models from disk:

```
lexicon = gensim.corpora.Dictionary.load_from_text('lexicon.txt')
tfidf = gensim.models.TfidfModel.load('tfidf.pkl')
```

One benefit of TF–IDF is that it naturally addresses the problem of *stopwords*, those words most likely to appear in all documents in the corpus (e.g., "a," "the," "of", etc.), and thus will accrue very small weights under this encoding scheme. This biases the TF–IDF model toward moderately rare words. As a result TF–IDF is widely used for bag-of-words models, and is an excellent starting point for most text analytics.

Distributed Representation

While frequency, one-hot, and TF–IDF encoding enable us to put documents into vector space, it is often useful to also encode the similarities between documents in the context of that same vector space. Unfortunately, these vectorization methods produce document vectors with non-negative elements, which means we won't be able to compare documents that don't share terms (because two vectors with a cosine distance of 1 will be considered far apart, even if they are semantically similar).

When document similarity is important in the context of an application, we instead encode text along a continuous scale with a distributed representation, as shown in Figure 4-5. This means that the resulting document vector is not a simple mapping from token position to token score. Instead, the document is represented in a feature space that has been embedded to represent word similarity. The complexity of this space (and the resulting vector length) is the product of how the mapping to that representation is learned. The complexity of this space (and the resulting vector length) is the product of how that representation is trained and not directly tied to the document itself.

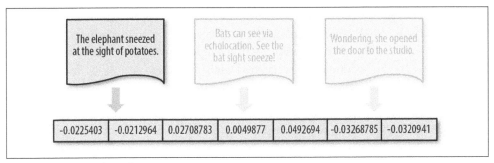

Figure 4-5. Distributed representation

Word2vec, created by a team of researchers at Google led by Tomáš Mikolov, implements a word embedding model that enables us to create these kinds of distributed representations. The word2vec algorithm trains word representations based on either a continuous bag-of-words (CBOW) or skip-gram model, such that words are embedded in space along with similar words based on their context. For example, Gensim's implementation uses a feedforward network.

The *doc2vec*[1] algorithm is an extension of *word2vec*. It proposes a *paragraph vector*— an unsupervised algorithm that learns fixed-length feature representations from variable length documents. This representation attempts to inherit the semantic properties of words such that "red" and "colorful" are more similar to each other than they are to "river" or "governance." Moreover, the paragraph vector takes into consideration the ordering of words within a narrow context, similar to an *n*-gram model. The combined result is much more effective than a bag-of-words or bag-of-*n*-grams model because it generalizes better and has a lower dimensionality but still is of a fixed length so it can be used in common machine learning algorithms.

The Gensim way

Neither NLTK nor Scikit-Learn provide implementations of these kinds of word embeddings. Gensim's implementation allows users to train both word2vec and doc2vec models on custom corpora and also conveniently comes with a model that is pretrained on the Google news corpus.

 To use Gensim's pretrained models, you'll need to download the model bin file, which clocks in at 1.5 GB. For applications that require extremely lightweight dependencies (e.g., if they have to run on an AWS lambda instance), this may not be practicable.

We can train our own model as follows. First, we use a list comprehension to load our corpus into memory. (Gensim supports streaming, but this will enable us to avoid exhausting the generator.) Next, we create a list of `TaggedDocument` objects, which extend the `LabeledSentence`, and in turn the distributed representation of word2vec. `TaggedDocument` objects consist of *words* and *tags*. We can instantiate the tagged document with the list of tokens along with a single tag, one that uniquely identifies the instance. In this example, we've labeled each document as `"d{}".format(idx)`, e.g. `d0`, `d1`, `d2` and so forth.

Once we have a list of tagged documents, we instantiate the `Doc2Vec` model and specify the size of the vector as well as the minimum count, which ignores all tokens that

---

1 Quoc V. Le and Tomas Mikolov, *Distributed Representations of Sentences and Documents*, (2014) *http://bit.ly/ 2GJBHjZ*

have a frequency less than that number. The `size` parameter is usually not as low a dimensionality as 5; we selected such a small number for demonstration purposes only. We also set the `min_count` parameter to zero to ensure we consider all tokens, but generally this is set between 3 and 5, depending on how much information the model needs to capture. Once instantiated, an unsupervised neural network is trained to learn the vector representations, which can then be accessed via the `docvecs` property.

```
from gensim.models.doc2vec import TaggedDocument, Doc2Vec

corpus = [list(tokenize(doc)) for doc in corpus]
corpus = [
    TaggedDocument(words, ['d{}'.format(idx)])
    for idx, words in enumerate(corpus)
]

model = Doc2Vec(corpus, size=5, min_count=0)
print(model.docvecs[0])
# [ 0.01797447 -0.01509272  0.0731937   0.06814702 -0.0846546 ]
```

Distributed representations will dramatically improve results over TF–IDF models when used correctly. The model itself can be saved to disk and retrained in an active fashion, making it extremely flexible for a variety of use cases. However, on larger corpora, training can be slow and memory intensive, and it might not be as good as a TF–IDF model with Principal Component Analysis (PCA) or Singular Value Decomposition (SVD) applied to reduce the feature space. In the end, however, this representation is breakthrough work that has led to a dramatic improvement in text processing capabilities of data products in recent years.

Again, the choice of vectorization technique (as well as the library implementation) tend to be use case- and application-specific, as summarized in Table 4-1.

Table 4-1. Overview of text vectorization methods

Vectorization Method	Function	Good For	Considerations
Frequency	Counts term frequencies	Bayesian models	Most frequent words not always most informative
One-Hot Encoding	Binarizes term occurrence (0, 1)	Neural networks	All words equidistant, so normalization extra important
TF–IDF	Normalizes term frequencies across documents	General purpose	Moderately frequent terms may not be representative of document topics
Distributed Representations	Context-based, continuous term similarity encoding	Modeling more complex relationships	Performance intensive; difficult to scale without additional tools (e.g., Tensorflow)

Later in this chapter we will explore the Scikit-Learn `Pipeline` object, which enables us to streamline vectorization together with later modeling phrases. As such, we often prefer to use vectorizers that conform to the Scikit-Learn API. In the next section, we will discuss how the API is organized and demonstrate how to integrate vectorization into a complete pipeline to construct the core of a fully operational (and customizable!) textual machine learning application.

The Scikit-Learn API

Scikit-Learn is an extension of SciPy (a scikit) whose primary purpose is to provide machine learning algorithms as well as the tools and utilities required to engage in successful modeling. Its primary contribution is an "API for machine learning" that exposes the implementations of a wide array of model families into a single, user-friendly interface. The result is that Scikit-Learn can be used to simultaneously train a staggering variety of models, evaluate and compare them, and then utilize the fitted model to make predictions on new data. Because Scikit-Learn provides a standardized API, this can be done with little effort and models can be prototyped and evaluated by simply swapping out a few lines of code.

The BaseEstimator Interface

The API itself is object-oriented and describes a hierarchy of interfaces for different machine learning tasks. The root of the hierarchy is an `Estimator`, broadly any object that can learn from data. The primary `Estimator` objects implement classifiers, regressors, or clustering algorithms. However, they can also include a wide array of data manipulation, from dimensionality reduction to feature extraction from raw data. The `Estimator` essentially serves as an interface, and classes that implement `Estimator` functionality must have two methods—`fit` and `predict`—as shown here:

```python
from sklearn.base import BaseEstimator

class Estimator(BaseEstimator):

    def fit(self, X, y=None):
        """
        Accept input data, X, and optional target data, y. Returns self.
        """
        return self

    def predict(self, X):
        """
        Accept input data, X and return a vector of predictions for each row.
        """
        return yhat
```

The `Estimator.fit` method sets the state of the estimator based on the training data, X and y. The training data X is expected to be matrix-like—for example, a two-dimensional NumPy array of shape (n_samples, n_features) or a Pandas `DataFrame` whose rows are the instances and whose columns are the features. Supervised estimators are also fit with a one-dimensional NumPy array, y, that holds the correct labels. The fitting process modifies the internal state of the estimator such that it is ready or able to make predictions. This state is stored in instance variables that are usually postfixed with an underscore (e.g., `Estimator.coefs_`). Because this method modifies an internal state, it returns `self` so the method can be chained.

The `Estimator.predict` method creates predictions using the internal, fitted state of the model on the new data, X. The input for the method must have the same number of columns as the training data passed to `fit`, and can have as many rows as predictions are required. This method returns a vector, yhat, which contains the predictions for each row in the input data.

 Extending Scikit-Learn's `BaseEstimator` automatically gives the Estimator a `fit_predict` method, which allows you to combine `fit` and `predict` in one simple call.

Estimator objects have parameters (also called hyperparameters) that define how the fitting process is conducted. These parameters are set when the `Estimator` is instantiated (and if not specified, they are set to reasonable defaults), and can be modified with the `get_param` and `set_param` methods that are also available from the `BaseEstimator` super class.

We engage the Scikit-Learn API by specifying the package and type of the estimator. Here we select the Naive Bayes model family, and a specific member of the family, a multinomial model (which is suitable for text classification). The model is defined when the class is instantiated and hyperparameters are passed in. Here we pass an alpha parameter that is used for additive smoothing, as well as prior probabilities for each of our two classes. The model is trained on specific data (documents and labels) and at that point becomes a fitted model. This basic usage is the same for every model (`Estimator`) in Scikit-Learn, from random forest decision tree ensembles to logistic regressions and beyond.

```
from sklearn.naive_bayes import MultinomialNB

model = MultinomialNB(alpha=0.0, class_prior=[0.4, 0.6])
model.fit(documents, labels)
```

Extending TransformerMixin

Scikit-Learn also specifies utilities for performing machine learning in a repeatable fashion. We could not discuss Scikit-Learn without also discussing the `Transformer` interface. A `Transformer` is a special type of `Estimator` that creates a new dataset from an old one based on rules that it has learned from the fitting process. The interface is as follows:

```
from sklearn.base import TransformerMixin

class Transfomer(BaseEstimator, TransformerMixin):

    def fit(self, X, y=None):
        """
        Learn how to transform data based on input data, X.
        """
        return self

    def transform(self, X):
        """
        Transform X into a new dataset, Xprime and return it.
        """
        return Xprime
```

The `Transformer.transform` method takes a dataset and returns a new dataset, X`, with new values based on the transformation process. There are several transformers included in Scikit-Learn, including transformers to normalize or scale features, handle missing values (imputation), perform dimensionality reduction, extract or select features, or perform mappings from one feature space to another.

Although both NLTK, Gensim, and even newer text analytics libraries like SpaCy have their own internal APIs and learning mechanisms, the scope and comprehensiveness of Scikit-Learn models and methodologies for machine learning make it an essential part of the modeling workflow. As a result, we propose to use the API to create our own `Transformer` and `Estimator` objects that implement methods from NLTK and Gensim. For example, we can create topic modeling estimators that wrap Gensim's LDA and LSA models (which are not currently included in Scikit-Learn) or create transformers that utilize NLTK's part-of-speech tagging and named entity chunking methods.

Creating a custom Gensim vectorization transformer

Gensim vectorization techniques are an interesting case study because Gensim corpora can be saved and loaded from disk in such a way as to remain decoupled from the pipeline. However, it is possible to build a custom transformer that uses Gensim vectorization. Our `GensimVectorizer` transformer will wrap a Gensim `Dictionary` object generated during `fit()` and whose `doc2bow` method is used during

---

transform(). The Dictionary object (like the TfidfModel) can be saved and loaded from disk, so our transformer utilizes that methodology by taking a path on instantiation. If a file exists at that path, it is loaded immediately. Additionally, a save() method allows us to write our Dictionary to disk, which we can do in fit().

The fit() method constructs the Dictionary object by passing already tokenized and normalized documents to the Dictionary constructor. The Dictionary is then immediately saved to disk so that the transformer can be loaded without requiring a refit. The transform() method uses the Dictionary.doc2bow method, which returns a *sparse* representation of the document as a list of (token_id, frequency) tuples. This representation can present challenges with Scikit-Learn, however, so we utilize a Gensim helper function, sparse2full, to convert the sparse representation into a NumPy array.

```python
import os
from gensim.corpora import Dictionary
from gensim.matutils import sparse2full

class GensimVectorizer(BaseEstimator, TransformerMixin):

    def __init__(self, path=None):
        self.path = path
        self.id2word = None
        self.load()

    def load(self):
        if os.path.exists(self.path):
            self.id2word = Dictionary.load(self.path)

    def save(self):
        self.id2word.save(self.path)

    def fit(self, documents, labels=None):
        self.id2word = Dictionary(documents)
        self.save()
            return self

    def transform(self, documents):
        for document in documents:
            docvec = self.id2word.doc2bow(document)
            yield sparse2full(docvec, len(self.id2word))
```

It is easy to see how the vectorization methodologies that we discussed earlier in the chapter can be wrapped by Scikit-Learn transformers. This gives us more flexibility in the approaches we take, while still allowing us to leverage the machine learning utilities in each library. We will leave it to the reader to extend this example and investigate TF–IDF and distributed representation transformers that are implemented in the same fashion.

Creating a custom text normalization transformer

Many model families suffer from "the curse of dimensionality"; as the feature space increases in dimensions, the data becomes more sparse and less informative to the underlying decision space. Text normalization reduces the number of dimensions, decreasing sparsity. Besides the simple filtering of tokens (removing punctuation and stopwords), there are two primary methods for text normalization: *stemming* and *lemmatization*.

Stemming uses a series of rules (or a model) to slice a string to a smaller substring. The goal is to remove word affixes (particularly suffixes) that modify meaning. For example, removing an `'s'` or `'es'`, which generally indicates plurality in Latin languages. Lemmatization, on the other hand, uses a dictionary to look up every token and returns the canonical "head" word in the dictionary, called a lemma. Because it is looking up tokens from a ground truth, it can handle irregular cases as well as handle tokens with different parts of speech. For example, the verb `'gardening'` should be lemmatized to `'to garden'`, while the nouns `'garden'` and `'gardener'` are both different lemmas. Stemming would capture all of these tokens into a single `'garden'` token.

Stemming and lemmatization have their advantages and disadvantages. Because it only requires us to splice word strings, stemming is faster. Lemmatization, on the other hand, requires a lookup to a dictionary or database, and uses part-of-speech tags to identify a word's root lemma, making it noticeably slower than stemming, but also more effective.

To perform text normalization in a systematic fashion, we will write a custom transformer that puts these pieces together. Our `TextNormalizer` class takes as input a language that is used to load the correct stopwords from the NLTK corpus. We could also customize the `TextNormalizer` to allow uses to choose between stemming and lemmatization, and pass the language into the `SnowballStemmer`. For filtering extraneous tokens, we create two methods. The first, `is_punct()`, checks if every character in the token has a Unicode category that starts with `'P'` (for punctuation); the second, `is_stopword()` determines if the token is in our set of stopwords.

```
import unicodedata
from sklearn.base import BaseEstimator, TransformerMixin

class TextNormalizer(BaseEstimator, TransformerMixin):

    def __init__(self, language='english'):
        self.stopwords  = set(nltk.corpus.stopwords.words(language))
        self.lemmatizer = WordNetLemmatizer()

    def is_punct(self, token):
        return all(
            unicodedata.category(char).startswith('P') for char in token
```

```
    )

    def is_stopword(self, token):
        return token.lower() in self.stopwords
```

We can then add a `normalize()` method that takes a single document composed of a list of paragraphs, which are lists of sentences, which are lists of (`token`, `tag`) tuples —the data format that we preprocessed raw HTML to in Chapter 3.

```
    def normalize(self, document):
        return [
            self.lemmatize(token, tag).lower()
            for paragraph in document
            for sentence in paragraph
            for (token, tag) in sentence
            if not self.is_punct(token) and not self.is_stopword(token)
        ]
```

This method applies the filtering functions to remove unwanted tokens and then lemmatizes them. The `lemmatize()` method first converts the Penn Treebank part-of-speech tags that are the default tag set in the `nltk.pos_tag` function to WordNet tags, selecting nouns by default.

```
    def lemmatize(self, token, pos_tag):
        tag = {
            'N': wn.NOUN,
            'V': wn.VERB,
            'R': wn.ADV,
            'J': wn.ADJ
        }.get(pos_tag[0], wn.NOUN)

        return self.lemmatizer.lemmatize(token, tag)
```

Finally, we must add the `Transformer` interface, allowing us to add this class to a Scikit-Learn pipeline, which we'll explore in the next section:

```
    def fit(self, X, y=None):
        return self

    def transform(self, documents):
        for document in documents:
            yield self.normalize(document)
```

Note that text normalization is only one methodology, and also utilizes NLTK very heavily, which may add unnecessary overhead to your application. Other options could include removing tokens that appear above or below a particular count threshold or removing stopwords and then only selecting the first five to ten thousand most common words. Yet another option is simply computing the cumulative frequency and only selecting words that contain 10%–50% of the cumulative frequency distribution. These methods would allow us to ignore both the very low frequency *hapaxes* (terms that appear only once) and the most common words, enabling us to identify the most potentially predictive terms in the corpus.

 The act of text normalization should be optional and applied carefully because the operation is destructive in that it removes information. Case, punctuation, stopwords, and varying word constructions are all critical to understanding language. Some models may require indicators such as case. For example, a named entity recognition classifier, because in English, proper nouns are capitalized.

An alternative approach is to perform dimensionality reduction with Principal Component Analysis (PCA) or Singular Value Decomposition (SVD), to reduce the feature space to a specific dimensionality (e.g., five or ten thousand dimensions) based on word frequency. These transformers would have to be applied following a vectorizer transformer, and would have the effect of merging together words that are similar into the same vector space.

Pipelines

The machine learning process often combines a series of transformers on raw data, transforming the dataset each step of the way until it is passed to the fit method of a final estimator. But if we don't vectorize our documents in the same exact manner, we will end up with wrong or, at the very least, unintelligible results. The Scikit-Learn `Pipeline` object is the solution to this dilemma.

`Pipeline` objects enable us to integrate a series of transformers that combine normalization, vectorization, and feature analysis into a single, well-defined mechanism. As shown in Figure 4-6, `Pipeline` objects move data from a loader (an object that will wrap our `CorpusReader` from Chapter 2) into feature extraction mechanisms to finally an estimator object that implements our predictive models. Pipelines are directed acyclic graphs (DAGs) that can be simple linear chains of transformers to arbitrarily complex branching and joining paths.

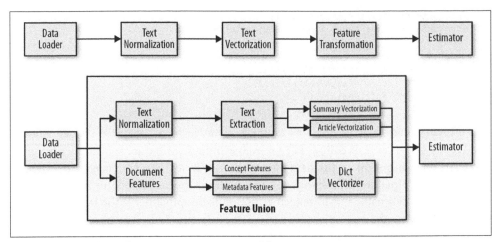

Figure 4-6. Pipelines for text vectorization and feature extraction

Pipeline Basics

The purpose of a `Pipeline` is to chain together multiple estimators representing a fixed sequence of steps into a single unit. All estimators in the pipeline, except the last one, must be transformers—that is, implement the `transform` method, while the last estimator can be of any type, including predictive estimators. Pipelines provide convenience; `fit` and `transform` can be called for single inputs across multiple objects at once. Pipelines also provide a single interface for grid search of multiple estimators at once. Most importantly, pipelines provide *operationalization* of text models by coupling a vectorization methodology with a predictive model.

Pipelines are constructed by describing a list of (`key, value`) pairs where the `key` is a string that names the step and the `value` is the estimator object. Pipelines can be created either by using the `make_pipeline` helper function, which automatically determines the names of the steps, or by specifying them directly. Generally, it is better to specify the steps directly to provide good user documentation, whereas `make_pipe line` is used more often for automatic pipeline construction.

`Pipeline` objects are a Scikit-Learn specific utility, but they are also the critical integration point with NLTK and Gensim. Here is an example that joins the `TextNormal izer` and `GensimVectorizer` we created in the last section together in advance of a Bayesian model. By using the `Transformer` API as discussed earlier in the chapter, we can use `TextNormalizer` to wrap NLTK `CorpusReader` objects and perform preprocessing and linguistic feature extraction. Our `GensimVectorizer` is responsible for vectorization, and Scikit-Learn is responsible for the integration via Pipelines, utilities like cross-validation, and the many models we will use, from Naive Bayes to Logistic Regression.

```
from sklearn.pipeline import Pipeline
from sklearn.naive_bayes import MultinomialNB

model = Pipeline([
    ('normalizer', TextNormalizer()),
    ('vectorizer', GensimVectorizer()),
    ('bayes', MultinomialNB()),
])
```

The Pipeline can then be used as a single instance of a complete model. Calling `model.fit` is the same as calling `fit` on each estimator in sequence, transforming the input and passing it on to the next step. Other methods like `fit_transform` behave similarly. The pipeline will also have all the methods the last estimator in the pipeline has. If the last estimator is a transformer, so too is the pipeline. If the last estimator is a classifier, as in the example above, then the pipeline will also have `predict` and `score` methods so that the entire model can be used as a classifier.

The estimators in the pipeline are stored as a list, and can be accessed by index. For example, `model.steps[1]` returns the tuple `('vectorizer', GensimVectorizer (path=None))`. However, common usage is to identify estimators by their names using the `named_steps` dictionary property of the `Pipeline` object. The easiest way to access the predictive model is to use `model.named_steps["bayes"]` and fetch the estimator directly.

Grid Search for Hyperparameter Optimization

In Chapter 5, we will talk more about model tuning and iteration, but for now we'll simply introduce an extension of the `Pipeline`, `GridSearch`, which is useful for hyperparameter optimization. Grid search can be implemented to modify the parameters of all estimators in the Pipeline as though it were a single object. In order to access the attributes of estimators, you would use the `set_params` or `get_params` pipeline methods with a dunderscore representation of the estimator and parameter names as follows: `estimator__parameter`.

Let's say that we want to one-hot encode only the terms that appear at least three times in the corpus; we could modify the `Binarizer` as follows:

```
model.set_params(onehot__threshold=3.0)
```

Using this principle, we could execute a grid search by defining the search parameters grid using the dunderscore parameter syntax. Consider the following grid search to determine the best one-hot encoded Bayesian text classification model:

```
from sklearn.model_selection import GridSearchCV

search = GridSearchCV(model, param_grid={
    'count__analyzer': ['word', 'char', 'char_wb'],
    'count__ngram_range': [(1,1), (1,2), (1,3), (1,4), (1,5), (2,3)],
    'onehot__threshold': [0.0, 1.0, 2.0, 3.0],
    'bayes__alpha': [0.0, 1.0],
})
```

The search nominates three possibilities for the `CountVectorizer` analyzer parameter (creating *n*-grams on word boundaries, character boundaries, or only on characters that are between word boundaries), and several possibilities for the *n*-gram ranges to tokenize against. We also specify the threshold for binarization, meaning that the *n*-gram has to appear a certain number of times before it's included in the model. Finally the search specifies two smoothing parameters (the `bayes_alpha` parameter): either no smoothing (add 0.0) or Laplacian smoothing (add 1.0).

The grid search will instantiate a pipeline of our model for each combination of features, then use cross-validation to score the model and select the best combination of features (in this case, the combination that maximizes the F1 score).

Enriching Feature Extraction with Feature Unions

Pipelines do not have to be simple linear sequences of steps; in fact, they can be arbitrarily complex through the implementation of *feature unions*. The `FeatureUnion` object combines several transformer objects into a new, single transformer similar to the `Pipline` object. However, instead of fitting and transforming data in sequence through each transformer, they are instead evaluated independently and the results are *concatenated* into a composite vector.

Consider the example shown in Figure 4-7. We might imagine an HTML parser transformer that uses BeautifulSoup or an XML library to parse the HTML and return the body of each document. We then perform a feature engineering step, where entities and keyphrases are each extracted from the documents and the results passed into the feature union. Using frequency encoding on the entities is more sensible since they are relatively small, but TF–IDF makes more sense for the keyphrases. The feature union then concatenates the two resulting vectors such that our decision space ahead of the logistic regression separates word dimensions in the title from word dimensions in the body.

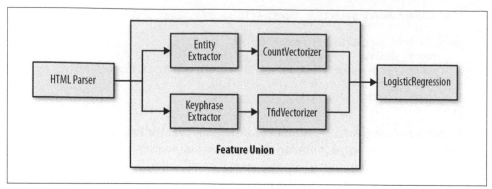

Figure 4-7. Feature unions for branching vectorization

FeatureUnion objects are similarly instantiated as Pipeline objects with a list of (key, value) pairs where the key is the name of the transformer, and the value is the transformer object. There is also a make_union helper function that can automatically determine names and is used in a similar fashion to the make_pipeline helper function—for automatic or generated pipelines. Estimator parameters can also be accessed in the same fashion, and to implement a search on a feature union, simply nest the dunderscore for each transformer in the feature union.

Given the unimplemented EntityExtractor and KeyphraseExtractor transformers mentioned above, we can construct our pipeline as follows:

```
from sklearn.pipeline import FeatureUnion
from sklearn.linear_model import LogisticRegression

model = Pipeline([
    ('parser', HTMLParser()),
    ('text_union', FeatureUnion(
        transformer_list = [
            ('entity_feature', Pipeline([
                ('entity_extractor', EntityExtractor()),
                ('entity_vect', CountVectorizer()),
            ])),
            ('keyphrase_feature', Pipeline([
                ('keyphrase_extractor', KeyphraseExtractor()),
                ('keyphrase_vect', TfidfVectorizer()),
            ])),
        ],
        transformer_weights= {
            'entity_feature': 0.6,
            'keyphrase_feature': 0.2,
        }
    )),
    ('clf', LogisticRegression()),
])
```

Note that the `HTMLParser`, `EntityExtractor` and `KeyphraseExtractor` objects are currently unimplemented but are used for illustration. The feature union is fit in sequence with respect to the rest of the pipeline, but each transformer within the feature union is fit *independently*, meaning that each transformer sees the same data as the input to the feature union. During transformation, each transformer is applied in parallel and the vectors that they output are concatenated together into a single larger vector, which can be optionally weighted, as shown in Figure 4-8.

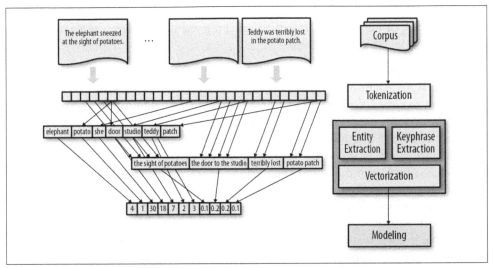

Figure 4-8. Feature extraction and union

In this example, we are weighting the `entity_feature` transformer more than the `keyphrase_feature` transformer. Using combinations of custom transformers, feature unions, and pipelines, it is possible to define incredibly rich feature extraction and transformation in a repeatable fashion. By collecting our methodology into a single sequence, we can repeatably apply the transformations, particularly on new documents when we want to make predictions in a production environment.

Conclusion

In this chapter, we conducted a whirlwind overview of vectorization techniques and began to consider their use cases for different kinds of data and different machine learning algorithms. In practice, it is best to select an encoding scheme based on the problem at hand; certain methods substantially outperform others for certain tasks.

For example, for recurrent neural network models it is often better to use one-hot encoding, but to divide the text space one might create a combined vector for the document summary, document header, body, etc. Frequency encoding should be normalized, but different types of frequency encoding can benefit probabilistic methods like Bayesian models. TF–IDF is an excellent general-purpose encoding and is often used first in modeling, but can also cover a lot of sins. Distributed representations are the new hotness, but are performance intensive and difficult to scale.

Bag-of-words models have a very high dimensionality, meaning the space is extremely sparse, leading to difficulty generalizing the data space. Word order, grammar, and other structural features are natively lost, and it is difficult to add knowledge (e.g., lexical resources, ontological encodings) to the learning process. Local encodings (e.g., nondistributed representations) require a lot of samples, which could lead to overtraining or underfitting, but distributed representations are complex and add a layer of "representational mysticism."

Ultimately, much of the work for language-aware applications comes from domain-specific feature analysis, not just simple vectorization. In the final section of this chapter we explored the use of `FeatureUnion` and `Pipeline` objects to create meaningful extraction methodologies by combining transformers. As we move forward, the practice of building pipelines of transformers and estimators will continue to be our primary mechanism of performing machine learning. In Chapter 5 we will explore classification models and applications, then in Chapter 6 we will take a look at clustering models, often called *topic modeling* in text analysis. In Chapter 7, we will explore some more complex methods for feature analysis and feature exploration that will assist in finetuning our vector-based models to achieve better results. Nonetheless, simple models that only consider word frequencies are often very successful. In our experience, a pure bag-of-words model works about 85% of the time!

## CHAPTER 5

Classification for Text Analysis

Imagine you were working at one of the large email providers in the late 1990s, handling increasingly large numbers of emails from servers all over the world. The prevalence and economy of email has made it a primary form of communication, and business is booming. Unfortunately, so is the rise of junk email. At the more harmless end of the spectrum, there are advertisements for internet products, which are nonetheless sent in deluges that severely tax your servers. Moreover, because email is unregulated, harmful messages are becoming increasingly common—more and more emails contain false advertising, pyramid schemes, and fake investments. What to do?

You might begin by blacklisting the email addresses or IP addresses of spammers or searching for keywords that might indicate that an email is spam. Unfortunately, since it is relatively easy to get a new email or IP address, spammers quickly circumvent even your most well-curated blacklists. Even worse, you're finding that the blacklists and whitelists do not do a good job of ensuring that valid email gets through, and users aren't happy. You need something better, a flexible and stochastic solution that will work at scale: enter machine learning.

Fast-forward a few decades, and spam filtering is the most common and possibly most commercially successful text classification model. The central innovation was that the content of an email is the primary determination of whether or not the email is spam. It is not simply the presence of the terms `"viagra"` or `"Nigerian prince"`, but their context, frequency, and misspellings. The collection of a corpus of *both* spam and ham emails allowed the construction of a Naive Bayes model—a model that uses a uniform prior to predict the probabilities of a word's presence in both spam and ham emails based on its frequency.

In this chapter we will start by exploring several real-world classification examples to see how to formulate these problems for applications. We will then explore the classifier workflow and extend the vectorization methodologies discussed in Chapter 4 to create modeling pipelines for topic classification using the Baleen corpus introduced in Chapter 2. Finally, we will begin to explore the next steps of our workflow, which build directly atop the foundational data layer we have established thus far. We will describe these next steps in the context of the "The model selection triple" on page 7 introduced in Chapter 1.

Text Classification

Classification is a primary form of text analysis and is widely used in a variety of domains and applications. The premise of classification is simple: given a categorical target variable, learn patterns that exist between instances composed of independent variables and their relationship to the target. Because the target is given ahead of time, classification is said to be *supervised* machine learning because a model can be trained to minimize error between predicted and actual categories in the training data. Once a classification model is fit, it assigns categorical labels to new instances based on the patterns detected during training.

This simple premise gives the opportunity for a huge number of possible applications, so long as the application problem can be formulated to identify either a yes/no (binary classification) or discrete buckets (multiclass classification). The most difficult part of applied text analytics is the curation and collection of a domain-specific corpus to build models upon. The second most difficult part is composing an analytical solution for an application-specific problem.

Identifying Classification Problems

It may not necessarily be immediately obvious how to compose application problems into classification solutions, but it helps to understand that most language-aware data products are actually composed of multiple models and submodels. For example, a recommendation system such as the one shown in Figure 5-1 may have classifiers that identify a product's target age (e.g., a youth versus an adult bicycle), gender (women's versus men's clothing), or category (e.g., electronics versus movies) by classifying the product's description or other attributes. Product reviews may then be classified to detect quality or to determine similar products. These classes then may be used as features in downstream models or may be used to create partitions for ensemble models.

The combination of multiple classifiers has been incredibly powerful, particularly in recent years, and for several types of text classification applications. From email clients that incorporate spam filtering to applications that can predict political bias of news articles, the uses for classification are almost as numerous as the number of categories that we assign to things—and humans are excellent taxonomists. Newer applications combine text and image learning to enhance newer forms of media—from automatic captioning to scene recognition, all of which leverage classification techniques.

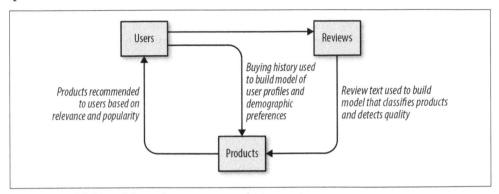

Figure 5-1. Multimodel product recommendation engine

The spam classification example has recently been displaced by a new vogue: sentiment analysis. Sentiment analysis models attempt to predict positive ("I love writing Python code") or negative ("I hate it when people repeat themselves") sentiment based on content and has gained significant popularity thanks to the expressiveness of social media. Because companies are involved in a more general dialogue where they do not control the information channel (such as reviews of their products and services), there is a belief that sentiment analysis can assist with targeted customer support or even model corporate performance. However, as we saw briefly in Chapter 1 and which we'll explore more fully in Chapter 12, the complexities and nuances inherent in language context make sentiment analysis less straightforward than spam detection.

If sentiment can be explored through textual content, what about other external labels, political bias, for example? Recent work has used expressions in the American presidential campaign to create models that can detect partisan polarity (or its absence). An interesting result from these efforts is that the use of per-user models (trained on specific users' data) provides more effective context than a global, generalizable model (trained on data pooled from many users).[1] Another real-world application is the automatic topic classification of text: by using blogs that publish content in a single domain (e.g., a cooking blog doesn't generally discuss cinema), it is possible to create classifiers that can detect topics in uncategorized sources such as news articles.

So what do all these examples have in common? First, a unique external target defined by the application: e.g., what do we want to measure? Whether we want to

---

1 Benjamin Bengfort, *Data Product Architectures*, (2016) *https://bit.ly/2vat7cN*

filter spam, detect sentiment or political polarity, a specific topic, or language being spoken, the application defines the classes. The second commonality is the observation that by reading the content of the document or utterance, it is possible to make a judgment about the class. With these two rules of thumb, it becomes possible to employ automatic classification in a variety of places: troll detection, reading level, product category, entertainment rating, name detection, author identification, and more.

Classifier Models

The nice thing about the Naive Bayesian method used in the classic spam identification problem is that both the construction of the model (requiring only a single pass through the corpus) and predictions (computation of a probability via the product of an input vector with the underlying truth table) are extremely fast. The performance of Naive Bayes meant a machine learning model that could keep up with email-sized applications. Accuracy could be further improved by adding nontext features like the IP or email address of the sender, the number of included images, the use of numbers in spelling "v14gr4", etc.

Naive Bayes is an *online* model, meaning that it can be updated in real time without retraining from scratch (simply update the underlying truth table and token probabilities). This meant that email service providers could keep up with spammer reactions by simply allowing the user to mark offending emails as spam—updating the underlying model for everyone.

There are a wide variety of classification models and mechanisms that are comparatively more mathematically diverse than the linear models primarily used for regression. From instance-based methods that use distance-based similarity, partitive schemes, and Bayesian probability, to linear and nonlinear approximation and neural modeling, text analysis applications have many choices for model families. However, all classifier model families have the same basic workflow, and with Scikit-Learn `Estimator` objects, they can be employed in a procedural fashion and compared using cross-validation to select the best performing predictor.

The classification workflow occurs in two phases: a build phase and an operational phase as shown in Figure 5-2. In the build phase, a corpus of documents is transformed into feature vectors. The document features, along with their annotated labels (the category or class we want the model to learn), are then passed into a classification algorithm that defines its internal state along with the learned patterns. Once trained or fitted, a new document can be vectorized into the same space as the training data and passed to the predictive algorithm, which returns the assigned class label for the document.

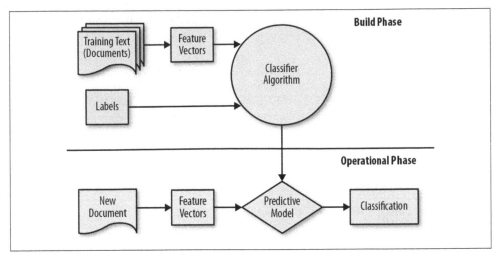

Figure 5-2. Classification workflow

Binary classifiers have two classes whose relationship is important: only the two classes are possible and one class is the opposite of the other (e.g., on/off, yes/no, etc.). In probabilistic terms, a binary classifier with classes A and B assumes that $P(B)$ = 1 - $P(A)$. However, this is frequently not the case. Consider sentiment analysis; if a document is not positive, is it necessarily negative? If some documents are neutral (which is often the case), adding a third class to our classifier may significantly increase its ability to identify the positive and negative documents. This then becomes a multiclass problem with multiple binary classes—for example, A and ¬A (not A) and B and ¬B (not B).

Building a Text Classification Application

Recall that in Chapters 2 and 3, we ingested, extracted, preprocessed, and stored HTML documents on disk to create our corpus. The Baleen ingestion engine requires us to configure a YAML file in which we organize RSS feeds into categories based on the kinds of documents they will contain. Feeds related to "gaming" are grouped together, as are those about "tech" and "books," etc. As such, the resulting ingested corpus is a collection of documents with human-generated labels that are essentially different categories of hobbies. This means we have the potential to build a classifier that can detect stories and news most relevant to a user's interests!

In the following section we will demonstrate the basic methodology for document-level classification by creating a text classifier to predict the label for a given document ("books," "cinema," "cooking," "DIY," "gaming," "sports," or "tech") given its text. Our implicit hypothesis is that each class will use language in distinctive ways, such that it should be possible to build a robust classifier that can distinguish and predict a document's category.

 In the context of our problem, each document is an *instance* that we will learn to classify. The end result of the steps described in Chapters 2 and 3 is a collection of files stored in a structured manner on disk—one document to a file, stored in directories named after their class. Each document is a pickled Python object composed of several nested `list` objects—for example, the document is a `list` of paragraphs, each paragraph is a `list` of sentences, and each sentence is a `list` of (`token`, `tag`) tuples.

Cross-Validation

One of the biggest challenges of applied machine learning is defining a stopping criterion upfront—how do we know when our model is good enough to deploy? When is it time to stop tuning? Which model is the best for our use case? Cross-validation is an essential tool for scoping these kinds of applications, since it will allow us to compare models using *training and test splits* and estimate in advance which model will be most performant for our use case.

Our primary goal is to fit a classifier that succeeds in detecting separability in the training data and is also generalizable to unseen data. Separability means that our feature space has been correctly defined such that a meaningful decision space can be constructed to delineate classes. Generalizability means that the model is mostly accurate on making predictions on unseen data that was not part of the training dataset.

The trick is to walk the line between *underfitting* and *overfitting*. An underfit model has low *variance*, generally making the same predictions every time, but with extremely high *bias*, because the model deviates from the correct answer by a significant amount. Underfitting is symptomatic of not having enough data points, or not training a complex enough model. An overfit model, on the other hand, has memorized the training data and is completely accurate on data it has seen before, but varies widely on unseen data. Neither an overfit nor underfit model is *generalizable*—that is, able to make meaningful predictions on unseen data.

There is a trade-off between bias and variance, as shown in Figure 5-3. Complexity increases with the number of features, parameters, depth, training epochs, etc. As complexity increases and the model overfits, the error on the training data decreases, but the error on test data increases, meaning that the model is less generalizable.

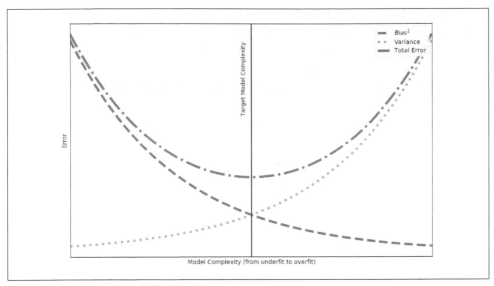

Figure 5-3. Bias–variance trade-off

The goal is therefore to find the optimal point with enough model complexity so as to avoid underfit (decreasing the bias) without injecting error due to variance. To find that optimal point, we need to evaluate our model on data that it was not trained on. The solution is cross-validation: a multiround experimental method that partitions the data such that part of the data is reserved for testing and not fit upon to reduce error due to overfit.

Figure 5-4. k-fold cross-validation

Cross-validation starts by shuffling the data (to prevent any unintentional ordering errors) and splitting it into k folds as shown in Figure 5-4. Then k models are fit on $\frac{k-1}{k}$ of the data (called the training split) and evaluated on $\frac{1}{k}$ of the data (called the test split). The results from each evaluation are averaged together for a final score, then the final model is fit on the entire dataset for operationalization.

A common question is what k should be chosen for k-fold cross-validation. We typically use 12-fold cross-validation as shown in Figure 5-4, though 10-fold cross-validation is also common. A higher k provides a more accurate estimate of model error on unseen data, but takes longer to fit, sometimes with diminishing returns.

Streaming access to k splits

It is essential to get into the habit of using cross-validation to ensure that our models perform well, particularly when engaging the model selection process. We consider it so important to applied text analytics that we start by creating a `CorpusLoader` object that wraps a `CorpusReader` in order to provide streaming access to k splits!

We'll construct the base class, `CorpusLoader`, which is instantiated with a `Corpus Reader`, the number of folds, and whether or not to shuffle the corpus, which is true by default. If folds is not `None`, we instantiate a Scikit-Learn `KFold` object that knows how to partition the corpus by the number of documents and specified folds.

```python
from sklearn.model_selection import KFold

class CorpusLoader(object):

    def __init__(self, reader, folds=12, shuffle=True, categories=None):
        self.reader = reader
        self.folds  = KFold(n_splits=folds, shuffle=shuffle)
        self.files  = np.asarray(self.reader.fileids(categories=categories))
```

The next step is to add a method that will allow us to access a listing of `fileids` by fold ID for either the train or the test splits. Once we have the `fileids`, we can return the documents and labels, respectively. The `documents()` method returns a generator to provide memory-efficient access to the documents in our corpus, and yields a list of tagged tokens for each `fileid` in the split, one document at a time. The `labels()` method uses the `corpus.categories()` to look up the label from the corpus and returns a list of labels, one per document.

```python
    def fileids(self, idx=None):
        if idx is None:
            return self.files
        return self.files[idx]
```

```
def documents(self, idx=None):
    for fileid in self.fileids(idx):
        yield list(self.reader.docs(fileids=[fileid]))

def labels(self, idx=None):
    return [
        self.reader.categories(fileids=[fileid])[0]
        for fileid in self.fileids(idx)
    ]
```

Finally, we add a custom iterator method that calls KFold's split() method, yielding training and test splits for each fold:

```
def __iter__(self):
    for train_index, test_index in self.folds.split(self.files):
        X_train = self.documents(train_index)
        y_train = self.labels(train_index)

        X_test = self.documents(test_index)
        y_test = self.labels(test_index)

        yield X_train, X_test, y_train, y_test
```

In "Model Evaluation" on page 91, we'll use this methodology to create 12-fold cross-validation that fits a model 12 times and collects a score each time, which we can then average and compare to select the most performant model.

Model Construction

As we learned in Chapter 4, Scikit-Learn Pipelines provide a mechanism for coordinating the vectorization process with the modeling process. We can start with a pipeline that normalizes our text, vectorizes it, and then passes it directly into a classifier. This will allow us to compare different text classification models such as Naive Bayes, Logistic Regression, and Support Vector Machines. Finally, we can apply a feature reduction technique such as Singular Value Decomposition to see if that improves our modeling.

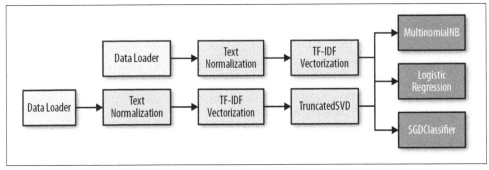

Figure 5-5. Simple classification pipelines

The end result is that we'll be constructing six classification models: one for each of the three models and for the two pipeline combinations as shown in Figure 5-5. We will go ahead and use the default *hyperparameters* for each of these models initially so that we can start getting results.

We'll add a `create_pipeline` function that takes an instantiated estimator as its first argument and a boolean indicating whether or not to apply decomposition to reduce the number of features. Our pipeline takes advantage of the `TextNormalizer` we built in Chapter 4 that uses WordNet lemmatization to reduce the number of overall word classes. Because we've already preprocessed and normalized the text, we must pass an `identity` function as the `TfidfVectorizer` tokenizer function; an `identity` function is simply a function that returns its arguments. Moreover, we can prevent preprocessing and lowercase by setting the appropriate arguments when instantiating the vectorizer.

```
from sklearn.pipeline import Pipeline
from sklearn.decomposition import TruncatedSVD
from sklearn.feature_extraction.text import TfidfVectorizer

def identity(words):
    return words

def create_pipeline(estimator, reduction=False):

    steps = [
        ('normalize', TextNormalizer()),
        ('vectorize', TfidfVectorizer(
            tokenizer=identity, preprocessor=None, lowercase=False
        ))
    ]

    if reduction:
        steps.append((
            'reduction', TruncatedSVD(n_components=10000)
        ))

    # Add the estimator
    steps.append(('classifier', estimator))
    return Pipeline(steps)
```

We can now quickly generate our models as follows:

```
from sklearn.linear_model import LogisticRegression
from sklearn.naive_bayes import MultinomialNB
from sklearn.linear_model import SGDClassifier

models = []
for form in (LogisticRegression, MultinomialNB, SGDClassifier):
    models.append(create_pipeline(form(), True))
    models.append(create_pipeline(form(), False))
```

The `models` list now contains six model forms—instantiated pipelines that include specific vectorization and feature extraction methods (feature analysis), a specific algorithm, and specific hyperparameters (currently set to the Scikit-Learn defaults).

Fitting the models given a training dataset of documents and their associated labels can be done as follows:

```
for model in models:
    model.fit(train_docs, train_labels)
```

By calling the `fit()` method on each model, the documents and labels from the training dataset are sent into the beginning of each pipeline. The transformers have their `fit()` methods called, then the data is passed into their `transform()` method. The transformed data is then passed to the `fit()` of the next transformer for each step in the sequence. The final estimator, in this case one of our classification algorithms, will have its `fit()` method called on the completely transformed data. Calling `fit()` will transform the input of preprocessed documents (lists of paragraphs that are lists of sentences, that are lists of tokens, tag tuples) into a two-dimensional numeric array, to which we can then apply optimization algorithms.

Model Evaluation

So which model was best? As with vectorization, model selection is data-, use case-, and application-specific. In our case, we want to know which model combination will be best at predicting the hobby category of a document based on its text. Because we have the correct target values from our test dataset, we can compare the predicted answers to the correct ones and determine the percent of the time the model is correct, effectively scoring each model with respect to its global accuracy.

Let's compare our models. We'll use the `CorpusLoader` we created in "Streaming access to k splits" on page 88 to get our `train_test_splits` for our cross-validation folds. Then, for each fold, we will fit the model on the training data and the accompanying labels, then create a prediction vector off the test data. Next, we will pass the actual and the predicted labels for each fold to a score function and append the score to a list. Finally, we will average the results across all folds to get a single score for the model.

```
import numpy as np

from sklearn.metrics import accuracy_score

for model in models:
    scores = [] # Store a list of scores for each split

    for X_train, X_test, y_train, y_test in loader:
        model.fit(X_train, y_train)
        y_pred = model.predict(X_test)
```

```
score  = accuracy_score(y_test, y_pred)
scores.append(score)

print("Accuracy of {} is {:0.3f}".format(model, np.mean(scores)))
```

The results are as follows:

```
Accuracy of LogisticRegression (TruncatedSVD) is 0.676
Accuracy of LogisticRegression is 0.685
Accuracy of SGDClassifier (TruncatedSVD) is 0.763
Accuracy of SGDClassifier is 0.811
Accuracy of MultinomialNB is 0.562
Accuracy of GaussianNB (TruncatedSVD) is 0.323
```

The way to interpret accuracy is to consider the global behavior of the model across all classes. In this case, for a 6-class classifier, the accuracy is the sum of the true classes divided by the total number of instances in the test data. Overall accuracy, however, does not give us much insight into what is happening in the model. It might be important to us to know if a certain classifier is better at detecting "sports" articles but worse at finding ones about "cooking."

Do certain models perform better for one class over another? Is there one poorly performing class that is bringing the global accuracy down? How often does the fitted classifier guess one class over another? In order to get insight into these factors, we need to look at a per-class evaluation: enter the confusion matrix.

The classification report prints out a per-class breakdown of performance of the model. Because this report is compiled by reporting true labels versus predicted labels, it is generally used without folds, but directly on train and test splits to better identify problem areas in the model.

```
from sklearn.metrics import classification_report

model = create_pipeline(SGDClassifier(), False)
model.fit(X_train, y_train)

y_pred = model.predict(X_test)
print(classification_report(y_test, y_pred, labels=labels))
```

The report itself is organized similarly to a confusion matrix, showing the breakdown in the precision, recall, F1, and support for each class as follows:

	precision	recall	f1-score	support
books	0.85	0.73	0.79	15
cinema	0.63	0.60	0.62	20
cooking	0.75	1.00	0.86	3
gaming	0.85	0.79	0.81	28
sports	0.93	1.00	0.96	26
tech	0.77	0.82	0.79	33
avg / total	0.81	0.81	0.81	125

The *precision* of a class, A, is computed as the ratio between the number of correctly predicted As (true As) to the total number of predicted As (true As plus false As). Precision shows how accurately a model predicts a given class according to the number of times it labels that class as true.

The *recall* of a class A is computed as the ratio between the number of predicted As (true As) to the total number of As (true As + false ¬As). Recall, also called sensitivity, is a measure of how often relevant classes are retrieved.

The *support* of a class shows how many test instances were involved in computing the scores. As we can see in the classification report above, the cooking class is potentially under-represented in our sample, meaning there are not enough documents to inform its score.

Finally, the *F1 score* is the harmonic mean of precision and recall and embeds more information than simple accuracy by taking into account how each class contributes to the overall score.

 In an application, we want to be able to retrain our models on some routine basis as new data is ingested. This training process will happen under the hood, and should result in updates to the deployed model depending on whichever model is currently most performant. As such, it is convenient to build these scoring mechanisms into the application's logs, so that we can go back and examine shifts in precision, recall, F1 score, and training time over time.

We can tabulate all the model scores and sort by F1 score in order to select the best model through some minor iteration and score collection.

```
import tabulate
import numpy as np

from collections import defaultdict
from sklearn.metrics import accuracy_score, f1_score
from sklearn.metrics import precision_score, recall_score

fields = ['model', 'precision', 'recall', 'accuracy', 'f1']
table  = []

for model in models:
    scores = defaultdict(list) # storage for all our model metrics

    # k-fold cross-validation
    for X_train, X_test, y_train, y_test in loader:
        model.fit(X_train, y_train)
        y_pred = model.predict(X_test)

        # Add scores to our scores
```

```
        scores['precision'].append(precision_score(y_test, y_pred))
        scores['recall'].append(recall_score(y_test, y_pred))
        scores['accuracy'].append(accuracy_score(y_test, y_pred))
        scores['f1'].append(f1_score(y_test, y_pred))

    # Aggregate our scores and add to the table.
    row = [str(model)]
    for field in fields[1:]:
        row.append(np.mean(scores[field]))

    table.append(row)

# Sort the models by F1 score descending
table.sort(key=lambda row: row[-1], reverse=True)
print(tabulate.tabulate(table, headers=fields))
```

Here we modify our earlier *k*-fold scoring to utilize a `defaultdict` and track precision, recall, accuracy, and F1 scores. After we fit the model on each fold, we take the mean score from each fold and add it to the table. We can then sort the table by F1 score and quickly identify the best performing model by printing it out with the Python `tabulate` module as follows:

```
model                              precision   recall   accuracy    f1
--------------------------------   ---------   ------   --------   -----
SGDClassifier                          0.821    0.811      0.811   0.81
SGDClassifier (TruncatedSVD)           0.81     0.763      0.763   0.766
LogisticRegression                     0.736    0.685      0.685   0.659
LogisticRegression (TruncatedSVD)      0.749    0.676      0.676   0.647
MultinomialNB                          0.696    0.562      0.562   0.512
GaussianNB (TruncatedSVD)              0.314    0.323      0.323   0.232
```

This allows us to quickly identify that the support vector machine trained using stochastic gradient descent without dimensionality reduction was the model that performed best. Note that for some models, like the `LogisticRegression`, use of the F1 score instead of accuracy has an impact on which model is selected. Through model comparison of this type, it becomes easy to test combinations of features, hyperparameters, and algorithms to find the best performing model for your domain.

Model Operationalization

Now that we have identified the best performing model, it is time to save the model to disk in order to *operationalize* it. Machine learning techniques are tuned toward creating models that can make predictions on *new* data in real time, without verification. To employ models in applications, we first need to save them to disk so that they can be loaded and reused. For the most part, the best way to accomplish this is to use the `pickle` module:

```
import pickle
from datetime import datetime

time = datetime.now().strftime("%Y-%m-%d")
path = 'hobby-classifier-{}'.format(time)

with open(path, 'wb') as f:
    pickle.dump(model, f)
```

The model is saved along with the date that it was built.

 In addition to saving the model, it is also important to save model metadata, which can be stored in an accompanying metadata file or database. Model fitting is a routine process, and generally speaking, models should be retrained at regular intervals appropriate to the velocity of your data. Graphing model performance over time and making determinations about data decay and model adjustments is a crucial part of machine learning applications.

To use the model in an application with new, incoming text, simply load the estimator from the pickle object, and use its `predict()` method.

```
import nltk

def preprocess(text):
    return [
        [
            list(nltk.pos_tag(nltk.word_tokenize(sent)))
            for sent in nltk.sent_tokenize(para)
        ] for para in text.split("\n\n")
    ]


with open(path, 'rb') as f:
    model = pickle.load(f)


model.predict([preprocess(doc) for doc in newdocs])
```

Because our vectorization process is embedded with our model via the `Pipeline` we need to ensure that the input to the pipeline is prepared in a manner identical to the training data input. Our training data was preprocessed text, so we need to include a function to preprocess strings into the same format. We can then open the pickle file, load the model, and use its `predict()` method to return labels.

Conclusion

As we've seen in this chapter, the process of selecting an optimal model is complex, iterative, and substantially more intricate than, say, the choice of a support vector machine over a decision tree classifier. Discussions of machine learning are frequently characterized by a singular focus on model selection. Be it logistic regression, random forests, Bayesian methods, or artificial neural networks, machine learning practitioners are often quick to express their preference. While model selection is important (especially in the context text classification), successful machine learning relies on significantly more than merely having picked the "right" or "wrong" algorithm.

When it comes to applied text analytics, the search for the most optimal model follows a common workflow: create a corpus, select a vectorization technique, fit a model, and evaluate using cross-validation. Wash, rinse, repeat, and compare results. At application time, select the model with the best result based on cross-validation and use it to make predictions.

Importantly, classification offers metrics such as precision, recall, accuracy, and F1 scores that can be used to guide our selection of algorithms. However, not all machine learning problems can be formulated as supervised learning problems. In the next chapter, we will discuss another prominent use of machine learning on text, *clustering*, which is an unsupervised technique. While somewhat more complex, we will illustrate that clustering can also be streamlined to produce impressive applications capable of discovering surprising and useful patterns in large amounts of data.

## CHAPTER 6

Clustering for Text Similarity

What would you do if you were handed a pile of papers—receipts, emails, travel itineraries, meeting minutes—and asked to summarize their contents? One strategy might be to read through each of the documents, highlighting the terms or phrases most relevant to each, and then sort them all into piles. If one pile started getting too big, you might split it into two smaller piles. Once you'd gone through all the documents and grouped them, you could examine each pile more closely. Perhaps you would use the main phrases or words from each pile to write up the summaries and give each a unique name—the topic of the pile.

This is, in fact, a task practiced in many disciplines, from medicine to law. At its core, this sorting task relies on our ability to compare two documents and determine their *similarity*. Documents that are similar to each other are grouped together and the resulting groups broadly describe the overall themes, topics, and patterns inside the corpus. Those patterns can be discrete (e.g., when the groups don't overlap at all) or fuzzy (e.g., when there is a lot of similarity and documents are hard to distinguish). In either case, the resultant groups represent a model of the contents of all documents, and new documents can be easily assigned to one group or another.

While most document sorting is currently done manually, it is possible to achieve these tasks in a fraction of the time with the effective integration of *unsupervised learning*, as we'll see in this chapter.

Unsupervised Learning on Text

Unsupervised approaches can be incredibly useful for exploratory text analysis. Oftentimes corpora do not arrive pretagged with labels ready for classification. In these cases, the only choice (aside from paying someone to label your data), or at least a necessary precursor for many natural language processing tasks, is an unsupervised approach.

Clustering algorithms aim to discover latent structure or themes in unlabeled data using features to organize instances into meaningfully dissimilar groups. With text data, each instance is a single document or utterance, and the features are its tokens, vocabulary, structure, metadata, etc.

In Chapter 5 we constructed our classification pipeline to compare and score many different models and select the most performant for use in predicting on new data. The behavior of unsupervised learning methods is fundamentally different; instead of learning a predefined pattern, the model attempts to find relevant patterns *a priori*.

As such, the integration of these techniques into a data product architecture is necessarily a bit different. As we see in the pipeline presented in Figure 6-1, a corpus is transformed into feature vectors and a clustering algorithm is employed to create groups or topic clusters, using a distance metric such that documents that are closer together in feature space are more similar. New incoming documents can then be vectorized and assigned to the nearest cluster. Later in this chapter, we'll employ this pipeline to conduct an end-to-end clustering analysis on a sample of the Baleen corpus introduced in Chapter 2.

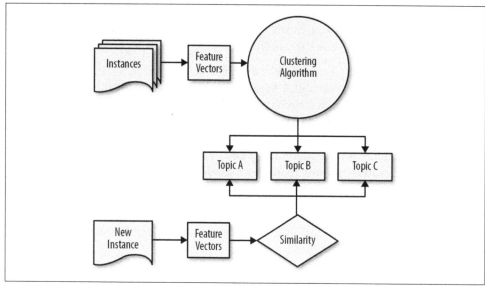

Figure 6-1. Clustering pipeline

First, we need a method for defining document similarity, and in the next section, we'll explore a range of distance metrics that can be used in determining the relative similarity between two given documents. Next, we will explore the two primary approaches to unsupervised learning, partitive clustering and hierarchical clustering, using methods implemented in NLTK and Scikit-Learn. With the resulting clusters, we'll experiment with using Gensim for topic modeling to describe and summarize our clusters. Finally, we will move on to exploring two alternative means of unsupervised learning for text: matrix factorization and Latent Dirichlet Allocation (LDA).

Clustering by Document Similarity

Many features of a document can inform similarity, from words and phrases to grammar and structure. We might group medical records by reported symptoms, saying two patients are similar if both have "nausea and exhaustion." We'd probably use a different method to sort personal websites and blogs differently, perhaps calling blogs similar if they feature recipes for pies and cookies. If a new blog features recipes for summer salads, it is probably more similar to the baking blogs than to ones with recipes for homemade explosives.

Effective clustering requires us to choose what it will mean for any two documents from our corpus to be similar or dissimilar. There are a number of different measures that can be used to determine document similarity; several are illustrated in Figure 6-2. Fundamentally, each relies on our ability to imagine documents as points in space, where the relative closeness of any two documents is a measure of their similarity.

String Matching	Distance Metrics	Relational Matching	Other Matching
Edit Distance - Levenstein - Smith-Waterman - Affine	- Euclidean - Manhattan - Minkowski	**Set Based** - Dice - Tanimoto (Jaccard) - Common Neighbors - Adar Weighted	- Numeric distance - Boolean equality - Fuzzy matching - Domain specific
Alignment - Jaro-Winkler - Soft-TFIDF - Monge-Elkan	**Text Analytics** - Jaccard - TFIDF - Cosine similarity	**Aggregates** - Average values - Max/Min values - Medians - Frequency (Mode)	**Gazettes** - Lexical matching - Named Entities (NER)
Phonetic - Soundex - Translation			

Figure 6-2. Spatializing similarity

Distance Metrics

When we think of how to measure the distance between two points, we usually think of a straight line, or *Euclidean distance*, represented in Figure 6-3 as the diagonal line.

Manhattan distance, shown in Figure 6-3 as the three stepped paths, is similar, computed as the sum of the absolute differences of the Cartesian coordinates. *Minkowski distance* is a generalization of Euclidean and Manhattan distance, and defines the distance between two points in a normalized vector space.

However, as the vocabulary of our corpus grows, so does its dimensionality—and rarely in an evenly distributed way. For this reason, these distance measures are not always a very effective measure, since they assume all data is symmetric and that distance is the same in all dimensions.

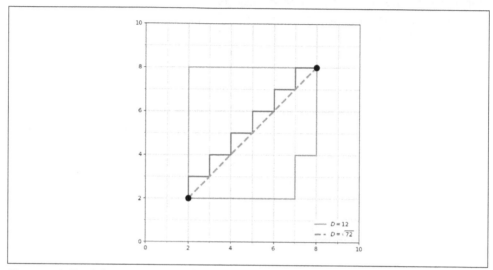

Figure 6-3. Euclidean versus Manhattan distance

By contrast, *Mahalanobis distance*, shown in Figure 6-4, is a multidimensional generalization of the measurement of how many standard deviations away a particular point is from a distribution of points. This has the effect of shifting and rescaling the coordinates with respect to the distribution. As such, Mahalanobis distance gives us a slightly more flexible way to define distances between documents; for instance, enabling us to identify similarities between utterances of different lengths.

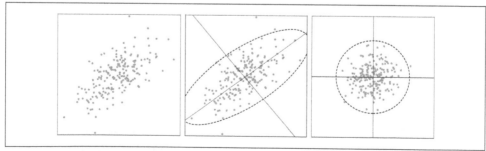

Figure 6-4. Mahalanobis distance

Jaccard distance defines similarity between finite sets as the quotient of their intersection and their union, as shown in Figure 6-5. For instance, we could measure the Jaccard distance between two documents A and B by dividing the number of unique words that appear in both A and B by the total number of unique words that appear in A and B. A value of 0 would indicate that the two documents have nothing in common, a 1 that they were the same document, and values between 0 and 1 indicating their relative degree of similarity.

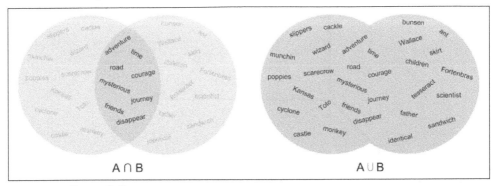

Figure 6-5. Jaccard distance

Edit distance measures the distance between two strings by the number of permutations needed to convert one into the other. There are multiple implementations of edit distance, all variations on Levenshtein distance, but with differing penalties for insertions, deletions, and substitutions, as well as potentially increased penalties for gaps and transpositions. In Figure 6-6 we can see that the edit distance between "woodman" and "woodland" includes penalties for one insertion and one substitution.

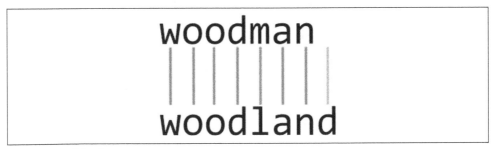

Figure 6-6. Edit distance

It is also possible to measure distances between vectors. For example, we can define two document vectors as similar by their *TF–IDF distance*; in other words, the magnitude to which they share the same unique terms relative to the rest of the words in the corpus. We can compute this using TF–IDF, as described in Chapter 4. We can also measure vector similarity with *cosine distance*, using the cosine of the angle between the two vectors to assess the degree to which they share the same orientation, as shown in Figure 6-7. In effect, the more parallel any two vectors are, the more similar the documents will be (regardless of their magnitude).

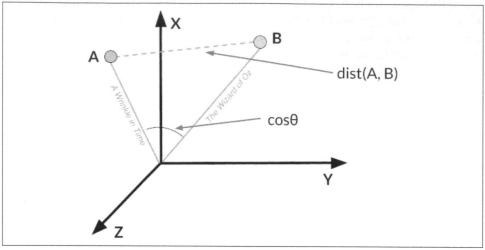

Figure 6-7. Cosine similarity

While Euclidean distance is often the default metric used in clustering model hyper-parameters (as we'll see in the next sections), we frequently find the most success using cosine distance.

Partitive Clustering

Now that we can quantify the similarity between any two documents, we can begin exploring unsupervised methods for finding similar groups of documents. *Partitive clustering* and *agglomerative clustering* are our two main approaches, and both separate documents into groups whose members share maximum similarity as defined by some distance metric. In this section, we will focus on partitive methods, which partition instances into groups that are represented by a central vector (the centroid) or described by a density of documents per cluster. Centroids represent an aggregated value (e.g., mean or median) of all member documents and are a convenient way to describe documents in that cluster.

As we saw in Chapter 5, the Baleen corpus is already categorized after a fashion, as each document is (human-)labeled with the categories of the RSS sources from which the data originated. However, some of these categories are not necessarily distinct (e.g., "tech" and "gaming") and others are significantly more diffuse. For instance, the "news" corpus contains news on a range of topics, including political news, entertainment, science, and other current events. In this section, we will use clustering to establish subcategories within the "news" corpus, which might then be employed as target values for subsequent classification tasks.

k-means clustering

Because it has implementations in familiar libraries like NLTK and Scikit-Learn, *k*-means is a convenient place to start. A popular method for unsupervised learning tasks, the *k*-means clustering algorithm starts with an arbitrarily chosen number of clusters, *k*, and partitions the vectorized instances into clusters according to their proximity to the centroids, which are computed to minimize the within-cluster sum of squares.

We will begin by defining a class, `KMeansClusters`, which inherits from `BaseEstimator` and `TransformerMixin` so it will function inside a Scikit-Learn `Pipeline`. We'll use NLTK's implementation of *k*-means for our `model`, since it allows us to define our own distance metric. We initialize the NLTK `KMeansClusterer` with our desired number of clusters (*k*) and our preferred distance measure (`cosine_distance`), and avoid a result with clusters that contain no documents.

```python
from nltk.cluster import KMeansClusterer
from sklearn.base import BaseEstimator, TransformerMixin


class KMeansClusters(BaseEstimator, TransformerMixin):

    def __init__(self, k=7):
        """
        k is the number of clusters
        model is the implementation of Kmeans
        """
        self.k = k
        self.distance = nltk.cluster.util.cosine_distance
        self.model = KMeansClusterer(self.k, self.distance,
                                     avoid_empty_clusters=True)
```

Now we'll add our no-op `fit()` method and a `transform()` method that calls the internal `KMeansClusterer` model's `cluster()` method, specifying that each document should be assigned a cluster. Our `transform()` method expects one-hot encoded documents, and by setting `assign_clusters=True`, it will return a list of the cluster assignments for each document:

```python
    def fit(self, documents, labels=None):
        return self

    def transform(self, documents):
        """
        Fits the K-Means model to one-hot vectorized documents.
        """
        return self.model.cluster(documents, assign_clusters=True)
```

To prepare our documents for our KMeansClusters class, we need to normalize and vectorize them first. For normalization, we'll use a version of the TextNormalizer class we defined in "Creating a custom text normalization transformer" on page 72, with one small change to the tranform() method. Instead of returning a representation of documents as bags-of-words, this version of the TextNormalizer will perform stopwords removal and lemmatization and return a string for each document:

```
class TextNormalizer(BaseEstimator, TransformerMixin):

    ...

    def transform(self, documents):
        return [' '.join(self.normalize(doc)) for doc in documents]
```

To vectorize our documents after normalization and ahead of clustering, we'll define a OneHotVectorizer class. For vectorization, we'll use Scikit-Learn's CountVector izer with binary=True, which will wrap both frequency encoding and binarization. Our transform() method will return a representation of each document as a one-hot vectorized array:

```
from sklearn.base import BaseEstimator, TransformerMixin
from sklearn.feature_extraction.text import CountVectorizer


class OneHotVectorizer(BaseEstimator, TransformerMixin):

    def __init__(self):
        self.vectorizer = CountVectorizer(binary=True)

    def fit(self, documents, labels=None):
        return self

    def transform(self, documents):
        freqs = self.vectorizer.fit_transform(documents)
        return [freq.toarray()[0] for freq in freqs]
```

Now, we can create a Pipeline inside our main() execution to perform k-means clustering. We'll initialize a PickledCorpusReader as defined in "Reading the Processed Corpus" on page 51, specifying that we want to use only the "news" category of our corpus. Then we'll initialize a pipeline to streamline our custom TextNormalizer, One HotVectorizer, and KMeansClusters classes. By calling fit_transform() on the pipeline, we perform each of these steps in sequence:

```
from sklearn.pipeline import Pipeline

corpus = PickledCorpusReader('../corpus')
docs = corpus.docs(categories=['news'])

model = Pipeline([
    ('norm', TextNormalizer()),
```

```
        ('vect', OneHotVectorizer()),
        ('clusters', KMeansClusters(k=7))
    ])

clusters = model.fit_transform(docs)
pickles = list(corpus.fileids(categories=['news']))
for idx, cluster in enumerate(clusters):
    print("Document '{}' assigned to cluster {}.".format(pickles[idx],cluster))
```

Our result is a list of cluster assignments corresponding to each of the documents from our news category, which we can easily map back to the `fileids` of the pickled documents:

```
Document 'news/56d62554c1808113ffb87492.pickle' assigned to cluster 0.
Document 'news/56d6255dc1808113ffb874f0.pickle' assigned to cluster 5.
Document 'news/56d62570c1808113ffb87557.pickle' assigned to cluster 4.
Document 'news/56d625abc1808113ffb87625.pickle' assigned to cluster 2.
Document 'news/56d63a76c1808113ffb8841c.pickle' assigned to cluster 0.
Document 'news/56d63ae1c1808113ffb886b5.pickle' assigned to cluster 3.
Document 'news/56d63af0c1808113ffb88745.pickle' assigned to cluster 5.
Document 'news/56d64c7ac1808115036122b4.pickle' assigned to cluster 6.
Document 'news/56d64cf2c1808115036125f5.pickle' assigned to cluster 2.
Document 'news/56d65c2ec1808116aade2f8a.pickle' assigned to cluster 2.
...
```

We now have a preliminary model for clustering documents based on text similarity; now we should consider what we can do to optimize our results. However, unlike the case of classification, we don't have a convenient measure to tell us if the "news" corpus has been correctly partitioned into subcategories—when it comes to unsupervised learning, we don't have a ground truth. Instead, generally we would look to some human validation to see if our clusters make sense—are they meaningfully distinct? Are they sufficiently focused? In the next section, we'll discuss what it might mean to "optimize" a clustering model.

Optimizing k-means

How can we "improve" a clustering model? In our case, this amounts to asking how we can make our results more interpretable and more useful. First, we can often make our results more interpretable by experimenting with different values of k. With k-means clustering, k-selection is often an iterative process; while there are rules of thumb, initial selection is often somewhat arbitrary.

In "Silhouette Scores and Elbow Curves" on page 177 we will discuss two visual techniques that can help guide experimentation with k-selection: silhouette scores and elbow curves.

We can also tune other parts of our pipeline; for example, instead of using one-hot encoding, we could switch to TF–IDF vectorization. Alternatively, in place of our `TextNormalizer`, we could introduce a feature selector that would select only a subset of the entire feature set (e.g., only the 5,000 most common tokens, excluding stop-words).

 Although the focus of this book is not big data, it is important to note that *k*-means does effectively scale for big data with the introduction of canopy clustering. Other text clustering algorithms, like LDA, are much more challenging to parallelize without additional tools (e.g., Tensorflow).

Keep in mind that *k*-means is not a lightweight algorithm and can be particularly slow with high-dimensional data such as text. If your clustering pipeline is very slow, you can optimize for speed by switching from the `nltk.cluster` module to using `sklearn.cluster`'s `MiniBatchKMeans` implementation. `MiniBatchKMeans` is a *k*-means variant that uses randomly sampled subsets (or "mini-batches") of the entire training dataset to optimize the same objective function, but with a much-reduced computation time.

```
from sklearn.cluster import MiniBatchKMeans
from sklearn.base import BaseEstimator, TransformerMixin


class KMeansClusters(BaseEstimator, TransformerMixin):

    def __init__(self, k=7):
        self.k = k
        self.model = MiniBatchKMeans(self.k)

    def fit(self, documents, labels=None):
        return self

    def transform(self, documents):
        return self.model.fit_predict(documents)
```

The trade-off is that our `MiniBatchKMeans` implementation, while faster, will use Euclidean distance, which is less effective for text. At the time of this writing, the Scikit-Learn implementations of `KMeans` and `MiniBatchKMeans` do not support the use of non-Euclidean distance measures.

Handling uneven geometries

The *k*-means algorithm makes several naive assumptions about data, presuming that it will be well-distributed, that clusters will have roughly comparable degrees of variance, and that they will be fundamentally spherical in nature. As such, there are many cases where *k*-means clustering will be unsuccessful; for instance, when outlier data points interfere with cluster coherence and when clusters have markedly different, or nonspherical densities. Using alternative distance measures, such as cosine or Mahalanobis distance, can help to address these cases.

 There are several other partitive techniques implemented in Scikit-Learn, such as affinity propagation, spectral clustering, and Gaussian mixtures, which may prove to be more performant in cases where k-means is not.

Ultimately, the advantages of using k-means make it an important tool in the natural language processing toolkit; k-means offers conceptual simplicity, producing tight, spherical clusters, convenient centroids that support model interpretability, and the guarantee of eventual convergence. In the rest of this chapter, we'll explore some of the other, more sophisticated techniques we have found useful for text, but there's no silver bullet, and a simple k-means approach is often a convenient place to start.

Hierarchical Clustering

In the previous section, we explored partitive methods, which divide points into clusters. By contrast, hierarchical clustering involves creating clusters that have a predetermined ordering from top to bottom. Hierarchical models can be either *agglomerative*, where clusters begin as single instances that iteratively aggregate by similarity until all belong to a single group, or *divisive*, where the data are gradually divided, beginning with all instances and finishing as single instances.

These methods create a dendrogram representation of the cluster structures, as shown in the lower left in Figure 6-8.

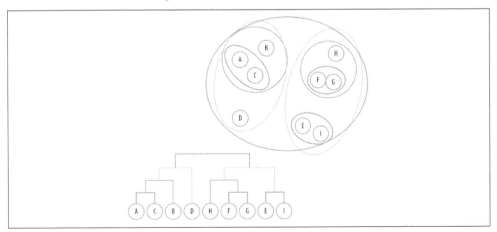

Figure 6-8. Hierarchical clustering

Agglomerative clustering

Agglomerative clustering iteratively combines the closest instances into clusters until all the instances belong to a single group. In the context of text data, the result is a hierarchy of variable-sized groups that describe document similarities at different levels or granularities.

We can switch our clustering implementation to an agglomerative approach fairly easily. We first define a `HierarchicalClusters` class, which initializes a Scikit-Learn `AgglomerativeClustering` model.

```
from sklearn.cluster import AgglomerativeClustering


class HierarchicalClusters(object):

    def __init__(self):
        self.model = AgglomerativeClustering()
```

We add our no-op `fit()` method and a `tranform()` method, which calls the internal model's `fit_predict` method, saving the resulting `children` and `labels` attributes for later use and returning the clusters.

```
    ...

    def fit(self, documents, labels=None):
        return self

    def transform(self, documents):
        """
        Fits the agglomerative model to the given data.
        """
        clusters = self.model.fit_predict(documents)
        self.labels = self.model.labels_
        self.children = self.model.children_

        return clusters
```

Next, we'll put the pieces together into a `Pipeline` and inspect the cluster labels and membership of each of the children of each nonleaf node.

```
model = Pipeline([
    ('norm', TextNormalizer()),
    ('vect', OneHotVectorizer()),
    ('clusters', HierarchicalClusters())
])

model.fit_transform(docs)
labels = model.named_steps['clusters'].labels
pickles = list(corpus.fileids(categories=['news']))
```

```
for idx, fileid in enumerate(pickles):
    print("Document '{}' assigned to cluster {}.".format(fileid,labels[idx]))
```

The results appear as follows:

```
Document 'news/56d62554c1808113ffb87492.pickle' assigned to cluster 1.
Document 'news/56d6255dc1808113ffb874f0.pickle' assigned to cluster 0.
Document 'news/56d62570c1808113ffb87557.pickle' assigned to cluster 1.
Document 'news/56d625abc1808113ffb87625.pickle' assigned to cluster 1.
Document 'news/56d63a76c1808113ffb8841c.pickle' assigned to cluster 1.
Document 'news/56d63ae1c1808113ffb886b5.pickle' assigned to cluster 0.
Document 'news/56d63af0c1808113ffb88745.pickle' assigned to cluster 1.
Document 'news/56d64c7ac1808115036122b4.pickle' assigned to cluster 1.
Document 'news/56d64cf2c1808115036125f5.pickle' assigned to cluster 0.
Document 'news/56d65c2ec1808116aade2f8a.pickle' assigned to cluster 0.
...
```

One of the challenges with agglomerative clustering is that we don't have the benefit of centroids to use in labeling our document clusters as we did with the *k*-means example. Therefore, to enable us to visually explore the resultant clusters of our AgglomerativeClustering model, we will define a method plot_dendrogram to create a visual representation.

Our plot_dendrogram method will use the dendrogram method from SciPy and will also require Matplotlib's pyplot. We use NumPy to compute a distance range between the child leaf nodes, and make an equal range of values to represent each child position. We then create a linkage matrix to hold the positions between each child and their distances. Finally we use SciPy's dendrogram method, passing in the linkage matrix and any keyword arguments that can later be passed in to modify the figure.

```python
import numpy as np
from matplotlib import pyplot as plt
from scipy.cluster.hierarchy import dendrogram

def plot_dendrogram(children, **kwargs):
    # Distances between each pair of children
    distance = position = np.arange(children.shape[0])

    # Create linkage matrix and then plot the dendrogram
    linkage_matrix = np.column_stack([
        children, distance, position]
    ).astype(float)

    # Plot the corresponding dendrogram
    fig, ax = plt.subplots(figsize=(10, 5))  # set size
    ax = dendrogram(linkage_matrix, **kwargs)
    plt.tick_params(axis='x', bottom='off', top='off', labelbottom='off')
    plt.tight_layout()
    plt.show()
```

```
children = model.named_steps['clusters'].children
plot_dendrogram(children)
```

We can see the resulting plot in Figure 6-9. The first documents to be aggregated into the same cluster, those with the shortest branches, are the ones that exhibited the least variations. Those with the longest branches illustrate those with more variance, which were clustered later in the process.

Just as there are multiple ways of quantifying the difference between any two documents, there are also multiple criteria for establishing the linkages between them. Agglomerative clustering requires both a distance function and a linkage criterion. Scikit-Learn's implementation defaults to the Ward criterion, which minimizes the within-cluster variance as each are successively merged. At each aggregation step, the algorithm finds the pair of clusters that contributes the least increase in total within-cluster variance after merging.

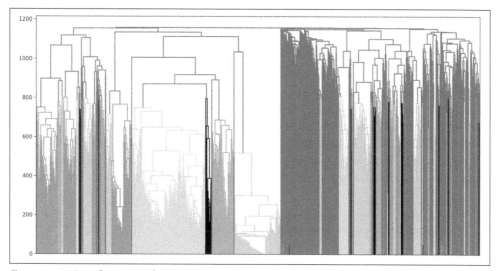

Figure 6-9. Dendrogram plot

 Other linkage criterion options in Scikit-Learn include `"average"`, which uses the average of the distances between points in the clusters, and `"complete"`, which uses the maximum distances between all points in the clusters.

As we can see from the results of our `KMeansClusters` and `HierarchicalClusters`, one of the challenges with both partitive and agglomerative clustering is that they don't give much insight into *why* a document ended up in a particular cluster. In the next section, we'll explore a different set of methods that expose strategies we can leverage not only to rapidly group our documents, but also to effectively describe their contents.

Modeling Document Topics

Now that we have organized our documents into piles, how should we go about labeling them and describing their contents? In this section, we'll explore *topic modeling*, an unsupervised machine learning technique for abstracting topics from collections of documents. While clustering seeks to establish groups of documents within a corpus, topic modeling aims to abstract core themes from a set of utterances; clustering is *deductive*, while topic modeling is *inductive*.

Methods for topic modeling, and convenient open source implementations, have evolved significantly over the last decade. In the next section, we'll compare three of these techniques: Latent Dirichlet Allocation (LDA), Latent Semantic Analysis (LSA), and Non-Negative Matrix Factorization (NNMF).

Latent Dirichlet Allocation

First introduced by David Blei, Andrew Ng, and Michael Jordan in 2003, *Latent Dirichlet Allocation* (LDA) is a topic discovery technique. It belongs to the generative probabilistic model family, in which topics are represented as the probability that each of a given set of terms will occur. Documents can in turn be represented in terms of a mixture of these topics. A unique feature of LDA models is that topics are not required to be distinct, and words may occur in multiple topics; this allows for a kind of topical fuzziness that is useful for handling the flexibility of language (Figure 6-10).

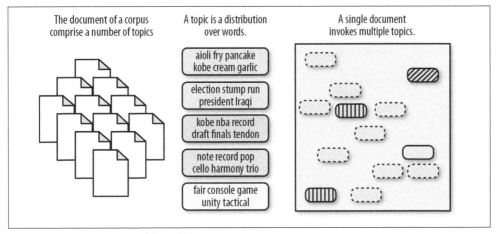

Figure 6-10. Latent Dirichlet Allocation

Blei et al. (2003) found that the Dirichlet prior, a continuous mixture distribution (a way of measuring a distribution over distributions), is a convenient way of discovering topics that occur across a corpus and also manifest in different mixtures within each document in the corpus.[1] In effect, with a Latent Dirichlet Allocation, we are given an observed word or token, from which we attempt to model the probability of topics, the distribution of words for each topic, and the mixture of topics within a document.

To use topic models in an application, we need a tunable pipeline that will extrapolate topics from unstructured text data, and a method for storing the best model so it can be used on new, incoming data. We'll do this first with Scikit-Learn and then with Gensim.

In Scikit-Learn

We begin by creating a class, SklearnTopicModels. The __init__ function instantiates a pipeline with our TextNormalizer, CountVectorizer, and Scikit-Learn's implementation of LatentDirichletAllocation. We must specify a number of topics (here 50), just as we did with *k*-means clustering.

```
from sklearn.pipeline import Pipeline
from sklearn.decomposition import LatentDirichletAllocation
from sklearn.feature_extraction.text import CountVectorizer

class SklearnTopicModels(object):

    def __init__(self, n_topics=50):
        """
        n_topics is the desired number of topics
        """
        self.n_topics = n_topics
        self.model = Pipeline([
            ('norm', TextNormalizer()),
            ('vect', CountVectorizer(tokenizer=identity,
                                     preprocessor=None, lowercase=False)),
            ('model', LatentDirichletAllocation(n_topics=self.n_topics)),
        ])
```

---

1 David M. Blei, Andrew Y. Ng, and Michael I. Jordan, *Latent Dirichlet Allocation*, (2003) *https://stanford.io/2GJBHR1*

In the rest of the examples in the chapter, we will want to use the original version of `TextNormalizer` from "Creating a custom text normalization transformer" on page 72, which returns a representation of documents as bags-of-words.

We then create a `fit_transform` method, which will call the internal `fit` and `transform` methods of each step of our pipeline:

```
def fit_transform(self, documents):
    self.model.fit_transform(documents)

    return self.model
```

Now that we have a way to create and fit the pipeline, we want some mechanism to inspect our topics. The topics aren't labeled, and we don't have a centroid with which to produce a label as we would with centroidal clustering. Instead, we will inspect each topic in terms of the words it has the highest probability of generating.

We create a `get_topics` method, which steps through our pipeline object to retrieve the fitted vectorizer and extracts the tokens from its `get_feature_names()` attribute. We loop through the `components_` attribute of the LDA model, and for each of the topics and its corresponding index, we reverse-sort the numbered tokens by weight such that the 25 highest weighted terms are ranked first. We then retrieve the corresponding tokens from the feature names and store our topics as a dictionary where the key is the index of one of the 50 topics and the values are the top words associated with that topic.

```
def get_topics(self, n=25):
    """
    n is the number of top terms to show for each topic
    """
    vectorizer = self.model.named_steps['vect']
    model = self.model.steps[-1][1]
    names = vectorizer.get_feature_names()
    topics = dict()

    for idx, topic in enumerate(model.components_):
        features = topic.argsort()[:-(n - 1): -1]
        tokens = [names[i] for i in features]
        topics[idx] = tokens

    return topics
```

We can now instantiate a `SklearnTopicModels` object, and fit and transform the pipeline on our corpus documents. We assign the result of the `get_topics()` attribute (a Python dictionary) to a `topics` variable and unpack the dictionary, printing out the corresponding topics and their most informative terms:

```
if __name__ == '__main__':
    corpus = PickledCorpusReader('corpus/')

    lda       = SklearnTopicModels()
    documents = corpus.docs()

    lda.fit_transform(documents)
    topics = lda.get_topics()
    for topic, terms in topics.items():
        print("Topic #{}:".format(topic+1))
        print(terms)
```

The results appear as follows:

```
Topic #1:
['science', 'scientist', 'data', 'daviau', 'human', 'earth', 'bayesian',
 'method', 'scientific', 'jableh', 'probability', 'inference', 'crater',
 'transhumanism', 'sequence', 'python', 'engineer', 'conscience',
 'attitude', 'layer', 'pee', 'probabilistic', 'radio']
Topic #2:
['franchise', 'rhoden', 'rosemary', 'allergy', 'dewine', 'microwave',
 'charleston', 'q', 'pike', 'relmicro', '($', 'wicket', 'infant',
 't20', 'piketon', 'points', 'mug', 'snakeskin', 'skinnytaste',
 'frankie', 'uninitiated', 'spirit', 'kosher']
Topic #3:
['cosby', 'vehicle', 'moon', 'tesla', 'module', 'mission', 'hastert',
 'air', 'mars', 'spacex', 'kazakhstan', 'accuser', 'earth', 'makemake',
 'dragon', 'model', 'input', 'musk', 'recall', 'buffon', 'stage',
 'journey', 'capsule']
...
```

The Gensim way

Gensim also exposes an implementation for Latent Dirichlet Allocation, which offers some convenient attributes over Scikit-Learn. Conveniently, Gensim (starting with version 2.2.0) provides a wrapper for its LDAModel, called ldamodel.LdaTransformer, which makes integration with a Scikit-Learn pipeline that much more convenient.

To use Gensim's LdaTransformer, we need to create a custom Scikit-Learn wrapper for Gensim's TfidfVectorizer so that it can function inside a Scikit-Learn Pipeline. GensimTfidfVectorizer will vectorize our documents ahead of LDA, as well as saving, holding, and loading a custom-fitted lexicon and vectorizer for later use.

```
class GensimTfidfVectorizer(BaseEstimator, TransformerMixin):

    def __init__(self, dirpath=".", tofull=False):
        """
        Pass in a directory that holds the lexicon in corpus.dict and the
        TF-IDF model in tfidf.model.

        Set tofull = True if the next thing is a Scikit-Learn estimator
        otherwise keep False if the next thing is a Gensim model.
```

```
        """
        self._lexicon_path = os.path.join(dirpath, "corpus.dict")
        self._tfidf_path = os.path.join(dirpath, "tfidf.model")

        self.lexicon = None
        self.tfidf = None
        self.tofull = tofull

        self.load()

    def load(self):
        if os.path.exists(self._lexicon_path):
            self.lexicon = Dictionary.load(self._lexicon_path)

        if os.path.exists(self._tfidf_path):
            self.tfidf = TfidfModel().load(self._tfidf_path)

    def save(self):
        self.lexicon.save(self._lexicon_path)
        self.tfidf.save(self._tfidf_path)
```

If the model has already been fit, we can initialize the GensimTfidfVectorizer with a lexicon and vectorizer that can be loaded from disk using the load method. We also implement a save() method, which we will call after fitting the vectorizer.

Next, we implement fit() by creating a Gensim Dictionary object, which takes as an argument a list of normalized documents. We instantiate a Gensim TfidfModel, passing in as an argument the list of documents, each of which have been passed through lexicon.doc2bow, and been transformed into bags of words. We then call the save method, which serializes our lexicon and vectorizer and saves them to disk. Finally, the fit() method returns self to conform with the Scikit-Learn API.

```
    def fit(self, documents, labels=None):
        self.lexicon = Dictionary(documents)
        self.tfidf = TfidfModel([
            self.lexicon.doc2bow(doc)
            for doc in documents],
            id2word=self.lexicon)
        self.save()
        return self
```

We then implement our transform() method, which creates a generator that loops through each of our normalized documents and vectorizes them using the fitted model and their bag-of-words representation. Because the next step in our pipeline will be a Gensim model, we initialized our vectorizer to set tofull=False, so that it would output a sparse document format (a sequence of 2-tuples). However, if we were going to use a Scikit-Learn estimator next, we would want to initialize our GensimTfidfVectorizer with tofull=True, which here in our transform method would convert the sparse format into the needed dense representation for Scikit-Learn, an np array.

```python
def transform(self, documents):
    def generator():
        for document in documents:
            vec = self.tfidf[self.lexicon.doc2bow(document)]
            if self.tofull:
                yield sparse2full(vec)
            else:
                yield vec
    return list(generator())
```

We now have a custom wrapper for our Gensim vectorizer, and here in GensimTopic Models, we put all of the pieces together:

```python
from sklearn.pipeline import Pipeline
from gensim.sklearn_api import ldamodel


class GensimTopicModels(object):

    def __init__(self, n_topics=50):
        """
        n_topics is the desired number of topics
        """
        self.n_topics = n_topics
        self.model = Pipeline([
            ('norm', TextNormalizer()),
            ('vect', GensimTfidfVectorizer()),
            ('model', ldamodel.LdaTransformer(num_topics = self.n_topics))
        ])

    def fit(self, documents):
        self.model.fit(documents)

        return self.model
```

We can now fit our pipeline with our corpus.docs:

```python
if __name__ == '__main__':
    corpus = PickledCorpusReader('../corpus')

    gensim_lda = GensimTopicModels()

    docs = [
        list(corpus.docs(fileids=fileid))[0]
        for fileid in corpus.fileids()
    ]

    gensim_lda.fit(docs)
```

In order to inspect the topics, we can retrieve them from the LDA step, which is the gensim_model attribute from the last step of our pipeline. We can then use the Gensim LDAModel show_topics method to view the topics and the token-weights for the top ten most influential tokens:

```
lda = gensim_lda.model.named_steps['model'].gensim_model
print(lda.show_topics())
```

We can also define a function get_topics, which given the fitted LDAModel and vectorized corpus, will retrieve the highest-weighted topic for each of the documents in the corpus:

```
def get_topics(vectorized_corpus, model):
    from operator import itemgetter

    topics = [
        max(model[doc], key=itemgetter(1))[0]
        for doc in vectorized_corpus
    ]

    return topics

lda = gensim_lda.model.named_steps['model'].gensim_model

corpus = [
    gensim_lda.model.named_steps['vect'].lexicon.doc2bow(doc)
    for doc in gensim_lda.model.named_steps['norm'].transform(docs)
]

topics = get_topics(corpus,lda)

for topic, doc in zip(topics, docs):
    print("Topic:{}".format(topic))
    print(doc)
```

Visualizing topics

Oftentimes with unsupervised learning techniques, it is helpful to be able to visually explore the results of a model, since traditional model evaluation techniques are useful only for supervised learning problems. Visualization techniques for text analytics will be discussed in greater detail in Chapter 8, but here we will briefly explore the use of the pyLDAvis library, which is designed to provide a visual interface for interpreting the topics derived from a topic model.

PyLDAvis works by extracting information from fitted LDA topic models to inform an interactive web-based visualization, which can easily be run from inside a Jupyter notebook or saved as HTML. In order visualize our document topics with pyLDAvis, we can fit our pipeline inside a Jupyter notebook as follows:

```
import pyLDAvis
import pyLDAvis.gensim

lda = gensim_lda.model.named_steps['model'].gensim_model

corpus = [
    gensim_lda.model.named_steps['vect'].lexicon.doc2bow(doc)
    for doc in gensim_lda.model.named_steps['norm'].transform(docs)
]

lexicon = gensim_lda.model.named_steps['vect'].lexicon

data = pyLDAvis.gensim.prepare(model,corpus,lexicon)
pyLDAvis.display(data)
```

The key method `pyLDAvis.gensim.prepare` takes as an argument the LDA model, the vectorized corpus, and the derived lexicon and produces, upon calling `display`, visualizations like the one shown in Figure 6-11.

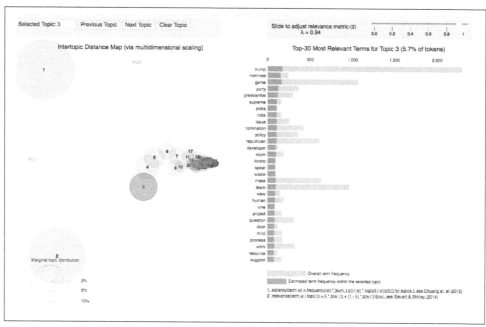

Figure 6-11. Interactive topic model visualization with pyLDAvis

Latent Semantic Analysis

Latent Semantic Analysis (LSA) is a vector-based approach first suggested as a topic modeling technique by Deerwester et al in 1990.[2]

While Latent Dirichlet Allocation works by abstracting topics from documents, which can then be used to score documents by their proportion of topical terms, Latent Semantic Analysis simply finds groups of documents with the same words. The LSA approach to topic modeling (also known as Latent Semantic Indexing) identifies themes within a corpus by creating a sparse term-document matrix, where each row is a token and each column is a document. Each value in the matrix corresponds to the frequency with which the given term appears in that document, and can be normalized using TF–IDF. *Singular Value Decomposition* (SVD) can then be applied to the matrix to factorize into matrices that represent the term-topics, the topic importances, and the topic-documents.

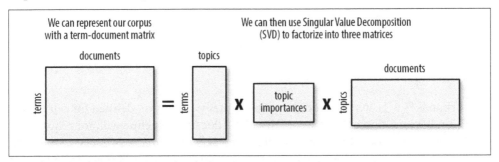

Figure 6-12. Latent Semantic Analysis

Using the derived diagonal topic importance matrix, we can identify the topics that are the most significant in our corpus, and remove rows that correspond to less important topic terms. Of the remaining rows (terms) and columns (documents), we can assign topics based on their highest corresponding topic importance weights.

In Scikit-Learn

To do Latent Semantic Analysis with Scikit-Learn, we will make a pipeline that normalizes our text, creates a term-document matrix using a `CountVectorizer`, and then employs `TruncatedSVD`, which is the Scikit-Learn implementation of Singular Value Decomposition. Scikit-Learn's implementation only computes the k largest singular values, where k is a hyperparameter that we must specify via the `n_components`

---

2 Scott Deerwester, Susan T. Dumais, George W. Furnas, Thomas K. Landauer, and Richard Harshman, *Indexing by Latent Semantic Analysis*, (1990) *http://bit.ly/2JHWx57*

attribute. Fortunately, this requires very little refactoring of the __init__ method we created for our SklearnTopicModels class!

```python
class SklearnTopicModels(object):

    def __init__(self, n_topics=50, estimator='LDA'):
        """
        n_topics is the desired number of topics
        To use Latent Semantic Analysis, set estimator to 'LSA',
        otherwise, defaults to Latent Dirichlet Allocation ('LDA').
        """
        self.n_topics = n_topics

        if estimator == 'LSA':
            self.estimator = TruncatedSVD(n_components=self.n_topics)
        else:
            self.estimator = LatentDirichletAllocation(n_topics=self.n_topics)

        self.model = Pipeline([
            ('norm', TextNormalizer()),
            ('tfidf', CountVectorizer(tokenizer=identity,
                                    preprocessor=None, lowercase=False)),
            ('model', self.estimator)
        ])
```

Our original fit_transform and get_topics methods that we defined for our Scikit-Learn implementation of the Latent Dirichlet Allocation pipeline will not require any modification to work with our newly refactored SklearnTopicModels class, so we can easily switch between the two algorithms to see which performs best according to our application and document context.

The Gensim way

Updating our GensimTopicModels class to enable a Latent Semantic Analysis pipeline is much the same. We again use our TextNormalizer, followed by the GensimTfidf Vectorizer we used in our Latent Dirichlet Allocation pipeline, and finally the Gensim LsiModel wrapper exposed through the gensim.sklearn_api module, lsimodel.LsiTransformer:

```python
from gensim.sklearn_api import lsimodel, ldamodel


class GensimTopicModels(object):

    def __init__(self, n_topics=50, estimator='LDA'):
        """
        n_topics is the desired number of topics

        To use Latent Semantic Analysis, set estimator to 'LSA'
        otherwise defaults to Latent Dirichlet Allocation.
```

```
"""
self.n_topics = n_topics

if estimator == 'LSA':
    self.estimator = lsimodel.LsiTransformer(num_topics=self.n_topics)
else:
    self.estimator = ldamodel.LdaTransformer(num_topics=self.n_topics)

self.model = Pipeline([
    ('norm', TextNormalizer()),
    ('vect', GensimTfidfVectorizer()),
    ('model', self.estimator)
])
```

We can now switch between the two Gensim algorithms with the `estimator` keyword argument.

Non-Negative Matrix Factorization

Another unsupervised technique that can be used for topic modeling is *non-negative matrix factorization* (NNMF). First introduced by Pentti Paatero and Unto Tapper (1994)[3] and popularized in a *Nature* article by Daniel Lee and H. Sebastian Seung (1999),[4] NNMF has many applications, including spectral data analysis, collaborative filtering for recommender systems, and topic extraction (Figure 6-13).

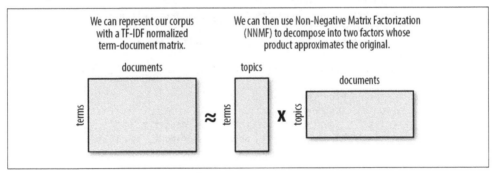

Figure 6-13. Non-negative matrix factorization

To apply NNMF for topic modeling, we begin by representing our corpus as we did with our Latent Semantic Analysis, as a TF–IDF normalized term-document matrix. We then decompose the matrix into two factors whose product approximates the

---

3 Pentti Paatero and Unto Tapper, *Positive matrix factorization: A non-negative factor model with optimal utilization of error estimates of data values,* (1994) *http://bit.ly/2GOFdJU*

4 Daniel D. Lee and H. Sebastian Seung, *Learning the parts of objects by non-negative matrix factorization,* (1999) *http://bit.ly/2GJBIV5*

original, such that every value in both factors is either positive or zero. The resulting matrices illustrate topics positively related to terms and documents of the corpus.

In Scikit-Learn

Scikit-Learn's implementation of non-negative matrix factorization is the `sklearn.decomposition.NMF` class. With a minor amount of refactoring to the `__init__` method of our `SklearnTopicModels` class, we can easily implement NNMF in our pipeline without any additional changes needed:

```python
from sklearn.decomposition import NMF


class SklearnTopicModels(object):

    def __init__(self, n_topics=50, estimator='LDA'):
        """
        n_topics is the desired number of topics
        To use Latent Semantic Analysis, set estimator to 'LSA',
        To use Non-Negative Matrix Factorization, set estimator to 'NMF',
        otherwise, defaults to Latent Dirichlet Allocation ('LDA').
        """
        self.n_topics = n_topics

        if estimator == 'LSA':
            self.estimator = TruncatedSVD(n_components=self.n_topics)
        elif estimator == 'NMF':
            self.estimator = NMF(n_components=self.n_topics)
        else:
            self.estimator = LatentDirichletAllocation(n_topics=self.n_topics)

        self.model = Pipeline([
            ('norm', TextNormalizer()),
            ('tfidf', CountVectorizer(tokenizer=identity,
                                      preprocessor=None, lowercase=False)),
            ('model', self.estimator)
        ])
```

So which topic modeling algorithm is best? Anecdotally,[5] LSA is sometimes considered better for learning descriptive topics, which is helpful with longer documents and more diffuse corpora. Latent Dirichlet Allocation and non-negative matrix factorization, on the other hand, can be better for learning compact topics, which is useful for creating succinct labels from topics.

---

5 Keith Stevens, Philip Kegelmeyer, David Andrzejewski, and David Buttler, *Exploring Topic Coherence over many models and many topics*, (2012) *http://bit.ly/2GNHg11*

Ultimately, the best model will depend a great deal on the corpus you are working with and the goals of your application. Now you are equipped with the tools to experiment with multiple models to determine which works best for your use case!

Conclusion

In this chapter, we've seen that unsupervised machine learning can be tricky since there is no surefire way to evaluate the performance of a model. Nonetheless, distance-based techniques that allow us to quantify the similarities between documents can be an effective and fast method of dealing with large corpora to present interesting and relevant information.

As we discussed, *k*-means is an effective general-purpose clustering technique that scales well to large corpora (particularly if using the NLTK implementation with cosine distance, or the Scikit-Learn `MiniBatchKMeans`), especially if there aren't too many clusters and the geometry isn't too complex. Agglomerative clustering is a useful alternative in cases where there are a large number of clusters and data is less evenly distributed.

We also learned that effectively summarizing a corpus of unlabeled documents often requires not only *a priori* categorization, but also a method for describing those categories. This makes topic modeling—whether with Latent Dirichlet Allocation, Latent Semantic Analysis, or non-negative matrix factorization—another essential tool for the applied text analytics toolkit.

Clusters can be an excellent starting point to begin annotating a dataset for supervised methods that can be evaluated upon. Creating collections of similar documents can lead to more complex structures like graph relationships (which we'll see more of in Chapter 9) that lead to more impactful downstream analysis. In Chapter 7, we'll take a closer look at some more advanced contextual feature engineering strategies that will allow us to capture some of those complex structures for more effective text modeling.

Context-Aware Text Analysis

The models we have seen in this book so far use a *bag-of-words* decomposition technique, enabling us to explore relationships between documents that contain the same mixture of individual words. This is incredibly useful, and indeed we've seen that the frequency of tokens can be very effective particularly in cases where the vocabulary of a specific discipline or topic is sufficient to distinguish it from or relate it to other text.

What we haven't taken into account yet, however, is the *context* in which the words appear, which we instinctively know plays a huge role in conveying meaning. Consider the following phrases: "she liked the smell of roses" and "she smelled like roses." Using the text normalization techniques presented in previous chapters such as stopwords removal and lemmatization, these two utterances would have identical bag-of-words vectors though they have completely different meanings.

This does not mean that bag-of-words models should be completely discounted, and in fact, bag-of-words models are usually very useful initial models. Nonetheless, lower performing models can often be significantly improved with the addition of contextual feature extraction. One simple, yet effective approach is to augment models with *grammars* to create templates that help us target specific types of phrases, which capture more nuance than words alone.

In this chapter, we will begin by using a grammar to extract *key phrases* from our documents. Next, we will explore *n-grams* and discover *significant collocations* we can use to augment our bag-of-words models. Finally, we will see how our *n*-gram model can be extended with *conditional frequency*, *smoothing*, and *back-off* to create a model that can generate language, a crucial part of many applications including machine translation, chatbots, smart autocomplete, and more.

Grammar-Based Feature Extraction

Grammatical features such as parts-of-speech enable us to encode more contextual information about language. One of the most effective ways of improving model performance is by combining *grammars* and *parsers*, which allow us to build up lightweight syntactic structures to directly target dynamic collections of text that could be significant.

To get information about the language in which the sentence is written, we need a set of grammatical rules that specify the components of well-structured sentences in that language; this is what a *grammar* provides. A grammar is a set of rules describing specifically how syntactic units (sentences, phrases, etc.) in a given language should be deconstructed into their constituent units. Here are some examples of these syntactic categories:

Symbol	Syntactic Category
S	Sentence
NP	Noun Phrase
VP	Verb Phrase
PP	Prepositional Phrase
DT	Determiner
N	Noun
V	Verb
ADJ	Adjective
P	Preposition
TV	Transitive Verb
IV	Intransitive Verb

Context-Free Grammars

We can use grammars to specify different rules that allow us to build up parts-of-speech into phrases or chunks. A *context-free grammar* is a set of rules for combining syntactic components to form sensical strings. For instance, the noun phrase "the castle" has a determiner (denoted DT using the Penn Treebank tagset) and a noun (N). The prepositional phrase (PP) "in the castle" has a preposition (P) and a noun phrase (NP). The verb phrase (VP) "looks in the castle" has a verb (V) and a prepositional phrase (PP). The sentence (S) "Gwen looks in the castle" has a proper noun (NNP) and verb phrase (VP). Using these tags, we can define a context-free grammar:

```
GRAMMAR = """
    S -> NNP VP
    VP -> V PP
    PP -> P NP
    NP -> DT N
    NNP -> 'Gwen' | 'George'
    V -> 'looks' | 'burns'
    P -> 'in' | 'for'
    DT -> 'the'
    N -> 'castle' | 'ocean'
    """
```

In NLTK, `nltk.grammar.CFG` is an object that defines a context-free grammar, specifying how different syntactic components can be related. We can use CFG to parse our grammar as a string:

```
from nltk import CFG
cfg = nltk.CFG.fromstring(GRAMMAR)

print(cfg)
print(cfg.start())
print(cfg.productions())
```

Syntactic Parsers

Once we have defined a grammar, we need a mechanism to systematically search out the meaningful syntactic structures from our corpus; this is the role of the *parser*. If a grammar defines the search criterion for "meaningfulness" in the context of our language, the parser executes the search. A *syntactic parser* is a program that deconstructs sentences into a parse tree, which consists of hierarchical constituents, or syntactic categories.

When a parser encounters a sentence, it checks to see if the structure of that sentence conforms to a known grammar. If so, it parses the sentence according to the rules of that grammar, producing a parse tree. Parsers are often used to identify important structures, like the subject and object of verbs in a sentence, or to determine which sequences of words in a sentence should be grouped together within each syntactic category.

First, we define a GRAMMAR to identify sequences of text that match a part-of-speech pattern, and then instantiate an NLTK `RegexpParser` that uses our grammar to chunk the text into subsections:

```
from nltk.chunk.regexp import RegexpParser

GRAMMAR = r'KT: {(<JJ>* <NN.*>+ <IN>)? <JJ>* <NN.*>+}'
chunker = RegexpParser(GRAMMAR)
```

The GRAMMAR is a regular expression used by the NLTK `RegexpParser` to create trees with the label KT (key term). Our chunker will match phrases that start with an optional component composed of zero or more adjectives, followed by one or more of any type of noun and a preposition, and end with zero or more adjectives followed by one more of any type of noun. This grammar will chunk phrases like "red baseball bat" or "United States of America."

Consider an example sentence from a news story about baseball: "Dusty Baker proposed a simple solution to the Washington National's early-season bullpen troubles Monday afternoon and it had nothing to do with his maligned group of relievers."

```
(S
  (KT Dusty/NNP Baker/NNP)
  proposed/VBD
  a/DT
  (KT simple/JJ solution/NN)
  to/TO
  the/DT
  (KT Washington/NNP Nationals/NNP)
  (KT
    early-season/JJ
    bullpen/NN
    troubles/NNS
    Monday/NNP
    afternoon/NN)
  and/CC
  it/PRP
  had/VBD
  (KT nothing/NN)
  to/TO
  do/VB
  with/IN
  his/PRP$
  maligned/VBN
  (KT group/NN of/IN relievers/NNS)
  ./.)
```

This sentence is parsed into keyphrase chunks with six key phrases, including "Dusty Baker," "early-season bullpen troubles Monday afternoon," and "group of relievers."

Extracting Keyphrases

Figure 4-8 depicted a pipeline that included a feature union with a `KeyphraseExtractor` and an `EntityExtractor`. In this section, we'll implement the `KeyphraseExtractor` class that will transform documents into a bag-of-keyphrase representation.

The *key terms* and *keyphrases* contained within our corpora often provide insight into the topics or entities contained in the documents being analyzed. Keyphrase extraction consists of identifying and isolating phrases of a dynamic size to capture as many nuances in the topics of documents as possible.

Our `KeyphraseExtractor` class is inspired by an excellent blog post written by Burton DeWilde.[1]

The first step in keyphrase extraction is to identify candidates for phrases (e.g., which words or phrases could best convey the topic or relationships of documents). We'll define our `KeyphraseExtractor` with a grammar and chunker to identify just the *noun phrases* using part-of-speech tagged text.

```
GRAMMAR = r'KT: {(<JJ>* <NN.*>+ <IN>)? <JJ>* <NN.*>+}'
GOODTAGS = frozenset(['JJ','JJR','JJS','NN','NNP','NNS','NNPS'])

class KeyphraseExtractor(BaseEstimator, TransformerMixin):
    """
    Wraps a PickledCorpusReader consisting of pos-tagged documents.
    """
    def __init__(self, grammar=GRAMMAR):
        self.grammar = GRAMMAR
        self.chunker = RegexpParser(self.grammar)
```

Since we imagine that this `KeyphraseExtractor` will be the first step in a pipeline after tokenization, we'll add a `normalize()` method that performs some lightweight text normalization, removing any punctuation and ensuring that all words are lowercase:

```
from unicodedata import category as unicat

def normalize(self, sent):
    """
    Removes punctuation from a tokenized/tagged sentence and
    lowercases words.
    """
    is_punct = lambda word: all(unicat(c).startswith('P') for c in word)
    sent = filter(lambda t: not is_punct(t[0]), sent)
    sent = map(lambda t: (t[0].lower(), t[1]), sent)
    return list(sent)
```

Now we will write an `extract_keyphrases()` method. Given a document, this method will first normalize the text and then use our chunker to parse it. The output of a parser is a tree with only some branches of interest (the keyphrases!). To get the phrases of interest, we use the `tree2conlltags` function to convert the tree into the CoNLL IOB tag format, a list containing (`word`, `tag`, `IOB-tag`) tuples.

---

1 Burton DeWilde, *Intro to Automatic Keyphrase Extraction*, (2014) *http://bit.ly/2GJBKwb*

An IOB tag tells you how a term is functioning in the context of the phrase; the term will either *begin* a keyphrase (B-KT), be *inside* a keyphrase (I-KT), or be *outside* a keyphrase (O). Since we're only interested in the terms that are part of a keyphrase, we'll use the groupby() function from the itertools package in the standard library to write a lambda function that continues to group terms so long as they are not O:

```python
from itertools import groupby
from nltk.chunk import tree2conlltags

    def extract_keyphrases(self, document):
        """
        For a document, parse sentences using our chunker created by
        our grammar, converting the parse tree into a tagged sequence.
        Yields extracted phrases.
        """
        for sents in document:
            for sent in sents:
                sent = self.normalize(sent)
                if not sent: continue
                chunks = tree2conlltags(self.chunker.parse(sent))
                phrases = [
                    " ".join(word for word, pos, chunk in group).lower()
                    for key, group in groupby(
                        chunks, lambda term: term[-1] != 'O'
                    ) if key
                ]
                for phrase in phrases:
                    yield phrase
```

Since our class is a transformer, we finish by adding a no-op fit method and a transform method that calls extract_keyphrases() on each document in the corpus:

```python
    def fit(self, documents, y=None):
        return self

    def transform(self, documents):
        for document in documents:
            yield self.extract_keyphrases(document)
```

Here's a sample result for one of our transformed documents:

```python
['lonely city', 'heart piercing wisdom', 'loneliness', 'laing',
 'everyone', 'feast later', 'point', 'own hermetic existence in new york',
 'danger', 'thankfully', 'lonely city', 'cry for connection',
 'overcrowded overstimulated world', 'blueprint of urban loneliness',
 'emotion', 'calls', 'city', 'npr jason heller', 'olivia laing',
 'lonely city', 'exploration of loneliness',
 'others experiences in new york city', 'rumpus', 'review', 'lonely city',
 'related posts']
```

In Chapter 12, we'll revisit this class with a different GRAMMAR to build a custom bag-of-keyphrase transformer for a neural network-based sentiment classifier.

Extracting Entities

Similarly to our `KeyphraseExtractor`, we can create a custom feature extractor to transform documents into bags-of-entities. To do this we will make use of NLTK's named entity recognition utility, ne_chunk, which produces a nested parse tree structure containing the syntactic categories as well as the part-of-speech tags contained in each sentence.

We begin by creating an `EntityExtractor` class that is initialized with a set of entity labels. We then add a `get_entities` method that uses ne_chunk to get a syntactic parse tree for a given document. The method then navigates through the subtrees in the parse tree, extracting entities whose labels match our set (consisting of people's names, organizations, facilities, geopolitical entities, and geosocial political entities). We append these to list of `entities`, which we yield after the method has finished traversing all the trees of the document:

```python
from nltk import ne_chunk

GOODLABELS = frozenset(['PERSON', 'ORGANIZATION', 'FACILITY', 'GPE', 'GSP'])

class EntityExtractor(BaseEstimator, TransformerMixin):
    def __init__(self, labels=GOODLABELS, **kwargs):
        self.labels = labels

    def get_entities(self, document):
        entities = []
        for paragraph in document:
            for sentence in paragraph:
                trees = ne_chunk(sentence)
                for tree in trees:
                    if hasattr(tree, 'label'):
                        if tree.label() in self.labels:
                            entities.append(
                                ' '.join([child[0].lower() for child in tree])
                                )
        return entities

    def fit(self, documents, labels=None):
        return self

    def transform(self, documents):
        for document in documents:
            yield self.get_entities(document)
```

A sample document from our transformed corpus looks like:

```python
['lonely city', 'loneliness', 'laing', 'new york', 'lonely city',
 'npr', 'jason heller', 'olivia laing', 'lonely city', 'new york city',
 'rumpus', 'lonely city', 'related']
```

We will revisit grammar-based feature extraction in Chapter 9, where we'll make use of our `EntityExtractor` for use with graph metrics to model the relative importances of different entities in documents.

n-Gram Feature Extraction

Unfortunately, grammar-based approaches, while very effective, do not always work. For one thing, they rely heavily on the success of part-of-speech tagging, meaning we must be confident that our tagger is correctly labeling nouns, verbs, adjectives, and other parts of speech. As we'll see in Chapter 8, it is very easy for out-of-the-box part-of-speech taggers to get tripped up by nonstandard or ungrammatical text.

Grammar-based feature extraction is also somewhat inflexible, because we must begin by defining a grammar. It is often very difficult to know in advance which grammar pattern will most effectively capture the high-signal terms and phrases within a text.

We can address these challenges iteratively, by experimenting with many different grammars or by training our own custom part-of-speech tagger. However, in this section we will explore another option, backing off from grammar to *n-grams*, which will give us a more general way of identifying sequences of tokens.

Consider the sentence "The reporters listened closely as the President of the United States addressed the room." By scanning a window of a fixed length, n, across the text, we can collect all possible contiguous subsequences of tokens. So far we've been working with *unigrams*, *n*-grams where n=1 (e.g., individual tokens). When n=2 we have *bigrams*, a tuple of tokens such as (`"The"`, `"reporters"`) and (`"reporters"`, `"listened"`). When n=3, *trigrams* are a three-tuple: (`"The"`, `"reporters"`, `"lis tened"`) and so on for any n. The windowing sequence for trigrams is shown in Figure 7-1.

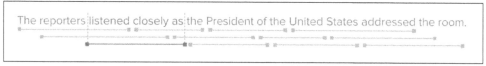

Figure 7-1. Windowing to select n-gram substrings

To identify all of the *n*-grams from our text, we simply slide a fixed-length window over a list of words until the window reaches the end of the list. We can do this in pure Python as follows:

```
def ngrams(words, n=2):
    for idx in range(len(words)-n+1):
        yield tuple(words[idx:idx+n])
```

This function ranges a start index from 0 to the position that is exactly one *n*-gram away from the end of the word list. It then slices the word list from the start index to *n*-gram length, returning an immutable tuple. When applied to our example sentence, the output is as follows:

```
words = [
    "The", "reporters", "listened", "closely", "as", "the", "President",
    "of", "the", "United", "States", "addressed", "the", "room", ".",
]

for ngram in ngrams(words, n=3):
    print(ngram)

('The', 'reporters', 'listened')
('reporters', 'listened', 'closely')
('listened', 'closely', 'as')
('closely', 'as', 'the')
('as', 'the', 'President')
('the', 'President', 'of')
('President', 'of', 'the')
('of', 'the', 'United')
('the', 'United', 'States')
('United', 'States', 'addressed')
('States', 'addressed', 'the')
('addressed', 'the', 'room')
('the', 'room', '.')
```

Not bad! However, these results do raise some questions. First, what do we do at the beginning and the end of sentences? And how do we decide what *n*-gram size to use? We'll address both questions in the next section.

An n-Gram-Aware CorpusReader

n-gram extraction is part of text preprocessing that occurs prior to modeling. As such, it would be convenient to include an `ngrams()` method as part of our custom `CorpusReader` and `PickledCorpusReader` classes. This will ensure it is easy to process our entire corpus for *n*-grams and retrieve them later. For example:

```
class HTMLCorpusReader(CategorizedCorpusReader, CorpusReader):

    ...

    def ngrams(self, n=2, fileids=None, categories=None):
        for sent in self.sents(fileids=fileids, categories=categories):
            for ngram in nltk.ngrams(sent, n):
                yield ngram

    ...
```

Because we are primarily considering *context* and because sentences represent discrete and independent thoughts, it makes sense to consider *n*-grams that do not cross over sentence boundaries.

The easiest way to handle more complex *n*-gram manipulation is to use the `ngrams()` method from NLTK, which can be used alongside NLTK segmentation and tokenization methods. This method will enable us to add padding before and after sentences such that *n*-grams generated also include sentence boundaries. This will allow us to identify which *n*-grams start sentences and which conclude them.

 Here we use XML symbols to demarcate the beginnings and ends of sentences because they are easily identified as markup and are likely not to be a unique token in the text. However, they are completely arbitrary and other symbols could be used. We frequently like to use ★ (`"\u2605"`) and ☆ (`"\u2606"`) when parsing text that does not contain symbols.

We'll begin with constants to define the start and end of the sentence as `<s>` and `</s>` (because English reads left to right, the `left_pad_symbol` and `right_pad_symbol`, respectively). In languages that read right to left, these could be reversed.

The second part of the code creates a function `nltk_ngrams` that uses the `partial` function to wrap the `nltk.ngrams` function with our code-specific keyword arguments. This ensures that every time we call `nltk_ngrams`, we get our expected behavior, without managing the call signature everywhere in our code that we use it. Finally our newly redefined `ngrams` function takes as arguments a string containing our text and *n*-gram size. It then applies the `sent_tokenize` and `word_tokenize` functions to the text before passing them into `nltk_ngrams` to get our padded *n*-grams:

```python
import nltk
from functools import partial

LPAD_SYMBOL = "<s>"
RPAD_SYMBOL = "</s>"

nltk_ngrams = partial(
    nltk.ngrams,
    pad_right=True, right_pad_symbol=RPAD_SYMBOL,
    left_pad=True, left_pad_symbol=LPAD_SYMBOL
)

    def ngrams(self, n=2, fileids=None, categories=None):
        for sent in self.sents(fileids=fileids, categories=categories):
            for ngram in nltk.ngrams(sent, n):
                yield ngram
```

For instance, given a size of n=4 and the sample text, "After, there were several follow-up questions. The *New York Times* asked when the bill would be signed," the resulting four-grams would be:

```
('<s>', '<s>', '<s>', 'After')
('<s>', '<s>', 'After', ',')
('<s>', 'After', ',', 'there')
('After', ',', 'there', 'were')
(',', 'there', 'were', 'several')
('there', 'were', 'several', 'follow')
('were', 'several', 'follow', 'up')
('several', 'follow', 'up', 'questions')
('follow', 'up', 'questions', '.')
('up', 'questions', '.', '</s>')
('questions', '.', '</s>', '</s>')
('.', '</s>', '</s>', '</s>')
('<s>', '<s>', '<s>', 'The')
('<s>', '<s>', 'The', 'New')
('<s>', 'The', 'New', 'York')
('The', 'New', 'York', 'Times')
('New', 'York', 'Times', 'asked')
('York', 'Times', 'asked', 'when')
('Times', 'asked', 'when', '</s>')
('asked', 'when', '</s>', '</s>')
('when', '</s>', '</s>', '</s>')
```

Note that the padding function adds padding to all possible sequences of *n*-grams. While this will be useful later in our discussion of *backoff*, if your application only requires identification of the start and end of the sentence, you can simply filter *n*-grams that contain more than one padding symbol.

Choosing the Right n-Gram Window

So how do we decide which n to choose? Consider an application where we are using *n*-grams to identify candidates for named entity recognition. If we consider a chunk size of n=2, our results include "The reporters," "the President," "the United," and "the room." While not perfect, this model successfully identifies three of the relevant entities as candidates in a lightweight fashion.

On the other hand, a model based on the small *n*-gram window of 2 would fail to capture some of the nuance of the original text. For instance, if our sentence is from a text that references multiple heads of state, "the President" could be somewhat ambiguous. In order to capture the entirety of the phrase "the President of the United States," we would have to set n=6:

```
('The', 'reporters', 'listened', 'closely', 'as', 'the'),
('reporters', 'listened', 'closely', 'as', 'the', 'President'),
('listened', 'closely', 'as', 'the', 'President', 'of'),
('closely', 'as', 'the', 'President', 'of', 'the'),
('as', 'the', 'President', 'of', 'the', 'United'),
```

```
('the', 'President', 'of', 'the', 'United', 'States'),
('President', 'of', 'the', 'United', 'States', 'addressed'),
('of', 'the', 'United', 'States', 'addressed', 'the'),
('the', 'United', 'States', 'addressed', 'the', 'room'),
('United', 'States', 'addressed', 'the', 'room', '.')
```

Unfortunately, as we can see in the results above, if we build a model based on an *n*-gram order that is too high, it will be very unlikely that we'll see any repeated entities. This will make it very difficult to assign likelihoods that capture the target of our analysis. Moreover, as n increases, the number of possible correct *n*-grams increases, thereby reducing the likelihood that we will observe all correct *n*-grams in our corpus. Too large of an n may add too much noise by overlapping independent contexts. If the window is larger than the sentence, it might not even produce any *n*-grams at all.

Choosing n can also be considered as balancing the trade-off between *bias* and *variance*. A small n leads to a simpler (weaker) model, therefore causing more error due to bias. A larger n leads to a more complex model (a higher-order model), thus causing more error due to variance. Just as with all supervised machine learning problems, we have to strike the right balance between the sensitivity and the specificity of our model. The more dependent words are on more distant precursors, the greater the complexity needed for an *n*-gram model to be predictive.

Significant Collocations

Now that our corpus reader is aware of *n*-grams, we can incorporate these features into our downstream models by vectorizing our text using *n*-grams as vector elements instead of simply vocabulary. However, using raw *n*-grams will produce many, many candidates, most of which will not be relevant. For example, the sentence "I got lost in the corn maze during the fall picnic" contains the trigram ('in', 'the', 'corn'), which is not a typical prepositional target, whereas the trigram ('I', 'got', 'lost') seems to make sense on its own.

In practice, this is too high a computational cost to be useful in most applications. The solution is to compute *conditional probability*. For example, what is the likelihood that the tokens ('the', 'fall') appear in the text given the token 'during'? We can compute empirical likelihoods by calculating the frequency of the (*n*-1)-gram conditioned by the first token of the *n*-gram. Using this technique we can value *n*-grams that are more often used together such as ('corn', 'maze') over rarer compositions that are less meaningful.

The idea of some *n*-grams having more value than others leads to another tool in the text analysis toolkit: *significant collocations*. Collocation is an abstract synonym for *n*-gram (without the specificity of the window size) and simply means a sequence of tokens whose likelihood of co-occurrence is caused by something other than random chance. Using conditional probability, we can test the hypothesis that a specified collocation is meaningful.

NLTK contains two tools to discover significant collocations: the `Collocation Finder`, which finds and ranks *n*-gram collocations, and `NgramAssocMeasures`, which contains a collection of metrics to score the significance of a collocation. Both utilities are dependent on the size of n and the module contains bigram, trigram, and quadgram ranking utilities. Unfortunately, 5-gram associations and above must be manually implemented by subclassing the correct base class and using one of the collocation tools as a template.

For now, let's explore the discovery of significant quadgrams. Because finding and ranking *n*-grams for a large corpus can take a lot of time, it is a good practice to write the results to a file on disk. We'll create a `rank_quadgrams` function that takes as input a corpus to read words from, as well as a metric from the `QuadgramAssocMeasures`, finds and ranks quadgrams, then writes the results as a tab-delimited file to disk:

```python
from nltk.collocations import QuadgramCollocationFinder
from nltk.metrics.association import QuadgramAssocMeasures


def rank_quadgrams(corpus, metric, path=None):
    """
    Find and rank quadgrams from the supplied corpus using the given
    association metric. Write the quadgrams out to the given path if
    supplied otherwise return the list in memory.
    """
    # Create a collocation ranking utility from corpus words.
    ngrams = QuadgramCollocationFinder.from_words(corpus.words())

    # Rank collocations by an association metric
    scored = ngrams.score_ngrams(metric)

    if path:
        # Write to disk as tab-delimited file
        with open(path, 'w') as f:
            f.write("Collocation\tScore ({})".format(metric.__name__))
            for ngram, score in scored:
                f.write("{}\t{}\n".format(repr(ngram), score))
    else:
        return scored
```

For example, we could use the likelihood ratios metric as follows:

```python
rank_quadgrams(
    corpus, QuadgramAssocMeasures.likelihood_ratio, 'quadgrams.txt'
)
```

This produces quadgrams with likelihood scores from our sample corpus, a few samples of which follow:

```
Collocation Score (likelihood_ratio)
('New', 'York', "'", 's') 156602.26742890902
('pictures', 'of', 'the', 'Earth')      28262.697780596758
('the', 'majority', 'of', 'users')      28262.36608379526
('numbed', 'by', 'the', 'mindlessness') 3091.139615301832
('There', 'was', 'a', 'time')    3090.2332736791095
```

The QuadgramAssocMeasures class gives several methods with which to rank significance via hypothesis testing. These methods assume that there is no association between the words (e.g., the null hypothesis), then compute the probability of the association occurring if the null hypothesis was true. If we can reject the null hypothesis because its significance level is too low we can accept the alternative hypothesis.

 NLTK's QuadgramAssocMeasures class exposes a number of significance testing tools such as the student T test, Pearson's Chi-square test, pointwise mutual information, the Poisson–Stirling measure, or even a Jaccard index. Bigram associations include even more methods such as Phi-square (the square of Pearson correlation), Fisher's Exact test, or Dice's coefficient.

Now we can conceive of a SignificantCollocations feature extraction transformer for use in a pipeline such as the one shown in Figure 7-2.

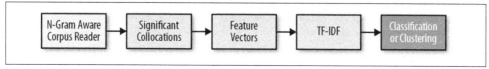

Figure 7-2. An n-gram feature extraction pipeline

On fit(), it would find and rank significant collocations, and then on transform() produce a vector that encoded the score for any significant collocation found in the document. These features could then be joined to your other vectors using the FeatureUnion.

```python
from sklearn.base import BaseEstimator, TransformerMixin


class SignificantCollocations(BaseEstimator, TransformerMixin):

    def __init__(self,
                 ngram_class=QuadgramCollocationFinder,
                 metric=QuadgramAssocMeasures.pmi):
        self.ngram_class = ngram_class
        self.metric = metric

    def fit(self, docs, target):
        ngrams = self.ngram_class.from_documents(docs)
        self.scored_ = dict(ngrams.score_ngrams(self.metric))
```

```
    def transform(self, docs):
        for doc in docs:
            ngrams = self.ngram_class.from_words(docs)
            yield {
                ngram: self.scored_.get(ngram, 0.0)
                for ngram in ngrams.nbest(QuadgramAssocMeasures.raw_freq, 50)
            }
```

The model could then be composed as follows:

```
from sklearn.linear_model import SGDClassifier
from sklearn.pipeline import Pipeline, FeatureUnion
from sklearn.feature_extraction import DictVectorizer
from sklearn.feature_extraction.text import TfidfVectorizer


model = Pipeline([
    ('union', FeatureUnion(
        transformer_list=[
            ('ngrams', Pipeline([
                ('sigcol', SignificantCollocations()),
                ('dsigcol', DictVectorizer()),
            ])),

            ('tfidf', TfidfVectorizer()),
        ]
    ))

    ('clf', SGDClassifier()),
])
```

Note that this is stub code only, but hopefully serves as a template so that context can be easily injected into a standard bag of words model.

n-Gram Language Models

Consider an application where a user will enter the first few words of a phrase, then suggest additional text based on the most likely next words (like a Google search). *n*-gram models utilize the statistical frequency of *n*-grams to make decisions about text. To compute an *n*-gram language model that predicts the next word after a series of words, we would first count all *n*-grams in the text and then use those frequencies to predict the likelihood of the last token in the *n*-gram given the tokens that precede it. Now we have reason to use our significant collocations not only as a feature extractor, but also as a model for language!

To build a language model that can generate text, our next step is to create a class that puts together the pieces we have stepped through in the above sections and implement one additional technique: *conditional frequency*.

NLTK once had a module that allowed for natural language generation, but it was removed following challenges to the method for computing *n*-gram models. The `NgramModel` and `NgramCounter` classes we implement in this section are inspired by a branch of NLTK that addressed many of these complaints, but is at the time of this writing still under development and not yet merged into master.

Frequency and Conditional Frequency

We first explored the concept of token frequency in Figure 4-2, where we used frequency representations with our bag-of-words model with the assumption that word count could sufficiently approximate a document's contents to differentiate it from others. Frequency is also a useful feature with *n*-gram modeling, where the frequency with which an *n*-gram occurs in the training corpus might reasonably lead us to expect to see that *n*-gram in new documents.

Imagine we are reading a book one word at a time and we want to compute the probability of the next word we'll see. A naive choice would be to assign the highest probability to the words that appear most frequently in the text, which we can visualize in Figure 7-3.

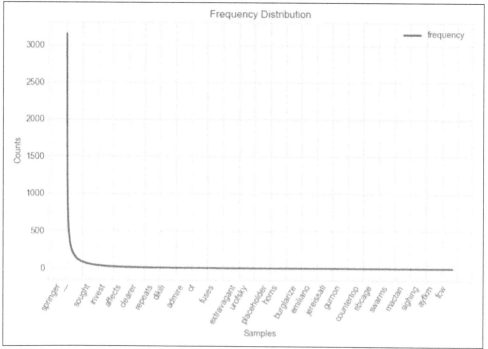

Figure 7-3. Frequency distribution plot of a text corpus

However, we know that this basic use of frequency is not enough; if we're starting a sentence some words have higher probability than other words and some words are much more likely given preceding words. For example, asking the question what is the probability of the word "chair" following "lawn" is very different than the probability of the word "chair" following "lava" (or "lamp"). These likelihoods are informed by *conditional probabilities* and are formulated as P(chair|lawn) (read as "the probability of chair given lawn"). To model these probabilities, we need to be able to compute the *conditional frequencies* of each of the possible *n*-gram windows.

We begin by defining an NgramCounter class that can keep track of conditional frequencies of all subgrams from unigrams up to *n*-grams using FreqDist and ConditionalFreqDist. Our class also implements the sentence padding we explored earlier in the chapter, and detects words that are not in the vocabulary of the original corpus.

```python
from nltk.util import ngrams
from nltk.probability import FreqDist, ConditionalFreqDist

from collections import defaultdict

# Padding Symbols
UNKNOWN = "<UNK>"
LPAD = "<s>"
RPAD = "</s>"


class NgramCounter(object):
    """
    The NgramCounter class counts ngrams given a vocabulary and ngram size.
    """

    def __init__(self, n, vocabulary, unknown=UNKNOWN):
        """
        n is the size of the ngram
        """
        if n < 1:
            raise ValueError("ngram size must be greater than or equal to 1")

        self.n = n
        self.unknown = unknown
        self.padding = {
            "pad_left": True,
            "pad_right": True,
            "left_pad_symbol": LPAD,
            "right_pad_symbol": RPAD,
        }

        self.vocabulary = vocabulary
        self.allgrams = defaultdict(ConditionalFreqDist)
```

```
        self.ngrams = FreqDist()
        self.unigrams = FreqDist()
```

Next, we will create a method for the NgramCounter class that enables us to systematically compute the frequency distribution and conditional frequency distribution for the requested *n*-gram window.

```
def train_counts(self, training_text):
    for sent in training_text:
        checked_sent = (self.check_against_vocab(word) for word in sent)
        sent_start = True
        for ngram in self.to_ngrams(checked_sent):
            self.ngrams[ngram] += 1
            context, word = tuple(ngram[:-1]), ngram[-1]
            if sent_start:
                for context_word in context:
                    self.unigrams[context_word] += 1
                sent_start = False

            for window, ngram_order in enumerate(range(self.n, 1, -1)):
                context = context[window:]
                self.allgrams[ngram_order][context][word] += 1
            self.unigrams[word] += 1

def check_against_vocab(self, word):
    if word in self.vocabulary:
        return word
    return self.unknown

def to_ngrams(self, sequence):
    """
    Wrapper for NLTK ngrams method
    """
    return ngrams(sequence, self.n, **self.padding)
```

Now we can define a quick method (outside of our NgramCounter class definition) that instantiates the counter and computes the relevant frequencies. Our count_ngrams function takes as parameters the desired *n*-gram size, the vocabulary, and a list of sentences represented as comma-separated strings.

```
def count_ngrams(n, vocabulary, texts):
    counter = NgramCounter(n, vocabulary)
    counter.train_counts(texts)
    return counter


if __name__ == '__main__':
    corpus = PickledCorpusReader('../corpus')
    tokens = [''.join(word[0]) for word in corpus.words()]
    vocab = Counter(tokens)
    sents = list([word[0] for word in sent] for sent in corpus.sents())
    trigram_counts = count_ngrams(3, vocab, sents)
```

For unigrams, we can get the frequency distribution using the `unigrams` attribute.

```
print(trigram_counts.unigrams)
```

For *n*-grams of higher order, we can retrieve a conditional frequency distribution from the `ngrams` attribute.

```
print(trigram_counts.ngrams[3])
```

The keys of the conditional frequency distribution show the possible contexts that might precede each word.

```
print(sorted(trigram_counts.ngrams[3].conditions()))
```

We can also use our model to get the list of possible next words:

```
print(list(trigram_counts.ngrams[3][('the', 'President')]))
```

Estimating Maximum Likelihood

Our `NgramCounter` class gives us the ability to transform a corpus into a conditional frequency distribution of *n*-grams. In the context of our hypothetical next word prediction application, we need a mechanism for scoring the possible candidates for next words after an *n*-gram so we can provide the most likely. In other words, we need a model that computes the probability of a token, `t`, given a preceding sequence, `s`.

One straightforward way to estimate the probability of the *n*-gram (`s,t`) is by computing its relative frequency. This is the number of times we see `t` appear as the next word after `s` in the corpus, divided by the total number of times we observe `s` in the corpus. The resulting ratio gives us a maximum likelihood estimate for the *n*-gram (`s,t`).

We will start by creating a class, `BaseNgramModel`, that will take as input an `Ngram Counter` object and produce a language model. We will initialize the `BaseNgramModel` model with attributes to keep track of the highest order *n*-grams from the trained `NgramCounter`, as well as the conditional frequency distributions of the *n*-grams, the *n*-grams themselves, and the vocabulary.

```
class BaseNgramModel(object):
    """
    The BaseNgramModel creates an n-gram language model.
    """

    def __init__(self, ngram_counter):
        """
        BaseNgramModel is initialized with an NgramCounter.
        """
        self.n = ngram_counter.n
        self.ngram_counter = ngram_counter
        self.ngrams = ngram_counter.ngrams[ngram_counter.n]
        self._check_against_vocab = self.ngram_counter.check_against_vocab
```

Next, inside our BaseNgramModel class, we create a score method to compute the relative frequency for the word given the context, checking first to make sure that the context is always shorter than the highest order *n*-grams from the trained Ngram Counter. Since the ngrams attribute of the BaseNgramModel is an NLTK Conditional FreqDist, we can retrieve the FreqDist for any given context, and get its relative frequency with freq:

```
def score(self, word, context):
    """
    For a given string representation of a word, and a string word context,
    returns the maximum likelihood score that the word will follow the
    context.

    fdist[context].freq(word) == fdist[(context, word)] / fdist[context]
    """
    context = self.check_context(context)

    return self.ngrams[context].freq(word)

def check_context(self, context):
    """
    Ensures that the context is not longer than or equal to the model's
    highest n-gram order.

    Returns the context as a tuple.
    """
    if len(context) >= self.n:
        raise ValueError("Context too long for this n-gram")

    return tuple(context)
```

In practice, *n*-gram probabilities tend to be pretty small, so they are often represented as log probabilities instead. For this reason, we'll create a logscore method that transforms the result of our score method into log format, unless the score is less than or equal to zero, in which case we'll return negative infinity:

```
def logscore(self, word, context):
    """
    For a given string representation of a word, and a word context,
    computes the log probability of the word in the context.
    """
    score = self.score(word, context)
    if score <= 0.0:
        return float("-inf")

    return log(score, 2)
```

Now that we have methods for scoring instances of particular *n*-grams, we want a method to score the language model as a whole, which we will do with *entropy*. We can create an `entropy` method for our `BaseNgramModel` by taking the average log probability of every *n*-gram from our `NgramCounter`.

```
def entropy(self, text):
    """
    Calculate the approximate cross-entropy of the n-gram model for a
    given text represented as a list of comma-separated strings.
    This is the average log probability of each word in the text.
    """
    normed_text = (self._check_against_vocab(word) for word in text)
    entropy = 0.0
    processed_ngrams = 0
    for ngram in self.ngram_counter.to_ngrams(normed_text):
        context, word = tuple(ngram[:-1]), ngram[-1]
        entropy += self.logscore(word, context)
        processed_ngrams += 1
    return - (entropy / processed_ngrams)
```

In Chapter 1 we encountered the concept of *perplexity*, and considered that within a given utterance, the previous few words might be enough to predict the next few subsequent words. The primary assumption is that meaning is very local, which is a variation of the Markov assumption. In the case of an *n*-gram model, we want to minimize perplexity by selecting the most likely (*n*+1)-gram, given an input *n*-gram. For that reason, it is common to evaluate the predictive power of a model by measuring its perplexity, which we can compute in terms of `entropy`, as 2 to the power entropy:

```
def perplexity(self, text):
    """
    Given list of comma-separated strings, calculates the perplexity
    of the text.
    """
    return pow(2.0, self.entropy(text))
```

Perplexity is a normalized way of computing probability; the higher the conditional probability of a sequence of tokens, the lower its perplexity will be. We should expect to see our higher-order models demonstrate less perplexity than our weaker models:

```
trigram_model = BaseNgramModel(count_ngrams(3, vocab, sents))
fivegram_model = BaseNgramModel(count_ngrams(5, vocab, sents))

print(trigram_model.perplexity(sents[0]))
print(fivegram_model.perplexity(sents[0]))
```

Unknown Words: Back-off and Smoothing

Because natural language is so flexible, it would be naive to expect even a very large corpus to contain all possible *n*-grams. Therefore our models must also be sufficiently flexible to deal with *n*-grams it has never seen before (e.g., "the President of California," "the United States of Canada"). Symbolic models deal with this problem of coverage through *backoff*—if the probability for an *n*-gram does not exist, the model looks for the probability of the (*n*-1)-gram ("the President of," "the United States of"), and so forth, until it gets to single tokens, or unigrams. As a rule of thumb, we should recursively back off to smaller *n*-grams until we have enough data to get a probability estimate.

Since our `BaseNgramModel` uses maximum likelihood estimation, some (perhaps many) *n*-grams will have a zero probability of occurring, resulting in a `score()` of zero and a perplexity score of + or - infinity. The means of addressing these zero-probability *n*-grams is to implement *smoothing*. Smoothing consists of donating some of the probability mass of frequent *n*-grams to unseen *n*-grams. The simplest type of smoothing is "add-one," or Laplace, smoothing, where the new term is assigned a frequency of 1 and the probabilities are recomputed, but there are many other types, such as "add-k," which is a generalization of Laplace smoothing.

We can easily implement both by creating an `AddKNgramModel` that inherits from our `BaseNgramModel` and overrides the `score` method by adding the smoothing value *k* to the *n*-gram count and dividing by the (*n*-1)-gram count, normalized by the unigram count multiplied by *k*:

```python
class AddKNgramModel(BaseNgramModel):
    """
    Provides add-k smoothed scores.
    """
    def __init__(self, k, *args):
        """
        Expects an input value, k, a number by which
        to increment word counts during scoring.
        """
        super(AddKNgramModel, self).__init__(*args)

        self.k = k
        self.k_norm = len(self.ngram_counter.vocabulary) * k

    def score(self, word, context):
        """
        With Add-k-smoothing, the score is normalized with
        a k value.
        """
        context = self.check_context(context)
        context_freqdist = self.ngrams[context]
        word_count = context_freqdist[word]
        context_count = context_freqdist.N()
        return (word_count + self.k) / \
                (context_count + self.k_norm)
```

Then we can create a `LaplaceNgramModel` class by passing in a value of k=1 to our `AddKNgramModel`:

```
class LaplaceNgramModel(AddKNgramModel):
    """
    Implements Laplace (add one) smoothing.
    Laplace smoothing is the base case of add-k smoothing,
    with k set to 1.
    """
    def __init__(self, *args):
        super(LaplaceNgramModel, self).__init__(1, *args)
```

NLTK's `probability` module exposes a number of ways of calculating probability, including some variations on maximum likelihood and add-*k* smoothing, as well as:

- `UniformProbDist`, which assigns equal probability to every sample in a given set, and a zero probability to all other samples.

- `LidstoneProbDist`, which smooths sample probabilities using a real number `gamma` between 0 and 1.

- `KneserNeyProbDist`, which implements a version of back-off that counts how likely an *n*-gram is provided the (n-1)-gram has been seen in training.

Kneser–Ney smoothing considers the frequency of a unigram not by itself but in relation to the *n*-grams it completes. While some words appear in many different contexts, others appear frequently, but only in certain contexts; we want to treat these differently.

We can create a wrapper for NLTK's convenient implementation of Kneser–Ney smoothing by creating a class `KneserNeyModel` that inherits from `BaseNgramModel` and overrides the `score` method to use `nltk.KneserNeyProbDist`. Note that NLTK's implementation, `nltk.KneserNeyProbDist`, requires trigrams:

```
class KneserNeyModel(BaseNgramModel):
    """
    Implements Kneser-Ney smoothing
    """
    def __init__(self, *args):
        super(KneserNeyModel, self).__init__(*args)
        self.model = nltk.KneserNeyProbDist(self.ngrams)

    def score(self, word, context):
        """
        Use KneserNeyProbDist from NLTK to get score
        """
        trigram = tuple((context[0], context[1], word))
        return self.model.prob(trigram)
```

Language Generation

Once we can assign probabilities to *n*-grams, we have a mechanism for preliminary language generation. In order to apply our `KneserNeyModel` to build a next word generator, we will create two additional methods, `samples` and `prob`, so that we can access the list of all trigrams with nonzero probabilities and the probability of each sample.

```python
def samples(self):
    return self.model.samples()

def prob(self, sample):
    return self.model.prob(sample)
```

Now, we can create a simple function that takes input text, retrieves the probability of each possible trigram continuation of the last two words, and appends the most likely next word. If fewer than two words are provided, we ask for more input. If our `KneserNeyModel` assigns zero probability, we try to change the subject:

```python
corpus = PickledCorpusReader('../corpus')
tokens = [''.join(word) for word in corpus.words()]
vocab = Counter(tokens)
sents = list([word[0] for word in sent] for sent in corpus.sents())

counter = count_ngrams(3, vocab, sents)
knm = KneserNeyModel(counter)

def complete(input_text):
    tokenized = nltk.word_tokenize(input_text)
    if len(tokenized) < 2:
        response = "Say more."
    else:
        completions = {}
        for sample in knm.samples():
            if (sample[0], sample[1]) == (tokenized[-2], tokenized[-1]):
                completions[sample[2]] = knm.prob(sample)
        if len(completions) == 0:
            response = "Can we talk about something else?"
        else:
            best = max(
                completions.keys(), key=(lambda key: completions[key])
            )
            tokenized += [best]
            response = " ".join(tokenized)

    return response

print(complete("The President of the United"))
print(complete("This election year will"))

The President of the United States
This election year will suddenly
```

While it's fairly easy to construct an application that does simple probabilistic language generation tasks, we can see that to build anything much more complex (e.g., something that generates full sentences), it will be necessary to encode more about language. This can be achieved with higher-order *n*-gram models and larger, domain-specific corpora.

So how do we decide if our model is good enough? We can evaluate *n*-gram models in two ways. The first is by using a probability measure like perplexity or entropy to evaluate the performance of the model on held-out or test data. In this case, whichever model maximizes entropy or minimizes perplexity for the test set is the better performing model. It is customary to describe the performance of symbolic models by their maximal context in terms of the size of *n*-grams and their smoothing mechanism. At the time of this writing, the best performing symbolic models are variations of the Kneser–Ney smoothed 5-gram model.[2]

On the other hand, it is sometimes more effective to evaluate an *n*-model by integrating it into the application and having users give feedback!

Conclusion

In this chapter we've explored several new methods of engineering context-aware features to improve simple bag-of-words models. The structure of text is essential in being able to understand text at a high level. By employing *context* through a grammar-based extraction of keyphrases or with significant collocations, we can considerably augment our models.

Our approach to text analysis in this chapter has been a *symbolic* approach, meaning we have modeled language as discrete chunks with probabilities of occurrence. By extending this model with *a priori* and a mechanism for *smoothing* when unknown words appeared we were able to create an *n*-gram language model for generating text. While this approach to language models may seem academic, the ability to statistically evaluate relationships between text has found popular use in a wide range of commercial applications including modern web search, chatbots, and machine translation.

Not discussed in this chapter, but relevant to the conclusion is a secondary approach: the neural, or *connectionist*, model of language, which utilizes neural networks as connected units with emergent behavior. While deep neural networks have been made widely available and very popular through tools like word2vec, Spacy, and TensorFlow, they can be very expensive to train and difficult to interpret and troubleshoot. For this reason, many applications employ more human understandable symbolic models, which can often be modified with more straightforward heuristics as we'll see in Chapter 10. In Chapter 12 we'll use the connectionist approach to build

---

2 Frankie James, Modified Kneser–Ney smoothing of *n*-gram models, (2000) *http://bit.ly/2JIc5pN*

a language classification model, and discuss use cases when it might be preferable in practice.

Before getting to these more advanced models, however, we'll first explore text visualization and visual model diagnostics in Chapter 8, using frequency and statistical computations to visualize exactly what's happening in our models.

Text Visualization

Machine learning is often associated with the automation of decision making, but in practice, the process of constructing a predictive model generally requires a human in the loop. While computers are good at fast, accurate numerical computation, humans are instinctively and instantly able to identify patterns. The bridge between these two necessary skill sets lies in *visualization*—the precise and accurate rendering of data by a computer in visual terms and the immediate assignation of meaning to that data by humans.

In Chapters 5 and 6 we examined several practical examples of applied machine learning models. Yet in the execution of these examples, we observed that the integration of machine learning is often not as straightforward as merely fitting a model. For one thing, the first model is rarely optimal, meaning that an iterative process of model fitting, evaluation, and tuning is frequently necessary.

Moreover, the evaluation, steering, and presentation of results from applied text analytics is significantly less straightforward than with numeric data. What is the best way to find the most informative features when features can be words, word fragments, or phrases? How do we know which classification model is best suited to our corpus? How can we know when we have selected the best value for k in a k-means clustering model?

It is these types of questions, coupled with our need to iterate toward an optimal, deployable solution as efficiently as possible, that have led us to adopt the *model selection triple* workflow as described in "The model selection triple" on page 7. In this chapter, we'll see how *visual diagnostics* extends this workflow with visual mechanisms to diagnose problems or to more easily qualify models with respect to each other. We'll explore a set of visual tools that can be useful in *steering* machine learning models, enabling more effective interventions in the modeling process led by our own innate abilities to see patterns in pictures.

We'll begin by building a variety of feature analysis and engineering techniques for text, from *n*-gram time series plots to stochastic neighbor embeddings. We'll then move toward visual analysis of text models and diagnostic tools for detecting model error, such as confusion matrices and class prediction error plots. Finally, we'll explore some visual methods for engaging in hyperparameter optimization to steer models toward higher performance.

Visualizing Feature Space

Within traditional numeric prediction pipelines, feature engineering, model evaluation, and tuning can be done in a fairly straightforward fashion. In low-dimensional space, we can identify a dataset's most informative features by fitting a model and computing how much of the observed variance is explained by each feature; such results can be visualized using bar charts or two-dimensional pairwise correlation heatmaps.

Visualizing feature space is not as easy when our data is text. This is in part because visualizing high-dimensional data is inherently more difficult, but also because visualizing text data in Python requires additional hoop-jumping compared to plotting purely numeric data. In this section, we'll explore a range of Matplotlib visualization routines we have found useful for *feature analysis* and *feature engineering*.

Visual Feature Analysis

In essence, feature analysis is the process by which we go about getting to know our data. With low-dimensional numeric data, the visual feature analysis techniques we might use would include box plots and violin plots, histograms, scatterplot matrices, radial visualizations, and parallel coordinates. Unfortunately, the high dimensionality of text data makes these techniques not only inconvenient, but also not always especially relevant.

In the context of text data, feature analysis amounts to building an understanding of what is in the corpus. For instance, how long are our documents and how big is our vocabulary? What patterns or combinations of *n*-grams tell us the most about our documents? For that matter, how grammatical is our text? Is it highly technical, composed of many domain-specific compound noun phrases? Has it been translated from another language? Is punctuation used in a predictable way?

These are the kinds of questions that enable us to begin forming sound hypotheses that will set us up for effective experimentation and efficient prototyping. In this section, we'll see a few specialized feature analysis techniques that are particularly well suited to text data: *n*-gram time series, network analyses, and projection plots.

n-gram viewer

In Chapter 7 we performed grammar-based feature extraction, aiming to identify significant patterns of tokens across many documents. In practice, we will have a much easier time steering this phase of the workflow if we can visually explore the frequency of combinations of tokens as a function of time. In this section, we'll illustrate how to create an *n*-gram viewer to support this kind of feature analysis.

 While the corpus readers we constructed in Chapters 3 and 4 did not have a `dates` method, this visualizer requires us to add some mechanism of mapping the timestamp of a document to its corresponding `fileid`.

Let's assume that the corpus data has been formatted as a dictionary where keys are corpus tokens and the values are (`token count, document datetime stamp`) tuples. Assume that we also have a comma-separated list, `terms`, with strings that correspond to the *n*-grams we would like to plot as a time series.

In order to explore *n*-grams over time, we begin by initializing a Matplotlib figure and axes, with the width and height dimensions specified in inches. For each term in our term list, we will plot the count of the target *n*-gram as the x-value and the datetime stamp of the document in which the term appeared as the y-value. We add a title to the plot, a color-coded legend, and labels for the y- and x-axes. We can also specify a particular date range to allow for zoom-and-filter functionality:

```
fig, ax = plt.subplots(figsize=(9,6))

for term in terms:
    data[term].plot(ax=ax)

ax.set_title("Token Frequency over Time")
ax.set_ylabel("word count")
ax.set_xlabel("publication date")
ax.set_xlim(("2016-02-29","2016-05-25"))
ax.legend()
plt.show()
```

The resulting plot, an example of which is shown in Figure 8-1, shows the frequency of mentions of political candidates (here represented by their unigrams) across news articles leading up to an election.

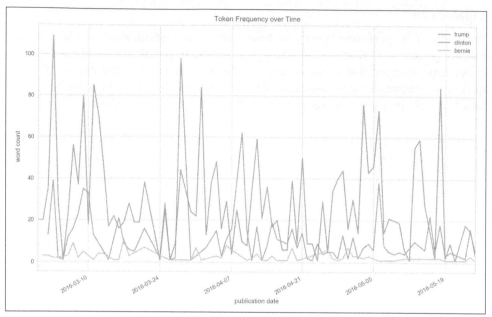

Figure 8-1. n-gram viewer displays token frequency over time

As such, time series plots can be a useful way to explore and compare the occurrences of *n*-grams in our corpus over time.

Network visualization

In practice, network visualizations are the current state of the art for text, as shown by the predominance of network style visualizations in a recent survey of text visualization.[1] This is because networks visually encode complex relationships that can only otherwise be expressed through natural language. They are particularly popular for social network analysis. Such graphs can be useful to illustrate relationships between entities, documents, and even concepts within a corpus, which we will explore more fully in Chapter 9. In this section, we'll create a plot that represents *The Wizard of Oz* by L. Frank Baum as a social network, where characters are nodes and their relationships are illustrated with edges that are shorter the closer their connection.

---

1 The ISOVIS Group. *Text Visualization Browser: A Visual Survey of Text Visualization Techniques*, (2015) *http:// textvis.lnu.se/*

In this section, we'll build a force-directed graph modeled on Mike Bostock's *Les Misérables character* co-occurrence network.[2] While such graphs are easier to render with D3 and other JavaScript frameworks, we will illustrate building them in Python using Matplotlib and NetworkX.

For our graph, we're using a postprocessed version of the Gutenberg edition stored in a JSON file that contains a dictionary with two items: first, a list of character names reverse-sorted by their frequency in the text, and second, a dictionary of chapters represented with {chapter heading: chapter text} key-value pairs. For simplicity, double newlines have been removed from the chapters (so each appears as a single paragraph), and all double quotation marks within the text (e.g., dialogue) have been converted to single quotes.

Since we will be representing the Oz characters as nodes in the graph, we need to establish the linkages between nodes. We can write a cooccurrence function that scans through each chapter, and for every possible pair of characters, checks how often both appear together. We initialize a dictionary with keys for each possible pair, then for each chapter, we use NLTK's sent_tokenize method to parse the text into sentences, and for each sentence that contains both characters' names, we increment the dictionary value by one:

```
import itertools
from nltk import sent_tokenize

def cooccurrence(text, cast):
    """
    Takes as input text, a dict of chapter {headings: text},
    and cast, a comma separated list of character names.
    Returns a dictionary of cooccurrence counts for each
    possible pair.
    """
    possible_pairs = list(itertools.combinations(cast, 2))
    cooccurring = dict.fromkeys(possible_pairs, 0)
    for title, chapter in text['chapters'].items():
        for sent in sent_tokenize(chapter):
            for pair in possible_pairs:
                if pair[0] in sent and pair[1] in sent:
                    cooccurring[pair] += 1
    return cooccurring
```

Next, we'll open our JSON file, load the text, extract the list of characters, and initialize a NetworkX graph. For each pair generated by our cooccurrence function with a nonzero value, we'll add an edge that stores the co-occurrence count as a property.

2 Mike Bostock, *Force-Directed Graph*, (2018) *http://bit.ly/2GNRKNU*

We'll then perform an `ego_graph` extraction on the graph that sets Dorothy as the center. We use a `spring_layout` to push nodes away from her in inverse proportion to their shared edge weight, specifying the desired distance between nodes using the *k* parameter (to avoid a hairball), and the number of iterations of spring-force relaxation with the `iterations` parameter. Finally, we use NetworkX's `draw` method to generate a Matplotlib figure with the desired node and edge colors and sizes, specifying that the node labels (the character names) be shown in a font that will be big enough to read:

```python
import json
import codecs
import networkx as nx
import matplotlib.pyplot as plt

with codecs.open('oz.json', 'r', 'utf-8-sig') as data:
    text = json.load(data)
    cast = text['cast']

    G = nx.Graph()
    G.name = "The Social Network of Oz"

    pairs = cooccurrence(text, cast)
    for pair, wgt in pairs.items():
        if wgt>0:
            G.add_edge(pair[0], pair[1], weight=wgt)

    # Make Dorothy the center
    D = nx.ego_graph(G, "Dorothy")
    edges, weights = zip(*nx.get_edge_attributes(D, "weight").items())

    # Push nodes away that are less related to Dorothy
    pos = nx.spring_layout(D, k=.5, iterations=40)
    nx.draw(D, pos, node_color="gold", node_size=50, edgelist=edges,
            width=.5, edge_color="orange", with_labels=True, font_size=12)
    plt.show()
```

The resulting plot shown in Figure 8-2 very effectively illustrates Dorothy's relationships in the book; the nodes closest to her include her closest allies—her dog, Toto, the Scarecrow, and the Tin Woodman, while those on the outer edges are characters with whom Dorothy interacts the least. The social graph also shows Dorothy's close promixity to Oz and the Wicked Witch, both of whom she has significant, albeit more complex, relationships.

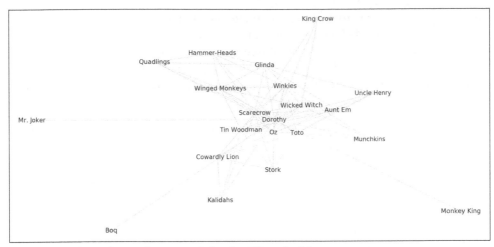

Figure 8-2. Force-directed ego graph for the Wizard of Oz

The construction and utility of property graphs as well as NetworkX's `add_edge`, `ego_graph` and `draw` methods will be discussed in greater detail in Chapter 9.

Co-occurrence plots

Co-occurrence is another way to quickly understand relationships between entities or other *n*-grams, in terms of the frequency with which they appear together. In this section we'll use Matplotlib to plot character co-occurrences in *The Wizard of Oz*.

First, we create a function `matrix` that will take in the text of the book and the list of characters. We initialize a multidimensional array that will be a list that contains a list for every character with the count of its co-occurrences with every other character:

```
from nltk import sent_tokenize

def matrix(text, cast):
    mtx = []
    for first in cast:
        row = []
        for second in cast:
            count = 0
            for title, chapter in text['chapters'].items():
                for sent in sent_tokenize(chapter):
                    if first in sent and second in sent:
                        count += 1
            row.append(count)
        mtx.append(row)
    return mtx
```

We can now plot our matrix. To approximate the D3 plots, we want to plot two co-occurrence matrices side by side; one with the characters ordered alphabetically and one where they are ordered by overall frequency in the text. We'll initialize a figure and axes, add a title and increase the default whitespace between the subplots to ensure there will be room for the characters names, and create enough x- and y-tick marks to correspond to every character.

We can then specify the modifications we'll be making to the first plot by referencing its index (121)—the number of rows (1), the number of columns (2), and the plot number (1) of the target subplot. We can then set the x- and y-tick marks and label the marks with the characters' names, reducing the default font size and rotating the labels by 90 degrees to ensure they will be easy to read. We'll specify that the x-ticks should appear on the top and add a label to our first axes plot. Finally, we'll call the imshow method to produce a heatmap with the interpolation parameter, specifying a yellow, orange, and brown colormap and using the lognorm of the frequency of each co-occurrence to ensure that very rare co-occurrences will not be too light to show up:

```
...

# First make the matrices
# By frequency
mtx = matrix(text,cast)

# Now create the plots
fig, ax = plt.subplots()
fig.suptitle('Character Co-occurrence in the Wizard of Oz', fontsize=12)
fig.subplots_adjust(wspace=.75)

n = len(cast)
x_tick_marks = np.arange(n)
y_tick_marks = np.arange(n)

ax1 = plt.subplot(121)
ax1.set_xticks(x_tick_marks)
ax1.set_yticks(y_tick_marks)
ax1.set_xticklabels(cast, fontsize=8, rotation=90)
ax1.set_yticklabels(cast, fontsize=8)
ax1.xaxis.tick_top()
ax1.set_xlabel("By Frequency")
plt.imshow(mtx,
           norm=matplotlib.colors.LogNorm(),
           interpolation='nearest',
           cmap='YlOrBr')
```

To create the alphabetic view of the co-occurrence plot, we begin by alphabetizing the list of characters and specifying that we want to work with the second subplot, (122), and add the axes elements much in the same way as for the first subplot:

```
...
# And alphabetically
alpha_cast = sorted(cast)
alpha_mtx = matrix(text,alpha_cast)

ax2 = plt.subplot(122)
ax2.set_xticks(x_tick_marks)
ax2.set_yticks(y_tick_marks)
ax2.set_xticklabels(alpha_cast, fontsize=8, rotation=90)
ax2.set_yticklabels(alpha_cast, fontsize=8)
ax2.xaxis.tick_top()
ax2.set_xlabel("Alphabetically")
plt.imshow(alpha_mtx,
            norm=matplotlib.colors.LogNorm(),
            interpolation='nearest',
            cmap='YlOrBr')
plt.show()
```

As with the network graph, the representation is only an approximation, as we are simply looking at the cast as though they are strings of characters, when in reality there are multiple ways in which characters can manifest ("Dorothy" and "the girl from Kansas," "Toto," and "her little dog, too"). Nonetheless, the resulting plot, shown in Figure 8-3, tells us a great deal about which characters interact the most within the text.

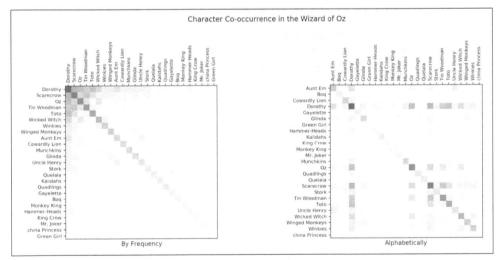

Figure 8-3. Character co-occurrences in the Wizard of Oz

Text x-rays and dispersion plots

While the network and co-occurrence plots do begin to elucidate the relationships between entities in a text (or characters in a plot), as well as which entities play some of the most important roles, they do not reflect very much about their various roles in the narrative. For this, we require something akin to Jeff Clark[3] and Trevor Stephen's[4] dispersion plots.

A dispersion plot provides a kind of "x-ray" of the text, plotting each character name along the y-axis and having the narrative plotted along the x-axis, such that a horizontal line can be added next to each character at the points in which he or she appears in the plot.

We can recreate a dispersion plot in Matplotlib using our *Wizard of Oz* text as follows. First, we need a list of `oz_words` of every word in the text in the order it occurs. We will also keep track of the lengths and headings of each chapter, so that we can later plot these along the x-axis to show where chapters begin and end:

```
...

from nltk import word_tokenize, sent_tokenize

    # Plot mentions of characters through chapters
    oz_words = []
    headings = []
    chap_lens = []
    for heading, chapter in text['chapters'].items():
        # Collect the chapter headings
        headings.append(heading)
        for sent in sent_tokenize(chapter):
            for word in word_tokenize(sent):
                # Collect all of the words
                oz_words.append(word)
        # Record the word lengths at each chapter
        chap_lens.append(len(oz_words))

    # Mark where chapters start
    chap_starts = [0] + chap_lens[:-1]
    # Combine with chapter headings
    chap_marks = list(zip(chap_starts,headings))
```

Now we want to search through the list of `oz_words` to look for places where the characters appear, adding these to a list of `points` for plotting. In our case, some of our characters have one-word names (e.g., "Dorothy," "Scarecrow," "Glinda"), while others have two-word names ("Cowardly Lion," "Monkey King"). To ensure we match types of strings, we'll first catalog the one-word name matches, checking for each word in the text to see if it matches a name, and then we'll look for the two-name characters by looking at each word together with its preceding word:

3 Jeff Clark, *Novel Views: Les Miserables,* (2013) *http://bit.ly/2GLzYKV*

4 Trevor Stephens, *Catch-22: Visualized,* (2014) *http://bit.ly/2GQKX6c*

```
...
        cast.reverse()
        points = []
        # Add a point for each time a character appears
        for y in range(len(cast)):
            for x in range(len(oz_words)):
                # Some characters have 1-word names
                if len(cast[y].split()) == 1:
                    if cast[y] == oz_words[x]:
                        points.append((x,y))
                # Some characters have 2-word names
                else:
                    if cast[y] == ' '.join((oz_words[x-1], oz_words[x])):
                        points.append((x,y))
        if points:
            x, y = list(zip(*points))
        else:
            x = y = ()
```

We will create a figure and axes, specifying a much wider x-axis than the default to ensure the plot will be easy to read. We will also add vertical lines to label the start of each chapter, and plot the names of each chapter as labels, adjusting them so that they will appear slightly below the axis, with a smaller font and a 90-degree rotation. We'll then plot our x and y points and modify the `tick_params` to turn off the default bottom ticks and labels. Then we add ticks along the y-axis for every character and label them with the character names, and finally, add a title:

```
...

        # Create the plot
        fig, ax = plt.subplots(figsize=(12,6))
        # Add vertical lines labeled for each chapter start
        for chap in chap_marks:
            plt.axvline(x=chap[0], linestyle='-',
                color='gainsboro')
            plt.text(chap[0], -2, chap[1], size=6, rotation=90)
        # Plot the character mentions
        plt.plot(x, y, "|", color="darkorange", scalex=.1)
        plt.tick_params(
            axis='x', which='both', bottom='off', labelbottom='off'
        )
        plt.yticks(list(range(len(cast))), cast, size=8)
        plt.ylim(-1, len(cast))
        plt.title("Character Mentions in the Wizard of Oz")
        plt.show()
```

The resulting plot, shown in Figure 8-4, provides a mini-map of the overall narrative of the text. Such a view not only enables us to see where certain characters (or, more generally, *n*-grams) enter and exit the story; it also emphasizes those characters who play a central role throughout the narrative, and even highlights some areas of interest in the text (e.g., those in which many characters are engaged simultaneously, or in which the cast shifts suddenly).

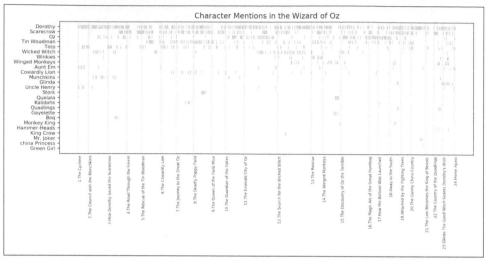

Figure 8-4. Dispersion plot of character mentions in the Wizard of Oz

Guided Feature Engineering

Once we have a more confident grasp on the raw content of our corpus, we must engineer the smallest and most predictive feature set for use in modeling. This engineered feature set must be as small as possible because each new dimension will inject noise and makes the decision space more difficult to model.

With text data, we need creative ways to dramatically reduce the dimensionality without sacrificing too much signal. Options such as Principal Component Analysis and linear discriminant analysis (and Doc2Vec in the case of text data) are all effective ways of compressing the dimensionality of the original data. However, these techniques can present problems later on if user stories require us to be able to retrieve the original features (e.g., the specific terms and phrases that make two documents similar).

In this section, we'll see a few visual techniques for steering feature engineering that we find are particularly well suited to text data: visual part-of-speech tagging and frequency distributions.

Part-of-speech tagging

As we learned in Chapter 3, parts of speech (e.g., verbs, nouns, prepositions, adjectives) indicate how a word is functioning within the context of a sentence. In English, as in many other languages, a single word can function in multiple ways, and we would like to be able to distinguish those uses (e.g., the words "ship" and "shop" can function as either verbs or nouns, depending on the context). Part-of-speech tagging lets us encode information not only about a word's definition, but also its use in context.

In Chapter 7, we used the part-of-speech tags together with a grammar to perform keyphrase extraction. One of the challenges of this kind of feature engineering is that it can be very difficult to know *a priori* which grammar to use to find significant keyphrases. Generally, our strategy is to use heuristics and experimentation until we land on a regular expression that does a good job at capturing the high-signal keyphrases. This strategy actually works quite well with grammatical English text. But what if the text with which we are working is ungrammatical, or rife with spelling and punctuation errors? In these cases, our out-of-the-box part-of-speech tagger may do more harm than good.

Consider if the text we are using does not encode the meaningful keyphrases according to the adjective-noun pattern? For example, there are numerous cases where the salient information could be captured not in the adjective phrases but instead in verbal or adverbial phrases, or in the proper nouns. In this case, even if our part-of-speech tagger is working properly and our keyphrase chunker looks something like...

```
grammar=r'KT: {(<JJ>* <NN.*>+ <IN>)? <JJ>* <NN.*>+}'
chunker = nltk.chunk.regexp.RegexpParser(grammar)
```

...we might indeed fail to capture the signal in our corpus!

It would be helpful to be able first to visually explore the parts-of-speech in a text before proceeding on to normalization, vectorization, and modeling (or perhaps as a diagnostic tool for understanding disappointing modeling results). For example, discovering that a large percentage of our text is not being labeled (or is being mislabeled) by our part-of-speech tagger might lead us to train our own regular expression–based tagger using our particular corpus. Alternatively, it might impact the way in which we choose to normalize our text (e.g., if there were many meaningful variations in the ways a certain root word was appearing, it might lead us to choose lemmatization over stemming, in spite of the increased computation time).

The Yellowbrick library offers a feature that enables the user to print out colorized text that illustrates different parts of speech. A PosTagVisualizer colorizes text to enable the user to visualize the proportions of nouns, verbs, etc., and to use this information to make decisions about part-of-speech tagging, text normalization (e.g., stemming versus lemmatization), and vectorization.

The transform method transforms the raw text input for the part-of-speech tagging visualization. Note that it requires that documents be in the form of (tag, token) tuples:

```
from nltk import pos_tag, word_tokenize
from yellowbrick.text.postag import PosTagVisualizer


pie = """
    In a small saucepan, combine sugar and eggs
    until well blended. Cook over low heat, stirring
    constantly, until mixture reaches 160° and coats
    the back of a metal spoon. Remove from the heat.
    Stir in chocolate and vanilla until smooth. Cool
    to lukewarm (90°), stirring occasionally. In a small
    bowl, cream butter until light and fluffy. Add cooled
    chocolate mixture; beat on high speed for 5 minutes
    or until light and fluffy. In another large bowl,
    beat cream until it begins to thicken. Add
    confectioners' sugar; beat until stiff peaks form.
    Fold into chocolate mixture. Pour into crust. Chill
    for at least 6 hours before serving. Garnish with
    whipped cream and chocolate curls if desired.
    """

tokens = word_tokenize(pie)
tagged = pos_tag(tokens)

visualizer = PosTagVisualizer()
visualizer.transform(tagged)

print(' '.join((visualizer.colorize(token, color)
            for color, token in visualizer.tagged)))
print('\n')
```

This code produces the results shown in Figure 8-5, when executed either in the command line or within a Jupyter Notebook.

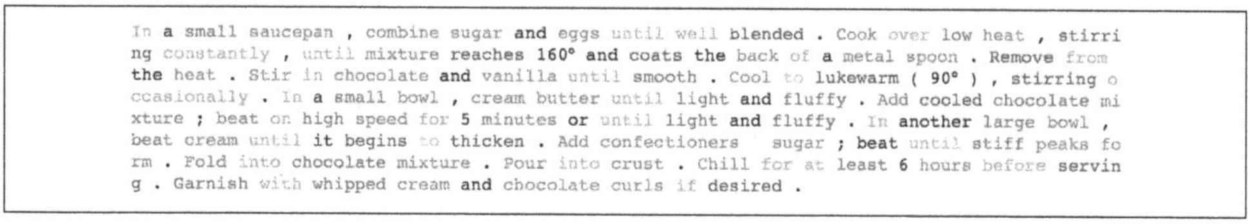

```
In a small saucepan , combine sugar and eggs until well blended . Cook over low heat , stirri
ng constantly , until mixture reaches 160° and coats the back of a metal spoon . Remove from
the heat . Stir in chocolate and vanilla until smooth . Cool to lukewarm ( 90° ) , stirring o
ccasionally . In a small bowl , cream butter until light and fluffy . Add cooled chocolate mi
xture ; beat on high speed for 5 minutes or until light and fluffy . In another large bowl ,
beat cream until it begins to thicken . Add confectioners  sugar ; beat until stiff peaks fo
rm . Fold into chocolate mixture . Pour into crust . Chill for at least 6 hours before servin
g . Garnish with whipped cream and chocolate curls if desired .
```

Figure 8-5. Part-of-speech tagged recipe

We can see from Figure 8-5 that the part-of-speech tagging has performed moderately well on the cookbook text, with only a few places where the tagger failed to tag or mistagged. However, we can see in the following example that the basic NLTK part-of-speech tagger does not perform equally well in all domains, such as in nursery rhymes (Figure 8-6).

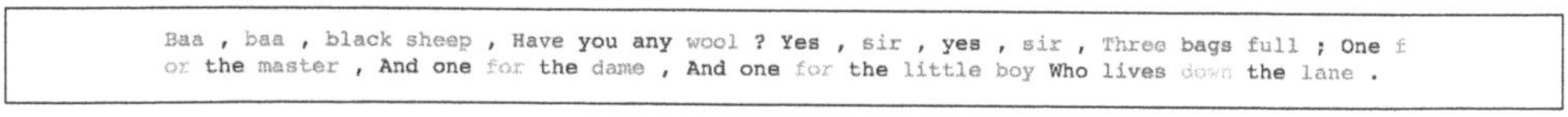

```
Baa , baa , black sheep , Have you any wool ? Yes , sir , yes , sir , Three bags full ; One f
or the master , And one for the dame , And one for the little boy Who lives down the lane .
```

Figure 8-6. Part-of-speech tagged nursery rhyme

Visual part-of-speech tagging can thus be used by the user as a tool for evaluating the efficacy of different preprocessing tasks (as described in Chapter 3) as well as for feature engineering and model diagnostics.

Most informative features

Identifying the most informative (i.e., predictive) features from a dataset is a key part of the model selection triple. Yet the techniques with which we are most familiar from numeric modeling (e.g., L1 and L2 regularization, Scikit-Learn utilities like `select_from_model`, etc.) are often less helpful when our data is comprised of text and our features are tokens or other linguistic characteristics. Once the data has been vectorized as in Chapter 4, the encoding makes it difficult to extract insights while keeping a natural narrative intact.

One method for visually exploring text is with frequency distributions. In the context of a text corpus, a frequency distribution tells us the prevalence of a vocabulary item or token.

In the next few examples, we'll use Yellowbrick to visually explore the "hobbies" subcorpus of Baleen, which can be downloaded along with the rest of Yellowbrick's datasets.

Loading Yellowbrick Datasets

How to load Yellowbrick datasets:

Yellowbrick provides several datasets wrangled from the UCI Machine Learning Repository. To download the data, clone the Yellowbrick library and run the download as follows:

```
$ git clone https://github.com/DistrictDataLabs/yellowbrick.git
$ cd yellowbrick/examples
$ python download.py
```

Note that this will create a directory called *data* that contains subdirectories with the given data.

Once downloaded, use the `sklearn.datasets.base.Bunch` object to load the corpus into features and target attributes, respectively, similarly to how Scikit-Learn's toy datasets are structured:

```
import os
import yellowbrick as yb
from sklearn.datasets.base import Bunch

## The path to the test datasets
FIXTURES  = os.path.join(os.getcwd(), "data")

## Corpus loading mechanisms
```

```
corpora = {
    "hobbies": os.path.join(FIXTURES, "hobbies")
}

def load_corpus(name):
    """
    Loads and wrangles the passed in text corpus by name.
    """

    # Get the path from the datasets
    path = corpora[name]

    # Read the directories in the directory as the categories.
    categories = [
        cat for cat in os.listdir(path)
        if os.path.isdir(os.path.join(path, cat))
    ]

    files  = [] # holds the filenames relative to the root
    data   = [] # holds the text read from the file
    target = [] # holds the string of the category

    # Load the data from the files in the corpus
    for cat in categories:
        for name in os.listdir(os.path.join(path, cat)):
            files.append(os.path.join(path, cat, name))
            target.append(cat)

            with open(os.path.join(path, cat, name), 'r') as f:
                data.append(f.read())

    # Return the data bunch for use similar to the newsgroups example
    return Bunch(
        categories=categories,
        files=files,
        data=data,
        target=target,
    )

corpus = load_corpus('hobbies')
```

Once we have our hobbies corpus loaded, we can use Yellowbrick to produce a frequency distribution to explore the vocabulary. NLTK also offers frequency distribution plots that show the top 50 tokens, but we'll use Yellowbrick here so that we can leverage its consistent API throughout a few examples. Note that neither the NLTK FreqDist method nor the Yellowbrick FreqDistVisualizer perform any normalization or vectorization on our behalf; both expect text that has already been count-vectorized.

We first instantiate a `FreqDistVisualizer` object and then call `fit()` on that object with the count vectorized documents and the features (i.e., the words from the corpus), which computes the frequency distribution. The visualizer then plots a bar chart of the top most frequent terms in the corpus (50 by default, but can be adjusted using the N parameter), with the terms listed along the x-axis and frequency counts depicted at y-axis values. We can then generate the finalized visualization by invoking Yellowbrick's `poof()` method:

```
from yellowbrick.text.freqdist import FreqDistVisualizer
from sklearn.feature_extraction.text import CountVectorizer

vectorizer = CountVectorizer()
docs = vectorizer.fit_transform(corpus.data)
features = vectorizer.get_feature_names()

visualizer = FreqDistVisualizer(features=features)
visualizer.fit(docs)
visualizer.poof()
```

In Figure 8-7, we can see the 50 most frequently occurring terms from the hobbies corpus. However, when we look at the words along the x-axis, we see that most of the terms are not particularly interesting (e.g., "the," "and," "to," "that," "of," "it"). Thus, while these are the most common terms, they likely aren't the most informative features.

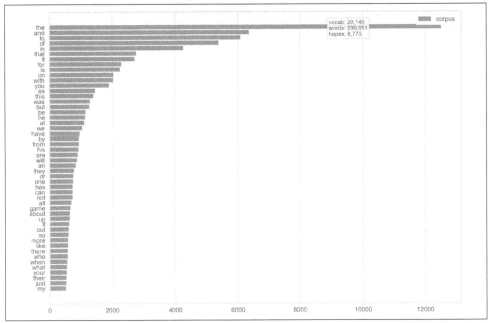

Figure 8-7. Frequency distribution of the Baleen corpus

In Chapter 4, we explored stopwords removal as a method for dimensionality reduction, and a means for arriving at the features that most likely encode salient information; here we'll use a frequency distribution to visualize the impact of removing the most common English words from our corpus, passing the `stop_words` parameter into Scikit-Learn's `CountVectorizer` in advance of `fit_transform`:

```
vectorizer = CountVectorizer(stop_words='english')
docs       = vectorizer.fit_transform(corpus.data)
features   = vectorizer.get_feature_names()

visualizer = FreqDistVisualizer(features=features)
visualizer.fit(docs)
visualizer.poof()
```

As we can see in Figure 8-8, now that the stopwords have been removed, the remaining features are somewhat more interesting (e.g., "game," "season," "team," "world," "film," "book," "week"). However, the diffuseness of the data is also evident. In Chapter 1 we learned that building language-aware data products relies on a domain-specific corpus rather than a generic one. What we need to determine now is whether the hobbies corpus is sufficiently domain specific to be modeled. We can continue to use frequency distribution plots to search within our corpus for more tightly focused subtopics and other patterns.

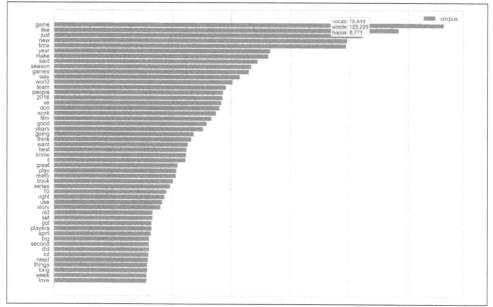

Figure 8-8. Frequency distribution of the Baleen corpus after stopwords removal

The hobbies corpus that comes with Yellowbrick has already been categorized (try `corpus['categories']`). Frequency distribution plots for two of the categories, "cooking" and "gaming," with stopwords removed are shown in Figures 8-9 and 8-10, respectively.

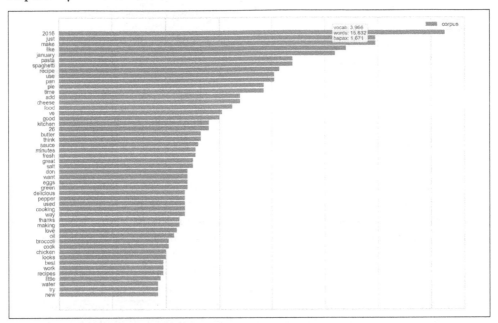

Figure 8-9. Frequency distribution for the cooking subcorpus

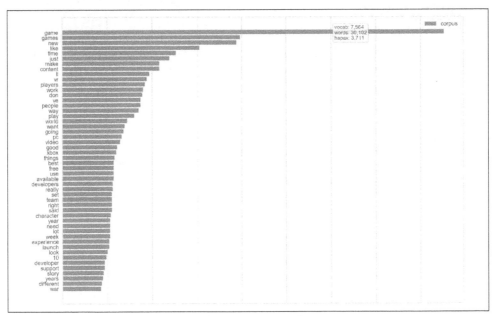

Figure 8-10. Frequency distribution for the gaming subcorpus

We can visually compare these plots, and instantly see how different they are; the most common words from the cooking corpus include "pasta," "pan," "broccoli," and "pepper," while the gaming corpus includes tokens like "players," "developers," "character," and "support."

Model Diagnostics

After feature analysis and engineering, the next phase of the model selection triple workflow is model selection. In practice, we will select and compare multiple models, since it is generally very difficult to predict in advance which model will be most effective with a new corpus. Thus, our next task is to determine when our models are performing well or poorly.

In a traditional machine learning context, we can rely on model performance scores —such as mean square error or coefficient of determination in the case of regression, and precision, accuracy, and F1 score for classification—to determine which models are strongest. These techniques can also be extended to the context of visual analytics. Regression problems are less common with text data, though we will see an example in Chapter 12, when we attempt to predict the floating-point scores of albums based purely on the text of their reviews. As discussed in Chapters 5 and 6, classification and clustering are more common learning approaches for text corpora, and in this section we will take a look at a few techniques for model evaluation in these contexts.

Visualizing Clusters

Model evaluation is not nearly as straightforward when it comes to clustering algorithms as it is in supervised learning problems, when we have the advantage of knowing the right and wrong answers *a priori*. With clustering, there is really no numeric score; instead, the relative success of a model is generally a function of how effectively it finds patterns that are distinguishable and meaningful to a human. For this reason, visualization becomes increasingly important.

Just as we looked for small-scale indications of separability and diffuseness using our frequency distribution plots, we should also investigate the degree of document similarity across all features. One very popular method for doing so is to use the nonlinear dimensionality reduction method t-distributed stochastic neighbor embedding, or *t-SNE*.

Scikit-Learn implements the t-SNE decomposition method as the `sklearn.mani fold.TSNE` transformer. By decomposing high-dimensional document vectors into two dimensions using probability distributions from both the original dimensionality and the decomposed dimensionality, t-SNE is able to effectively cluster similar documents. By decomposing to two or three dimensions, the documents can be visualized with a scatterplot.

Unfortunately, t-SNE is very computationally expensive, so typically a simpler decomposition method such as SVD or PCA is applied ahead of time. The Yellow-brick library exposes a `TSNEVisualizer`, which creates an inner transformer pipeline that applies such a decomposition first (SVD with 50 components by default), then performs the t-SNE embedding. The `TSNEVisualizer` expects document vectors, so we will use the `TfidfVectorizer` from Scikit-Learn in advance of passing the documents into the `TSNEVisualizer` fit method:

```
from yellowbrick.text import TSNEVisualizer
from sklearn.feature_extraction.text import TfidfVectorizer

tfidf = TfidfVectorizer()
docs  = tfidf.fit_transform(corpus.data)

tsne = TSNEVisualizer()
tsne.fit(docs)
tsne.poof()
```

What we're looking for in such graphs are spatial similarities between the points (documents) and any other discernible patterns. Figure 8-11 displays a projection of the vectorized Baleen hobbies corpus in two dimensions using t-SNE. The result is a scatterplot of the vectorized corpus, where each point represents a document or utterance. The distance between two points in the visual space is embedded using the probability distribution of pairwise similarities in the higher dimensionality; thus our `TSNEVisualizer` shows clusters of similar documents in the hobbies corpus and the relationships between groups of documents.

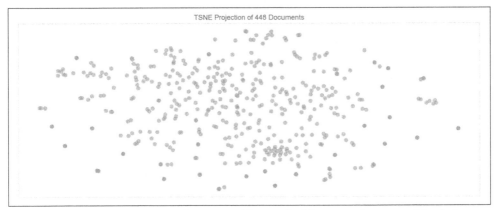

Figure 8-11. A t-distributed stochastic neighbor embedding visualization of the Baleen hobbies corpus

As mentioned before, the `TSNEVisualizer` expects vectorized text as input, and in this case, we have used TF–IDF, though we could have used any of the vectorization techniques described in Chapter 4 and then generated t-SNE visualization to compare the results. To speed the rendering, the `TSNEVisualizer` also employs decomposition ahead of the stochastic neighbor embedding, defaulting to using a sparse method (`TruncatedSVD`); we might also experiment with a dense method like PCA, which we can do by passing `decompose = "pca"` into `TSNEVisualizer()` upon initialization.

When used in conjunction with a clustering algorithm, `TSNEVisualizer` can also be used for visualizing clusters. Used this way, the technique can help to assess the efficacy of one clustering method over another. Here, we'll use `sklearn.clus ter.KMeans`, set the number of clusters to 5, and then pass the resulting `cluster.labels_` attribute as y into the `TSNEVisualizer fit()` method:

```
# Apply clustering instead of class names.
from sklearn.cluster import KMeans

clusters = KMeans(n_clusters=5)
clusters.fit(docs)

tsne = TSNEVisualizer()
tsne.fit(docs, ["c{}".format(c) for c in clusters.labels_])
tsne.poof()
```

Now, not only are all points in the same cluster grouped together, the points are also colored based on *k*-means similarity (Figure 8-12). We could experiment with different clustering methods here, or with different values of *k*, which we'll explore more fully later in the section on hyperparameter tuning.

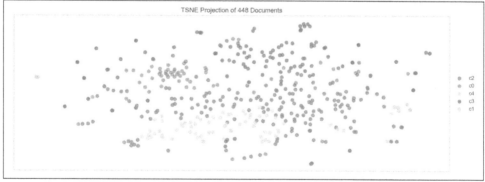

Figure 8-12. A t-SNE visualization of the Baleen hobbies corpus after k-means clustering

Visualizing Classes

For classification problems, we can simply provide a target value (stored in `corpus.target` here) to our `TSNEVisualizer` to produce a version of the graph where the colors of points are associated with the categorical labels corresponding to the documents. By specifying these labels as an argument for the classes when we call fit() on our t-SNE visualizer, we can colorize our dimensionality-reduced points with respect to their category:

```
from yellowbrick.text import TSNEVisualizer
from sklearn.feature_extraction.text import TfidfVectorizer

tfidf  = TfidfVectorizer()
docs   = tfidf.fit_transform(corpus.data)
labels = corpus.target

tsne = TSNEVisualizer()
tsne.fit(docs, labels)
tsne.poof()
```

As we can see in the scatterplot in Figure 8-13, this view extends our neighbor embedding with more information about similarity, which can allow for better interpretation of our classes. If we were interested in exploring only a few of the categories within our corpus, this is as easy as passing in a `classes` parameter into the `TSNEVisualizer` upon instantiation, with a list of the strings representing the different subcategories (e.g., TSNEVisualizer(classes=['sports', 'cinema', 'gaming'])).

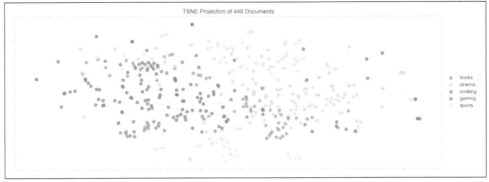

Figure 8-13. A t-distributed stochastic neighbor embedding visualization of the Baleen hobbies corpus with category labels

Visually iterating through these plots can enable us to see the categories whose documents are more tightly grouped, as well as those that are comparatively more diffuse, which might complicate the modeling process.

Diagnosing Classification Error

In traditional classification pipelines, fitted models can be optimized and then described with respect to their precision, recall, and F1 scores. We can visualize these measures using confusion matrices, classification heatmaps, and ROC-AUC curves.

In Chapter 5, we used cross-validation to test our models' performance on different train and test splits within the corpus. We also created a method to test a number of different models, so that their results could be compared using classification reports and confusion matrices. We were able to use the metrics to identify which of our models performed best, but the metrics alone did not provide much insight into why a certain model (or train test split) performed the way it did.

In this section, we'll explore two of our favorite techniques for visually analyzing and comparing the performance of classifiers on text: classification heatmaps and confusion matrices.

Classification report heatmaps

A classification report is a text summary of the main metrics for assessing the success of a classifier: *precision*, the ability not to label an instance positive that is actually negative; *recall*, the ability to find all positive instances; and *f1 score*, a weighted harmonic mean of precision and recall. While the Scikit-Learn `metrics` module does expose a `classification_report` method, we find that the Yellowbrick version, which integrates numerical scores with a color-coded heatmap, supports easier interpretation and problem detection.

To use Yellowbrick to create a classification heatmap, we load our corpus as in "Loading Yellowbrick Datasets" on page 165, TF–IDF vectorize the documents and create train and test splits. We then instantiate a `ClassificationReport`, pass in the desired classifier, and the names of the classes, the call `fit` and `score`, which call the internal Scikit-Learn fitting and scoring mechanisms for the model. Finally, we call `poof` on the visualizer, which adds the requisite labeling and coloring to the plot and then calls Matplotlib's `draw`:

```
from sklearn.naive_bayes import GaussianNB
from sklearn.model_selection import train_test_split
from yellowbrick.classifier import ClassificationReport

corpus = load_corpus('hobbies')
docs   = TfidfVectorizer().fit_transform(corpus.data)
labels = corpus.target

X_train, X_test, y_train, y_test = train_test_split(
    docs.toarray(), labels, test_size=0.2
)

visualizer = ClassificationReport(GaussianNB(), classes=corpus.categories)

visualizer.fit(X_train, y_train)
visualizer.score(X_test, y_test)
visualizer.poof()
```

The resulting classification heatmap, shown in Figure 8-14, displays the precision, recall, and F1 scores for the fitted model, where the darker zones show the model's highest areas of performance. In this example, we see that the Gaussian model successfully classifies most of the categories, but struggles with false negatives for the "books" category.

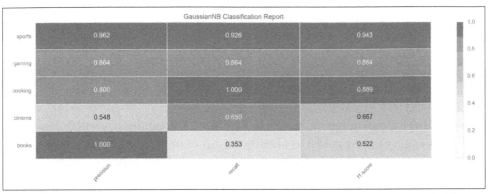

Figure 8-14. Classification heatmap for Gaussian Naive Bayes classifier on the hobbies corpus

We can compare the Gaussian model to another model simply by importing a different Scikit-Learn classifier and passing it into the `ClassificationReport` on instantiation. By comparison, the `SGDClassifier`, shown in Figure 8-15, is less successful at classifying the hobbies corpus, struggling with false positives for "gaming" and false negatives for "books."

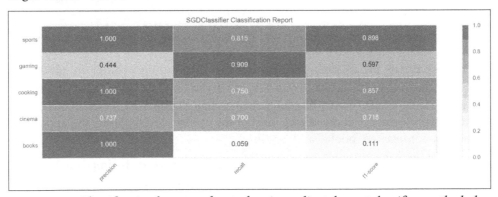

Figure 8-15. Classification heatmap for stochastic gradient descent classifier on the hobbies corpus

Confusion matrices

A confusion matrix provides similar information as what is available in a classification report, but rather than top-level scores, it provides more detailed information.

In order to use Yellowbrick to create this type of visualization, we instantiate a `ConfusionMatrix` and pass in the desired classifier and the names of the classes, as we did with the `ClassificationReport`, and call the `fit`, `score`, `poof` sequence:

```
from yellowbrick.classifier import ConfusionMatrix
from sklearn.linear_model import LogisticRegression

...

visualizer = ConfusionMatrix(LogisticRegression(), classes=corpus.categories)

visualizer.fit(X_train, y_train)
visualizer.score(X_test, y_test)
visualizer.poof()
```

The resulting confusion matrix, shown in Figure 8-16, demonstrates which classes are most challenging for the model to identify. In this example, the `LogisticRegression` model is successful at identifying "sports" and "gaming," but appears to struggle with the other categories.

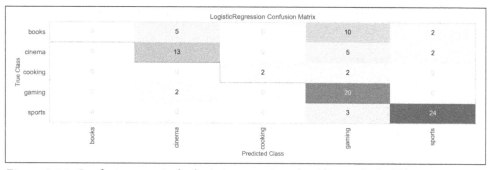

Figure 8-16. Confusion matrix for logistic regression classifier on the hobbies corpus

We can compare the model's performance by substituting a different model on instantiation of the `ConfusionMatrix`, just as we did for the `ClassificationReport`. By comparison, a `MultinomialNB` classifier, shown in Figure 8-17, seems to have similarly weak performance at classifying most of the hobby subcategories, and appears to frequently confuse the "books" and "gaming."

Overall performance is highly context-dependent, and it is important to set application-specific benchmarks rather than relying on high-level metrics like F1 score to determine if a model is adequate for deployment. For instance, if our hypothetical application will depend on successfully identifying sports-related content, these models may be sufficient. If we're intending to find book reviews, though, the consistently poor performance of these classifiers suggests we may need to revisit our original dataset.

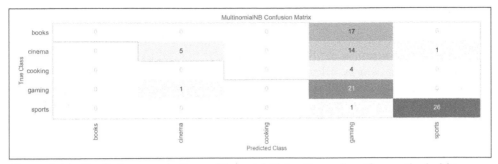

Figure 8-17. Confusion matrix for multinomial Naive Bayes classifier on the hobbies corpus

Visual Steering

When we call `fit` on a Scikit-Learn estimator, the model learns the parameters of the algorithm that best fit the data it has been provided. However, some parameters are not directly learned within an estimator. These are the ones we provide on instantiation, the *hyperparameters*.

Hyperparameters are model-specific, but include things such as the amount of penalty to use for a regularization, the kernel function for a support vector machine, the number of leaves or depth of a decision tree, the number of neighbors used in a nearest neighbor classifier, or the number of clusters in *k*-means clustering.

Scikit-Learn models are often surprisingly successful with little to no modification of the default hyperparameters. Rather than a matter of luck, this is a signal of the substantial amount of experience and domain expertise that have been contributed to the library. Nonetheless, after we have arrived at the suite of models we find most successful for our problem, the next step of the process is to experiment with tuning the hyperparameters so that we can arrive at the most optimal settings for each model.

In this section, we will demonstrate how to explore hyperparameters visually, specifically to steer *k*-selection for *k*-means clustering problems.

Silhouette Scores and Elbow Curves

As we saw in Chapter 6, *k*-means is a simple unsupervised machine learning algorithm that groups data into a specified number *k* of clusters. Because the user must specify in advance what *k* to choose, the algorithm is somewhat naive—it assigns all members to *k* clusters whether or not it is the right *k* for the dataset. The Yellowbrick library provides two mechanisms for selecting an optimal *k* parameter for centroidal clustering, *silhouette scores* and *elbow curves*, which we'll explore in this section.

Silhouette scores

The silhouette coefficient is used when the ground-truth about the dataset is unknown, instead computing the density of clusters produced by the model. A silhouette score can then be calculated by averaging the silhouette coefficient for each sample, computed as the difference between the average intracluster distance and the mean nearest-cluster distance for each sample, normalized by the maximum value.

This produces a score between 1 and -1, where 1 is highly dense clusters, -1 is completely incorrect clustering, and values near zero indicate overlapping clusters. The higher the score the better, because the clusters are denser and more separate. Negative values imply that samples have been assigned to the wrong cluster, and positive values mean that there are discrete clusters. The scores can then be plotted to display a measure of how close each point in one cluster is to points in the neighboring clusters.

The Yellowbrick `SilhouetteVisualizer` can be used to visualize the silhouette scores of each cluster in a single model. Because it is very difficult to score a clustering model, Yellowbrick visualizers wrap Scikit-Learn "clusterer" estimators via their `fit()` method. Once the clustering model is trained, the visualizer can call `poof()` to display the clustering evaluation metric. In order to create the visualization, we first train the clustering model, instantiate the visualizer, fit it on the corpus, and then call the visualizer's `poof()` method:

```
from sklearn.cluster import KMeans
from yellowbrick.cluster import SilhouetteVisualizer

# Instantiate the clustering model and visualizer
visualizer = SilhouetteVisualizer(KMeans(n_clusters=6))
visualizer.fit(docs)
visualizer.poof()
```

The `SilhouetteVisualizer` displays the silhouette coefficient for each sample on a per-cluster basis, visualizing which clusters are dense and which are not. The vertical thickness of the plotted cluster indicates its size, and the dashed red line is the global average. This is particularly useful for determining cluster imbalance, or for selecting a value for k by comparing multiple visualizers. We can see from Figure 8-18 that several clusters are vertically thick but low scoring, suggesting that we should pick a higher k.

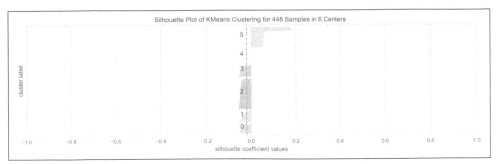

Figure 8-18. A visualization of the silhouette scores for k-means clustering

Elbow curves

Another visual technique that can be used for *k* selection is the elbow method. The elbow method visualizes multiple clustering models with different values for *k*. Model selection is based on whether or not there is an "elbow" in the curve (i.e., if the curve looks like an arm with a clear change in angle from one part of the curve to another).

In Yellowbrick, the KElbowVisualizer implements the elbow method of selecting the optimal number of clusters for *k*-means clustering. The user instantiates the visualizer, passing in the unfitted KMeans() model and a range of values for *k* (say, from 4 to 10). Then, when fit() is called on the model with the documents from the corpus (we assume below the corpus has already been TF–IDF vectorized), the elbow method runs *k*-means clustering on the dataset for each value of *k* and computes the silhouette_score, the mean silhouette coefficient for all samples. When poof() is called, the silhouette score for each *k* is plotted:

```
from sklearn.cluster import KMeans
from yellowbrick.cluster import KElbowVisualizer

# Instantiate the clustering model and visualizer
visualizer = KElbowVisualizer(KMeans(), metric='silhouette', k=[4,10])
visualizer.fit(docs)
visualizer.poof()
```

If the line chart looks like an arm, then the "elbow" (the point of inflection on the curve) is the best value of *k*; we want as small a *k* as possible such that the clusters do not overlap. If the data isn't very clustered, the elbow method may not always work well, resulting either in a smooth curve or a very jumpy line. Such results might lead us to use the SilhouetteScore visualizer instead, or to reconsider the partitive clustering approach for our data. While fairly jumpy, our plot in Figure 8-19 suggests that setting the number of clusters to 7 might improve the density and separability of our document clusters.

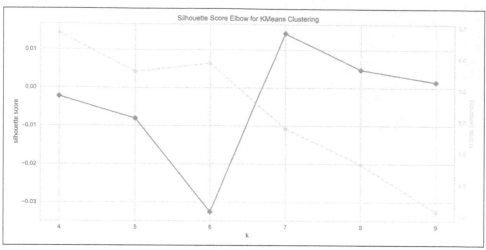

Figure 8-19. A visualization of the elbow curve for k-means clustering

Conclusion

Regardless of whether our data consists of numbers or text (or of image pixels or acoustic notes, for that matter), a single score, or even a single plot, is often insufficient to support the construction of model selection triples. For exploratory analysis, feature engineering, model selection, and evaluation, visualizations are very useful for diagnostic purposes. In combination with numeric scores, they can help build better intuition around performance. However, text data can present some special challenges for visualization, particularly with regards to dimensionality and interpretability.

In our experience, steering leads to better models (e.g., higher F1 scores, more distinct clusters, etc.), arrived at more quickly and with greater overall insight. Thanks to the visual cortex, we are frequently much better at detecting such patterns visually than we are using numeric outputs alone. Thus, using visual steering we can more effectively engage the modeling process.

While there are as yet not a wide variety of Python libraries to support visual diagnostics for modeling on text data, the techniques demonstrated in this chapter can prove to be very good resources, lowering the barrier between the human level and the computational layer by providing an interactive interface for machine learning on text. Of the visualization libraries available, two very useful tools are Matplotlib and Yellowbrick, which together enable visual filtering, aggregation, indexing, and formatting, to help render large corpora and feature space more interpretable and interactive.

One of the most effective text visualizations we saw in this chapter are graphs, which enable us to distill tremendous amounts of information in very intuitive ways. In

Chapter 9, we will explore graph models more deeply, both to the extent to which they enable effective visual aggregation, but also their capacity to model information that would otherwise require significantly more complex feature engineering efforts.

Graph Analysis of Text

Up until this point, we have been applying traditional classification and clustering algorithms to text. By allowing us to measure distances between terms, assign weights to phrases, and calculate probabilities of utterances, these algorithms enable us to reason about the relationships between documents. However, tasks such as machine translation, question answering, and instruction-following often require more complex, semantic reasoning.

For instance, given a large number of news articles, how would you build a model of the narratives they contain—of actions taken by key players or enacted upon others, of the sequence of events, of cause and effect? Using the techniques in Chapter 7, you could extract the entities or keyphrases or look for themes using the topic modeling methods described in Chapter 6. But to model information about the *relationships* between those entities, phrases, and themes, you would need a different kind of data structure.

Let's consider how such relationships may be expressed in the headlines of some of our articles:

```
headlines = ['FDA approves gene therapy',
             'Gene therapy reduces tumor growth',
             'FDA recalls pacemakers']
```

Traditionally, phrases like these are encoded using *text meaning representations* (TMRs). TMRs take the form of (*'subject'*, *'predicate'*, *'object'*) triples (e.g., (`'FDA'`, `'recalls'`, `'pacemakers'`)), to which first-order logic or lambda calculus can be applied to achieve semantic reasoning.

Unfortunately, the construction of TMRs often requires substantial prior knowledge. For instance, we need to know not only that the acronym "FDA" is an actor, but that "recalling" is an action that can be taken by some entities against others. For most language-aware data products, building a sufficient number of TMRs to support meaningful semantic analysis will not be practical.

However, if we shift our thinking slightly, we might also think of this subject-predicate-object as a *graph*, where the predicates are *edges* between subject and object *nodes*, as shown in Figure 9-1. By extracting co-occurring entities and keyphrases from the headlines, we can construct a graph representation of the relationships between the "who," the "what," and even the "where," "how," and "when" of an event. This will allow us to use graph traversal to answer analytical questions like "Who are the most influential actors to an event?" or "How do relationships change over time?" While not necessarily a complete semantic analysis, this approach can produce useful insights.

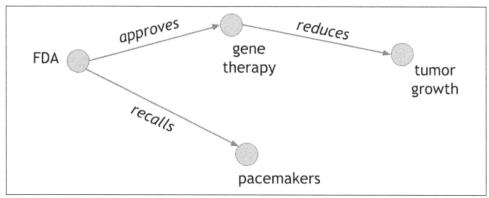

Figure 9-1. Semantic reasoning on text using graphs

In this chapter, we will analyze text data in this way, using graph algorithms. First, we will build a graph-based thesaurus and identify some of the most useful graph metrics. We will then extract a social graph from our Baleen corpus, connecting actors that appear in the same documents together and employing some simple techniques for extracting and analyzing *subgraphs*. Finally, we will introduce a graph-based approach to *entity resolution* called *fuzzy blocking*.

NetworkX and Graph-tool are the two primary Python libraries that implement graph algorithms and the property graph model (which we'll explore later in this chapter). Graph-tool scales significantly better than NetworkX, but is a C++ implementation that must be compiled from source. For graph-based visualization, we frequently leverage non-Python tools, such as Gephi, D3.js, and Cytoscape.js. To keep things simple in this chapter, we will stick to NetworkX.

Graph Computation and Analysis

One of the primary exercises in graph analytics is to determine what exactly the nodes and edges should be. Generally, nodes represent the real-world entities we would like to analyze, and edges represent the different types (and magnitudes) of relationships that exist between nodes.

Once a schema is determined, graph extraction is fairly straightforward. Let's consider a simple example that models a thesaurus as a graph. A traditional thesaurus maps words to sets of other words that have similar meanings, connotations, and usages. A graph-based thesaurus, which instead represents words as nodes and synonyms as edges, could add significant value, modeling semantic similarity as a function of the path length and weight between any two connected terms.

Creating a Graph-Based Thesaurus

To implement the graph-based thesaurus just described, we will use WordNet,[1] a large lexical database of English-language words that have been grouped into interlinked *synsets*, collections of cognitive synonyms that express distinct concepts. For our thesaurus, nodes will represent words from the WordNet synsets (which we can access via NLTK's WordNet interface) and edges will represented synset relationships and interlinkages.

We will define a function, `graph_synsets()`, to construct the graph and add all the nodes and edges. Our function accepts a list of terms as well as a maximum depth, creates an undirected graph using NetworkX, and assigns it the `name` property for quick identification later. Then, an internal `add_term_links()` function adds synonyms by looking up the NLTK `wn.synsets()` function, which returns all possible definitions for the given word.

For each definition, we loop over the synonyms returned by the internal `lemma_names()` method, adding nodes and edges in a single step with the NetworkX `G.add_edge()` method. If we are not at the depth limit, we recurse, adding the links for the terms in the `synset`. Our `graph_synsets` function then loops through each of the terms provided and uses our recursive `add_term_links()` function to retrieve the synonyms and build the edges, finally returning the graph:

---

1 George A. Miller and Christiane Fellbaum, *WordNet: A Lexical Database for English*, (1995) *http://bit.ly/2GQKXmI*

```
import networkx as nx
from nltk.corpus import wordnet as wn

def graph_synsets(terms, pos=wn.NOUN, depth=2):
    """
    Create a networkx graph of the given terms to the given depth.
    """

    G = nx.Graph(
        name="WordNet Synsets Graph for {}".format(", ".join(terms)), depth=depth,
    )

    def add_term_links(G, term, current_depth):
        for syn in wn.synsets(term):
            for name in syn.lemma_names():
                G.add_edge(term, name)
                if current_depth < depth:
                    add_term_links(G, name, current_depth+1)

    for term in terms:
        add_term_links(G, term, 0)

    return G
```

To get the descriptive statistical information from a NetworkX graph, we can use the info() function, which will return the number of nodes, the number of edges, and the average degree of the graph. Now we can test our function by extracting the graph for the word "trinket" and retrieving these basic graph statistics:

```
G = graph_synsets(["trinket"])
print(nx.info(G))
```

The results are as follows:

```
Name: WordNet Synsets Graph for trinket
Type: Graph
Number of nodes: 25
Number of edges: 49
Average degree:   3.9200
```

We now have a functional thesaurus! You can experiment by creating graphs with a different target word, a list of target words, or by changing the depth of synonyms collected.

Analyzing Graph Structure

By experimenting with different input terms for our graph_synsets function, you should see that the resulting graphs can be very big or very small, and structurally more or less complex depending on how terms are connected. When it comes to analysis, graphs are described by their structure. In this section, we'll go over the set of standard metrics for describing the structure of a graph.

In the last section, the results of our `nx.info` call provided us with the graph's number of nodes (or *order*), its number of edges (or *size*), and its average *degree*. A node's *neighborhood* is the set of nodes that are reachable from that specific node via edge traversal, and the size of the neighborhood identifies the node's *degree*. The average degree of a graph reflects the average size of all the neighborhoods within that graph.

The *diameter* of a graph is the number of nodes traversed in the *shortest path* between the two most distant nodes. We can use the `diameter()` function to get this statistic:

```
>>> nx.diameter(G)
4
```

In the context of our "trinket" thesaurus graph, a shortest path of 4 may suggest a more narrowly used term (see Table 9-1), as opposed to other terms that have more interpretations (e.g., "building") or are used in more contexts ("bank").

Table 9-1. Shortest paths for common terms

Term	trinket	bank	hat	building	boat	whale	road	tickle
Diameter	4	6	2	6	1	5	3	6

When analyzing a graph structure, some key questions to consider are:

- What is the depth or diameter of the graph?
- Is it fully connected (meaning is there a pathway between every possible pair of nodes)?
- If there are disconnected components, what are their sizes and other features?
- Can we extract a subgraph (or *ego-graph*, which we'll explore a bit later) for a particular node of interest?
- Can we create a subgraph that filters for a specific amount or type of information? For example, of the 25 possible results, can we return only the top 5?
- Can we insert nodes or edges of different types to create different styles of structures? For example, can we represent antonyms as well as synonyms?

Visual Analysis of Graphs

We can also analyze graphs visually, though the default layout may result in "hairballs" that are difficult to unpack (more on this later). One popular mechanism for graph layouts is the spring block model. The spring block model visualizes every node as a mass (or block) and the edges between them as springs that push and pull based on their strength. This prevents the nodes they connect from overlapping and often results in graph visualizations that are more manageable.

Using the built-in `nx.spring_layout` from NetworkX, we can draw our trinket synset graph as follows. First, we get the positions of the nodes with a spring layout. Then we draw the nodes as very large white circles with very thin linewidths so that text will be readable. Next, we draw the text labels and the edges with the specified positions (making sure the font size is big enough to read and that the edges are lighter grey so that the text is readable). Finally, we remove the ticks and labels from the plot, as they are not meaningful in the context of our thesaurus graph, and show the plot (Figure 9-2):

```python
import matplotlib.pyplot as plt

def draw_text_graph(G):
    pos = nx.spring_layout(G, scale=18)
    nx.draw_networkx_nodes(
        G, pos, node_color="white", linewidths=0, node_size=500
    )
    nx.draw_networkx_labels(G, pos, font_size=10)
    nx.draw_networkx_edges(G, pos, edge_color='lightgrey')

    plt.tick_params(
        axis='both',        # changes apply to both the x- and y-axis
        which='both',       # both major and minor ticks are affected
        bottom='off',       # turn off ticks along bottom edge
        left='off',         # turn off ticks along left edge
        labelbottom='off',  # turn off labels along bottom edge
        labelleft='off')    # turn off labels along left edge

    plt.show()
```

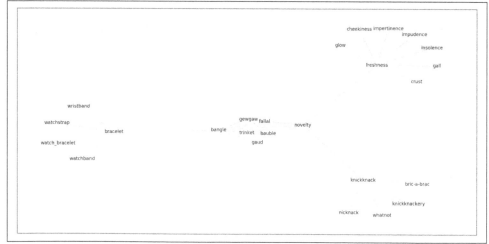

Figure 9-2. A spring layout helps to make visualization more manageable

In the next section, we will explore graph extraction and analysis techniques as they apply specifically to text.

Extracting Graphs from Text

One major challenge presents itself when the core dataset is text: where does the graph come from? The answer will usually depend on your problem domain, and generally speaking, the search for structural elements in semistructured or unstructured data will be guided by context-specific analytical questions.

To break this problem down into smaller substeps, we propose a simple graph analytics workflow for text as shown in Figure 9-3.

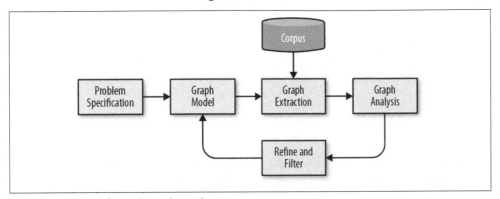

Figure 9-3. Workflow of graph analysis on text

In this workflow, we first use a problem statement to determine entities and their relationships. Using this schema, we can create a graph extraction methodology that uses the corpus, metadata, documents in the corpus, and phrases or tokens in the corpus' documents to extract and link our data. The extraction method is a batch process that can run on the corpus and generate a graph that can be written to disk or stored in memory for analytical processing.

The graph analysis phase conducts computations on the extracted graph such as clustering, structural analysis, filtering, or querying and returns a new graph that is used as output for applications. Inspecting the results of the analytical process allows us to iterate on our method and schema, extracting or collapsing groups of nodes or edges as needed to ensure accurate, usable results.

Creating a Social Graph

Consider our corpus of news articles and our task of modeling relationships between different entities contained in the text. If our questions concern variations in coverage by different news outlets, we might build graph elements related to publication titles, author names, and syndication sources. However, if our goal is to aggregate multiple mentions of a single entity across many articles, our networks might encode forms of address like honorifics, in addition to demographic details. As such, entities of interest may reside in the structure of the documents themselves, or they may simply be contained in the text itself.

Let's assume that our goal is merely to understand which people, places, and things are related to each other in our documents. In other words, we want to build a social network, which we can do with a series of transformations, as shown in Figure 9-4. We will begin constructing our graph using the `EntityExtractor` class we built in Chapter 7. Then we'll add a custom transformer that finds pairs of related entities, followed by another custom transformer that transforms the paired entities into a graph.

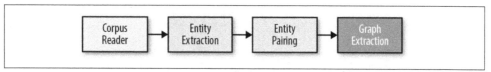

Figure 9-4. Entity graph extraction pipeline

Finding entity pairs

Our next step is to create an `EntityPairs` class that will expect documents that are represented as lists of entities (which is the result of a transform using the `EntityExtractor` class defined in Chapter 7). We want our class to function as a transformer inside a Scikit-Learn `Pipeline`, so it must inherit from `BaseEstimator` and `TransformerMixin`, as described in Chapter 4. We expect entities inside a single document to be related to each other, so we will add a `pairs` method, which uses the `itertools.permutations` function to identify every pair of entities that co-occur in the same document. Our `transform` method will call the `pairs` method on each document in the transformed corpus:

```
import itertools
from sklearn.base import BaseEstimator, TransformerMixin

class EntityPairs(BaseEstimator, TransformerMixin):
    def __init__(self):
        super(EntityPairs, self).__init__()

    def pairs(self, document):
        return list(itertools.permutations(set(document), 2))

    def fit(self, documents, labels=None):
        return self

    def transform(self, documents):
        return [self.pairs(document) for document in documents]
```

Now we can systematically extract entities from documents and identify pairs. However, we don't have a convenient way to differentiate pairs of entities that co-occur very frequently from those that appear together only once. We need a way of encoding the strength of the relationships between entities, which we'll explore in the next section.

Property graphs

The mathematical model of a graph considers only sets of nodes and edges and can be represented as an adjacency matrix, which is useful for a large range of computations. However, it does not provide us with a mechanism for modeling the strength or type of any given relationship. Do the two actors appear in only one document together, or in many? Do they co-occur more frequently in certain genres of articles? In order to support this type of reasoning, we require some way of storing meaningful properties on our nodes and edges.

The *property graph model* allows us to embed more information into the graph, thereby extending computational ability. In a property graph, nodes are objects with incoming and outgoing edges and usually contain a `type` field, similar to a table in a relational database. Edges are objects with a source and target, and they typically contain a `label` field that identifies the type of relationship and a `weight` field that identifies the strength of the relationship. For graph-based text analytics, we generally use nodes to represent nouns and edges for verbs. Then later, when we move into a modeling phase, this allows us to describe the *types* of nodes, the *labels* of links, and the expected structure of the graph.

Implementing the graph extraction

We can now define a class, `GraphExtractor`, that will not only transform the entities into nodes, but also assign weights to their edges based on the frequency with which those entities co-occur in our corpus. Our class will initialize a NetworkX graph, and then our `transform` method will iterate through each document (which is a list of entity pairs), checking to see if there is already an edge between them in the graph. If there is, we will increment the edge's `weight` property by 1. If the edge does not already exist in the graph, we use the `add_edge` method to create one with a `weight` of 1. As with our thesaurus graph construction, the `add_edge` method will also add a new node to the graph if it encounters a member of a pair that does not already exist in the graph:

```
import networkx as nx

class GraphExtractor(BaseEstimator,TransformerMixin):
    def __init__(self):
        self.G = nx.Graph()
```

```
def fit(self, documents, labels=None):
    return self

def transform(self, documents):
    for document in documents:
        for first, second in document:
            if (first, second) in self.G.edges():
                self.G.edges[(first, second)]['weight'] += 1
            else:
                self.G.add_edge(first, second, weight=1)
    return self.G
```

We can now streamline our entity extraction, entity pairing, and graph extraction steps in a Scikit-Learn `Pipeline` as follows:

```
if __name__ == '__main__':
    from reader import PickledCorpusReader
    from sklearn.pipeline import Pipeline

    corpus = PickledCorpusReader('../corpus')
    docs = corpus.docs()

    graph = Pipeline([
        ('entities', EntityExtractor()),
        ('pairs', EntityPairs()),
        ('graph', GraphExtractor())
    ])

    G = graph.fit_transform(docs)
    print(nx.info(G))
```

On a sample of the Baleen corpus, the graph that is constructed has the following statistics:

```
Name: Entity Graph
Type: Graph
Number of nodes: 29176
Number of edges: 1232644
Average degree:  84.4971
```

Insights from the Social Graph

We now have a graph model of the relationships between different entities from our corpus, so we can begin asking interesting questions about these relationships. For instance, is our graph a social network? In a social network, we would expect to see some very specific structures in the graph, such as *hubs*, or certain nodes that have many more edges than average.

In this section, we'll see how we can leverage graph theory metrics like centrality measures, degree distributions, and clustering coefficients to support our analyses.

Centrality

In a network context, the most important nodes are *central* to the graph because they are connected directly or indirectly to the most nodes. Because centrality gives us a means of understanding a particular node's relationship to its immediate neighbors and extended network, it can help us identify entities with more prestige and influence. In this section we will compare several ways of computing centrality, including *degree centrality*, *betweenness centrality*, *closeness centrality*, *eigenvector centrality*, and *pagerank*.

First, we'll write a function that accepts an arbitrary centrality measure as a keyword argument and uses this measure to rank the top n nodes and assign each node a property with a score. NetworkX implements centrality algorithms as top-level functions that take a graph, G, as its first input and return dictionaries of scores for each node in the graph. This function uses the nx.set_node_attributes() function to map the scores computed by the metric to the nodes:

```python
import heapq
from operator import itemgetter

def nbest_centrality(G, metrics, n=10):
    # Compute the centrality scores for each vertex
    nbest = {}
    for name, metric in metrics.items():
        scores = metric(G)

        # Set the score as a property on each node
        nx.set_node_attributes(G, name=name, values=scores)

        # Find the top n scores and print them along with their index
        topn = heapq.nlargest(n, scores.items(), key=itemgetter(1))
        nbest[name] = topn

    return nbest
```

We can use this interface to assign scores automatically to each node in order to save them to disk or employ them as visual weights.

The simplest centrality metric, *degree centrality*, measures popularity by computing the neighborhood size (degree) of each node and then normalizing by the total number of nodes in the graph. Degree centrality is a measure of how connected a node is, which can be a signifier of influence or significance. If degree centrality measures how connected a given node is, *betweenness centrality* indicates how connected the graph is as a result of that node. Betweenness centrality is computed as the ratio of shortest paths that include a particular node to the total number of *shortest paths*.

Here we can use our entity extraction pipeline and nbest_centrality function to compare the top 10 most central nodes, with respect to degree and betweenness centrality:

```
from tabulate import tabulate

corpus = PickledCorpusReader('../corpus')
docs = corpus.docs()

graph = Pipeline([
        ('entities', EntityExtractor()),
        ('pairs', EntityPairs()),
        ('graph', GraphExtractor())
    ])

G = graph.fit_transform(docs)

centralities = {"Degree Centrality" : nx.degree_centrality,
                "Betweenness Centrality" : nx.betweenness_centrality}

centrality = nbest_centrality(G, centralities, 10)

for measure, scores in centrality.items():
    print("Rankings for {}:".format(measure))
    print((tabulate(scores, headers=["Top Terms", "Score"])))
    print("")
```

In our results, we see that degree and betweenness centrality overlap significantly in their ranks of the most central entities (e.g., "american," "new york," "trump," "twitter"). These are the influential, densely connected nodes whose entities appear in more documents and also sit at major "crossroads" in the graph:

```
Rankings for Degree Centrality:
Top Terms      Score
----------    ----------
american      0.054093
new york      0.0500643
washington    0.16096
america       0.156744
united states 0.153076
los angeles   0.139537
republican    0.130077
california    0.120617
trump         0.116778
twitter       0.114447

Rankings for Betweenness Centrality:
Top Terms      Score
----------    ----------
american      0.224302
new york      0.214499
america       0.0258287
united states 0.0245601
washington    0.0244075
los angeles   0.0228752
twitter       0.0191998
```

```
follow        0.0181923
california    0.0181462
new           0.0180939
```

While degree and betweenness centrality might be used as a measure of overall celebrity, we frequently find that the most connected node has a large neighborhood, but is disconnected from the majority of nodes in the graph.

Let's consider the context of a particular *egograph*, or subgraph, of our full graph that reframes the network from the perspective of one particular node. We can extract this egograph using the NetworkX method `nx.ego_graph`:

```
H = nx.ego_graph(G, "hollywood")
```

Now we have a graph that distills all the relationships to one specific entity ("Hollywood"). Not only does this dramatically reduce the size of our graph (meaning that subsequent searches will be much more efficient), this transformation will also enable us to reason about our entity.

Let's say we want to identify entities that are closer on average to other entities in the Hollywood graph. *Closeness centrality* (implemented as `nx.closeness_centrality` in NetworkX) uses a statistical measure of the outgoing paths for each node and computes the average path distance to all other nodes from a single node, normalized by the size of the graph. The classic interpretation of closeness centrality is that it describes how fast information originating at a specific node will spread throughout the network.

By contrast, *eigenvector centrality* says that the more important nodes you are connected to, the more important you are, expressing "fame by association." This means that nodes with a small number of very influential neighbors may outrank nodes with high degrees. Eigenvector centrality is the basis of several variants, including *Katz centrality* and the famous *PageRank* algorithm.

We can use our `nbest_centrality` function to see how each of these centrality measures produces differing determinations of the most important entities in our Hollywood egograph:

```
hollywood_centralities = {"closeness" : nx.closeness_centrality,
                          "eigenvector" : nx.eigenvector_centrality_numpy,
                          "katz" : nx.katz_centrality_numpy,
                          "pagerank" : nx.pagerank_numpy,}

hollywood_centrality = nbest_centrality(H, hollywood_centralities, 10)
for measure, scores in hollywood_centrality.items():
    print("Rankings for {}:".format(measure))
    print((tabulate(scores, headers=["Top Terms", "Score"])))
    print("")
```

Our results show that the entities with the highest closeness centrality (e.g., "video," "british," "brooklyn"), are not particularly ostentatious, perhaps instead serving as the hidden forces connecting more prominent celebrity structures. Eigenvector, PageRank, and Katz centrality all reduce the impact of degree (e.g., the most commonly occurring entities) and have the effect of showing "the power behind the scenes," highlights well-connected entities ("republican," "obama") and sidekicks:

```
Rankings for Closeness Centrality:
Top Terms       Score
----------      ---------
hollywood       1
new york        0.687801
los angeles     0.651051
british         0.6356
america         0.629222
american        0.625243
video           0.621315
london          0.612872
china           0.612434
brooklyn        0.607227


Rankings for Eigenvector Centrality:
Top Terms       Score
----------      ---------
hollywood       0.0510389
new york        0.0493439
los angeles     0.0485406
british         0.0480387
video           0.0480122
china           0.0478956
london          0.0477556
twitter         0.0477143
new york city   0.0476534
new             0.0475649


Rankings for PageRank Centrality:
Top Terms       Score
----------      ---------
hollywood       0.0070501
american        0.00581407
new york        0.00561847
trump           0.00521602
republican      0.00513387
america         0.00476237
donald trump    0.00453808
washington      0.00417929
united states   0.00398346
obama           0.00380977


Rankings for Katz Centrality:
Top Terms       Score
----------      ---------
video           0.107601
washington      0.104191
```

chinese	0.1035
hillary	0.0893112
cleveland	0.087653
state	0.0876141
muslims	0.0840494
editor	0.0818608
paramount pictures	0.0801545
republican party	0.0787887

 For both betweenness and closeness centrality, all shortest paths in the graph must be computed, meaning they can take a long time to run and may not scale well to larger graphs. The primary mechanism of improving performance is to use a lower-level implementation that may also parallelize the computation. Graph-tool has mechanisms for both betweenness and closeness centrality, and is a good option for computing against larger graphs.

Structural analysis

As we saw earlier in this chapter, visual analysis of graphs enables us to detect interesting patterns in their structure. We can plot our Hollywood egograph to explore this structure as we did earlier with our thesaurus graph, using the nx.spring_layout method, passing in a *k* value to specify the minimum distance between nodes, and an iterations keyword argument to ensure the nodes are separate enough to be legible (Figure 9-5).

```
H = nx.ego_graph(G, "hollywood")
edges, weights = zip(*nx.get_edge_attributes(H, "weight").items())
pos = nx.spring_layout(H, k=0.3, iterations=40)

nx.draw(
    H, pos, node_color="skyblue", node_size=20, edgelist=edges,
    edge_color=weights, width=0.25, edge_cmap=plt.cm.Pastel2,
    with_labels=True, font_size=6, alpha=0.8)
plt.show()
```

Many larger graphs will suffer from the "hairball effect," meaning that the nodes and edges are so dense as to make it difficult to effectively discern meaningful structures. In these cases, we often instead try to inspect the degree distribution for all nodes in a network to inform ourselves about its overall structure.

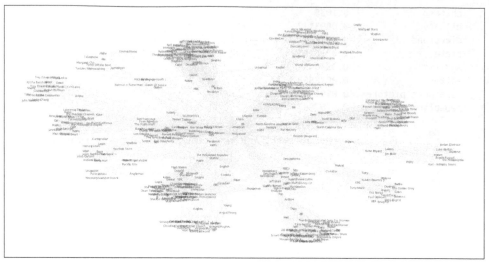

Figure 9-5. Relationships to Hollywood in the Baleen corpus

We can examine this distribution using Seaborn's `distplot` method, setting the `norm_hist` parameter to `True` so that the height will display degree density rather than raw count:

```
import seaborn as sns

sns.distplot([G.degree(v) for v in G.nodes()], norm_hist=True)
plt.show()
```

In most graphs, the majority of nodes have relatively low degree, so we generally expect to observe a high amount of right-skew in their degree distributions, such as in the Baleen Entity Graph plot shown in the upper left of Figure 9-6. The small number of nodes with the highest degrees are *hubs* due to their frequent occurrence and large number of connections across the corpus.

 Certain social networks, called *scale-free networks*, exhibit power law distributions, and are associated with particularly high *fault-tolerance*. Such structures indicate a resilient network that doesn't rely on any single node (in our case, perhaps a person or organization) to keep the others connected.

Interestingly, the degree distributions for certain ego graphs display remarkably different behavior, such as with the Hollywood ego graph exhibiting a nearly symmetric probability distribution, as shown in the upper right of Figure 9-6.

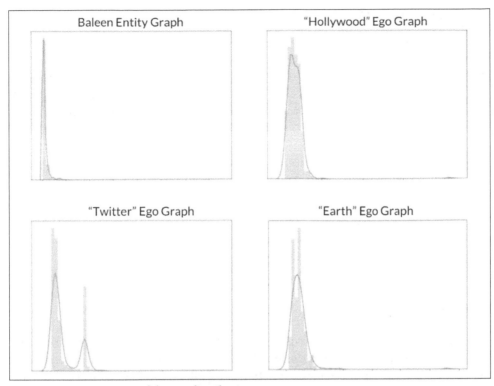

Figure 9-6. Histograms of degree distributions

Other useful structural measures of a network are its *clustering coefficient* (nx.aver age_clustering) and *transitivity* (nx.transitivity), both of which can be used to assess how social a network is. The clustering coefficient is a real number that is 0 when there is no clustering and 1 when the graph consists entirely of disjointed *cliques* (nx.graph_number_of_cliques). Transitivity tells us the likelihood that two nodes with a common connection are neighbors:

```python
print("Baleen Entity Graph")
print("Average clustering coefficient: {}".format(nx.average_clustering(G)))
print("Transitivity: {}".format(nx.transitivity(G)))
print("Number of cliques: {}".format(nx.graph_number_of_cliques(G)))

print("Hollywood Ego Graph")
print("Average clustering coefficient: {}".format(nx.average_clustering(H)))
print("Transitivity: {}".format(nx.transitivity(H)))
print("Number of cliques: {}".format(nx.graph_number_of_cliques(H)))

Baleen Entity Graph
Average clustering coefficient: 0.7771459590548481
Transitivity: 0.29504798606584176
Number of cliques: 51376
```

```
Hollywood Ego Graph
Average clustering coefficient: 0.9214236425410913
Transitivity: 0.6502420989124886
Number of cliques: 348
```

In the context of our entity graph, the high clustering and transitivity coefficients suggest that our network is extremely social. For instance, in our "Hollywood" ego graph, the transitivity suggests that there is a 65 percent chance that any two entities who share a common connection are themselves neighbors!

 The *small world phenomenon* can be observed in a graph where, while most nodes are not direct neighbors, nearly all can be reached from every other node within a few hops. Small world networks can be identified from structural features, namely that they often contain many cliques, have a high clustering coefficient, and have a high degree of transitivity. In the context of our entity graph, this would suggest that even in a network of strangers, most are nevertheless linked through a very short chain of acquaintances.

Entity Resolution

One challenge we have yet to discuss is the multiplicity of ways in which our entities can appear. Because we have performed little or no normalization on our extracted entities, we can expect to see many variations in spelling, forms of address, and naming conventions, such as nicknames and acronyms. This will result in multiple nodes that reference a single entity (e.g., "America," "US," and "the United States" all appear as nodes in the graph).

In Figure 9-7, we see multiple, often ambiguous references to "Hilton," which refers not only to the family as a whole, but also to individual members of the family, to the corporation, and to specific hotel facilities in different cities. Ideally we would like to identify nodes that correspond to multiple references so that we can resolve them into unique entity nodes.

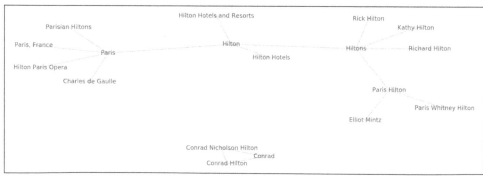

Figure 9-7. Multiple entity references within a graph

Entity resolution refers to computational techniques that identify, group, or link digital *mentions* (records) of some object in the real world (an entity). Part of the data wrangling process is performing entity resolution to ensure that all mentions to a single, unique entity are collected together into a single reference.

Tasks like deduplication (removing duplicate entries), record linkage (joining two records together), and canonicalization (creating a single, representative record for an entity) rely on computing the *similarity* of (or *distance* between) two records and determining whether they are a match.

Entity Resolution on a Graph

As Bhattacharya and Getoor (2005)[2] explain, a graph with multiple nodes corresponding to single entities is not actually an entity graph, but a reference graph. Reference graphs are very problematic for semantic reasoning tasks, as they can distort and misrepresent the relationships between entities.

Entity resolution will get us closer to analyzing and extracting useful information about the true structure of a real-world network, reducing the obscurity caused by the many ways language allows us to refer to the same entity. In this section we'll explore a methodology where we include entity resolution as an added step in our graph extraction pipeline, as shown in Figure 9-8.

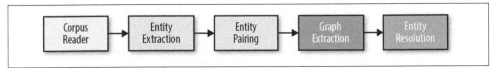

Figure 9-8. Entity graph extraction pipeline

To begin resolving the entities in our Hilton graph, we will first define a function `pairwise_comparisons` that takes as input a NetworkX graph and uses the `iter tools.combinations` method to create a generator with every possible pair of nodes:

```
import networkx as nx
from itertools import combinations

def pairwise_comparisons(G):
    """
    Produces a generator of pairs of nodes.
    """
    return combinations(G.nodes(), 2)
```

Unfortunately, even a very small dataset such as our Hilton graph of 18 nodes will generate 153 pairwise comparisons. Given that similarity comparison is usually an

---

2 Indrajit Bhattacharya and Lise Getoor, *Entity Resolution in Graph Data*, (2005) *http://bit.ly/2GQKXDe*

expensive operation involving dynamic programming and other resource-intensive computing techniques, this clearly will not scale well. There are a few simple things we can do, such as eliminating pairs that will never match, to reduce the number of pairwise comparisons. In order to make decisions like these, either in an automatic fashion or by proposing pairs of records to a user, we first need some mechanism to expose likely similar matches and weed out the obvious nonduplicates. One method we can use is blocking.

Blocking with Structure

Blocking is the strategic reduction of the number of pairwise comparisons that are required using the structure of a natural graph. Blocking provides entity resolution with two primary benefits: increasing the performance by reducing the number of computations and reducing the search space to propose possible duplicates to a user.

One reasonable assumption we might make is that if two nodes both have an edge to the same entity (e.g., "Hilton Hotels" and "Hilton Hotels and Resorts" both have edges to "Hilton"), they are more likely to be references to the same entity. If we can inspect only the most likely matches, that could dramatically reduce the number of comparisons we have to make. We can use the NetworkX `neighbors` method to compare the edges of any two given nodes and highlight only the pairwise comparisons that have very similar neighborhoods:

```
def edge_blocked_comparisons(G):
    """
    A generator of pairwise comparisons, that highlights comparisons
    between nodes that have an edge to the same entity.
    """
    for n1, n2 in pairwise_comparisons(G):
        hood1 = frozenset(G.neighbors(n1))
        hood2 = frozenset(G.neighbors(n2))
        if hood1 & hood2:
            yield n1,n2
```

Fuzzy Blocking

Even with blocking, there are still some unnecessary comparisons. For example, even though "Kathy Hilton" and "Richard Hilton" both have an edge to "Hiltons," they do not refer to the same person. We want to be able to further uncomplicate the graph by identifying the most likely approximate matches using some kind of similarity measure that can compute the distance between "Kathy Hilton" and "Richard Hilton."

There are a number of methods for computing string distance, many of which depend on the use case. Here we will demonstrate an implementation that leverages the `partial_ratio` method from the Python library `fuzzywuzzy`, which uses

Levenshtein distance to compute the number of deletions, insertions, and substitutions required to transform the first string into the second.

We will define a `similarity` function that takes as input two NetworkX nodes. Our function will score the distance between the string name labels for each node, the distance between their Spacy entity types (stored as a node attributes), and return their mean:

```
from fuzzywuzzy import fuzz

def similarity(n1, n2):
    """
    Returns the mean of the partial_ratio score for each field in the two
    entities. Note that if they don't have fields that match, the score will
    be zero.
    """
    scores = [
        fuzz.partial_ratio(n1, n2),
        fuzz.partial_ratio(G.node[n1]['type'], G.node[n2]['type'])
    ]

    return float(sum(s for s in scores)) / float(len(scores))
```

If two entities have almost the same name (e.g., "Richard Hilton" and "Rick Hilton"), and are also both of the same type (e.g., PERSON), they will get a higher score than if they have the same name but are of different types (e.g., one PERSON and one ORG).

Now that we have a way to identify high-probability matches, we can incorporate it as a filter into a new function, `fuzzy_blocked_comparison`. This function will iterate through each possible pair of nodes and determine the amount of structural overlap between them. If there is significant overlap, it will compute their `similarity` and yield pairs with similar neighborhoods who are sufficiently similar (above some threshold, which we implement as a keyword argument that defaults to a 65 percent match):

```
def fuzzy_blocked_comparisons(G, threshold=65):
    """
    A generator of pairwise comparisons, that highlights comparisons between
    nodes that have an edge to the same entity, but filters out comparisons
    if the similarity of n1 and n2 is below the threshold.
    """
    for n1, n2 in pairwise_comparisons(G):
        hood1 = frozenset(G.neighbors(n1))
        hood2 = frozenset(G.neighbors(n2))
        if hood1 & hood2:
            if similarity(n1, n2) > threshold:
                yield n1,n2
```

This is a very efficient way of reducing pairwise comparisons, because we use the computationally less intensive neighborhood comparison first, and only then proceed to the more expensive string similarity measure. The reduction in total comparisons is significant:

```
def info(G):
    """
    Wrapper for nx.info with some other helpers.
    """
    pairwise = len(list(pairwise_comparisons(G)))
    edge_blocked = len(list(edge_blocked_comparisons(G)))
    fuzz_blocked = len(list(fuzzy_blocked_comparisons(G)))

    output = [""]
    output.append("Number of Pairwise Comparisons: {}".format(pairwise))
    output.append("Number of Edge Blocked Comparisons: {}".format(edge_blocked))
    output.append("Number of Fuzzy Blocked Comparisons: {}".format(fuzz_blocked))

    return nx.info(G) + "\n".join(output)
```

```
Name: Hilton Family
Type: Graph
Number of nodes: 18
Number of edges: 17
Average degree:   1.8889
Number of Pairwise Comparisons: 153
Number of Edge Blocked Comparisons: 32
Number of Fuzzy Blocked Comparisons: 20
```

We have now identified the 20 pairs of nodes with the highest likelihood of being references to the same entity, a more than 85 percent reduction in the total possible pairwise comparisons.

Now we can imagine creating a custom transformer that we can chain together with the rest of our pipeline to transform our reference graph into a list of fuzzy edge blocked comparisons. For instance, a `FuzzyBlocker` might begin with these methods and add others depending on the specific requirements of the entity resolution problem:

```
from sklearn.base import BaseEstimator, TransformerMixin

class FuzzyBlocker(BaseEstimator, TransformerMixin):

    def __init__(self, threshold=65):
        self.threshold = threshold

    def fit(self, G, y=None):
        return self

    def transform(self, G):
        return fuzzy_blocked_comparisons(G, self.threshold)
```

Depending on the context and the fuzzy match threshold we have specified, these blocked nodes could be collapsed into single nodes (updating the edge properties as necessary), or be passed to a domain expert for manual inspection. In either case, entity resolution will often be a critical first step in building quality data products, and as we've seen in this section, graphs can make this process both more efficient and effective.

Conclusion

Graphs are used to represent and model complex systems in the real world, such as communication networks and biological ecosystems. However, they can also be used more generally to structure problems in meaningful ways. With a little creativity, almost any problem can be structured as a graph.

While graph extraction may seem challenging initially, it is just another iterative process that requires clever language processing and creative modeling of the target data. Just as with the other model families we have explored in this book, iterative refinement and analysis is part of the *model selection triple*, and techniques like normalization, filtering, and aggregation can be added to improve performance.

However, in contrast to other model families we have explored in previous chapters, the graph model family contains algorithms whose computations are composed of traversals. From a local node, the computation can use information from neighboring nodes extracted by traveling along the edges that connect any two nodes. Such computations expose nodes that are connected, show how connections form, and identify which nodes are most central to the network. Graph traversals enable us to extract meaningful information from documents without requiring vast amounts of prior knowledge and ontologies.

Graphs can embed complex semantic representations in a compact form. As such, modeling data as networks of related entities is a powerful mechanism for analytics, both for visual analyses and machine learning. Part of this power comes from performance advantages of using a graph data structure, and the other part comes from an inherent human ability to intuitively interact with small networks.

The lesson of graph analytics is an important one; text analysis applications are made and broken by their interpretability—if the user doesn't understand it, it doesn't matter how insightful the result is. Next, in Chapter 10 we will continue to follow the thread of human–computer interaction we began in Chapter 8 and pursued in this chapter, considering instead how the application of chatbots to everyday language-based tasks can augment the user's experience.

Chatbots

In this chapter we will explore one of the fastest-growing language-aware applications: conversational agents. From Slackbot to Alexa to BMW's Dragon Drive, conversational agents are quickly becoming an indispensable part of our everyday experiences, integrated into an ever broader range of contexts. They enhance our lives with extended memory (e.g., looking stuff up on the internet), increased computation (e.g., making conversions or navigating our commute), and more fluid communication and control (e.g., sending messages, managing smart homes).

The primary novelty of such agents is not the information or assistance they provide (as that has been available in web and mobile applications using point-and-click interfaces for a long time); rather, it is their interface that makes them so compelling. Natural language interactions provide a low-friction, low-barrier, and highly intuitive method of accessing computational resources. Because of this, chatbots represent an important step forward in user experience, such as inlining commands naturally with text-based applications thereby minimizing poorly designed menu-based interfaces. Importantly, they also allow new human–computer interactions in new computational contexts, such as in devices not well suited to a screen like in-car navigation.

So why is this rise happening now, given the long history of conversational agents in reality (with early models like Eliza and PARRY) and in fiction ("Computer" from *Star Trek* or "Hal" from *2001: A Space Odyssey*)? Partly it's because the "killer app" for such interfaces requires ubiquitous computing enabled by today's Internet of Things. More importantly, it's because modern conversational agents are empowered by user data, which enriches their *context*, and in turn, their value to us. Mobile devices leverage GPS data to know where we are and propose localized recommendations; gaming consoles adapt play experiences based on the number of people they can see and hear. To do this effectively, such applications must not only process natural language, they must also maintain *state*, remembering information provided by the user and situational context.

In this chapter we propose a conversational framework for building chatbots, the purpose of which is to manage state and use that state to produce meaningful conversations within a specific context. We will demonstrate this framework by constructing a kitchen helper bot that can greet new users, perform measurement conversions, and recommend good recipes. Through the lens of this prototype, we'll sketch out three features—a rule-based system that uses regular expressions to match utterances; a question-and-answer system that uses pretrained syntax parsers to filter incoming questions and determine what answers are needed; and finally, a recommendation system that uses unsupervised learning to determine relevant suggestions.

Fundamentals of Conversation

In the 1940s, Claude Shannon and Warren Weaver, pioneers of information theory and machine translation, developed a model of communication so influential it is still used to understand conversation today.[1] In their model, communication comes down to a series of encodings and transformations, as messages pass through channels with varying levels of noise and entropy, from initial source to destination.

Modern notions of *conversation*, as shown in Figure 10-1, extend the Shannon–Weaver model, where two (or more) parties take turns responding to each other's messages. Conversations take place over time and are generally bounded by a fixed length. During a conversation, a participant can either be listening or speaking. Effective conversation requires at any given time a single speaker communicating and other participants listening. Finally, the time-ordered record of the conversation must be consistent such that each statement makes sense given the previous statement in the conversation.

To you, our human reader, this description of a conversation probably seems obvious and natural, but it has important computational implications (consider how garbled and confusing a conversation would be if any of the requirements were not satisfied). One simple way to satisfy conversational requirements is to have each participant in the conversation switch between speaking and listening by taking turns. In each turn, the *initiative* is granted to the speaker who gets to decide where the conversation goes next based on what was last said. Turn taking and the back-and-forth transfer of initiative keeps the conversation going until one or more of the participants decides to end it. The resulting conversation meets all the requirements described here and is consistent.

---

1 Claude Shannon, *A Mathematical Theory of Communication*, (1948) *http://bit.ly/2JJnVjd*

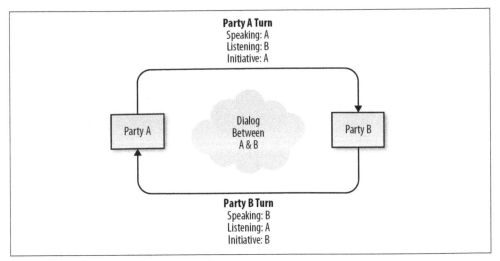

Figure 10-1. Structure of a conversation

A *chatbot* is a program that participates in turn-taking conversations and whose aim is to interpret input text or speech and to output appropriate, useful responses. Unlike the humans with whom they interact, chatbots must rely on heuristics and machine learning techniques to achieve these results. For this reason, they require a computational means of grappling with the ambiguity of language and situational context in order to effectively parse incoming language and produce the most appropriate reply.

A chatbot's architecture, shown in Figure 10-2, is comprised of two primary components. The first component is a user-facing interface that handles the mechanics of receiving user input (e.g., microphones for speech transcription or a web API for an app) and delivering interpretable output (speakers for speech generation or a mobile frontend). This outer component wraps the second component, an internal *dialog system* that interprets text input, maintains an internal state, and produces responses.

The outer user interface component obviously can vary widely depending on the use and requirements of the application. In this chapter we will focus on the internal dialog component and show how it can be easily generalized to any application and composed of multiple subdialogs. To that end we will first create an abstract base class that formally defines the fundamental behavior or interface of the dialog. We will then explore three implementations of this base class for state management, questions and answers, and recommendations and show how they can be composed as a single conversational agent.

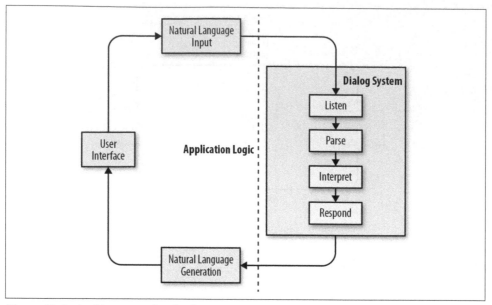

Figure 10-2. Architecture of a chatbot

Dialog: A Brief Exchange

To create a generalizable and composable conversational system, we must first define the smallest unit of work during an interaction between chatbot and user. From the architecture described in the last section, we know that the smallest unit of work must accept natural language text as input and produce natural language text as output. In a conversation many types of parses and responses are required, so we will think of a conversation agent as composed of many internal dialogs that each handle their own area of responsibility.

To ensure dialogs work together in concert, we must describe a single interface that defines how dialogs operate. In Python no formal interface type exists, but we can use an *abstract base class* via the abc standard library module to list the methods and signatures expected of all subclasses (if a subclass does not implement the abstract methods, an exception is raised). In this way we can ensure that all subclasses of our Dialog interface behave in an expected way.

Generally, Dialog is responsible for listening to utterances, parsing the text, interpreting the parse, updating its internal state, and then formulating a response on demand. Because we assume that the system will sometimes misinterpret incoming text, Dialog objects must also return a relevance score alongside the response to quantify how successfully the initial utterance has been interpreted. To create our interface, we'll break this behavior into several methods that will be specifically defined in our subclasses. However, we'll first start by describing a nonabstract method, listen, the primary entry point for a `Dialog` object that implements the general dialog behavior using (soon-to-be-implemented) abstract methods:

```python
import abc


class Dialog(abc.ABC):
    """
    A dialog listens for utterances, parses and interprets them, then updates
    its internal state. It can then formulate a response on demand.
    """

    def listen(self, text, response=True, **kwargs):
        """
        A text utterance is passed in and parsed. It is then passed to the
        interpret method to determine how to respond. If a response is
        requested, the respond method is used to generate a text response
        based on the most recent input and the current Dialog state.
        """
        # Parse the input
        sents = self.parse(text)

        # Interpret the input
        sents, confidence, kwargs = self.interpret(sents, **kwargs)

        # Determine the response
        if response:
            reply = self.respond(sents, confidence, **kwargs)
        else:
            reply = None

        # Return initiative
        return reply, confidence
```

The `listen` method contains a global implementation, which unifies our (soon-to-be-defined) abstract functionality. The `listen` signature accepts text as a string, as well as a `response` boolean that indicates if initiative has passed to the `Dialog` and a response is required (if `False`, the `Dialog` simply listens and updates its internal state). Finally, `listen` also takes arbitrary keyword arguments (`kwargs`) that may contain other contextual information such as the user, session id, or transcription score.

The output of this method is a response if required (`None` if not) as well as a *confidence* score, a floating-point value between 0.0 and 1.0. Since we may not always be able to successfully parse and interpret incoming text, or formulate an appropriate response, this metric expresses a `Dialog` object's confidence in its interpretation, where 1.0 is extremely confident in the response and 0 is completely confused. Confidence can be computed or updated at any point during the `Dialog.listen` execution, which we have defined by three abstract steps: `parse`, `interpret`, and `respond`, though generally speaking confidence is produced during the `interpret` phase:

```
@abc.abstractmethod
def parse(self, text):
    """
    Every dialog may need its own parsing strategy, some dialogs may need
    dependency vs. constituency parses, others may simply require regular
    expressions or chunkers.
    """
    return []
```

The `parse` method allows `Dialog` subclasses to implement their own mechanism for handling raw strings of data. For instance, some `Dialog` subclasses may require dependency or constituency parsing while others may simply require regular expressions or chunkers. The abstract method defines the parse signature: a subclass should implement `parse` to expect a string as input and return a list of data structures specific to the needs of the particular `Dialog` behavior. Ideally, in a real-world implementation, we'd also include optimizations to ensure that computationally expensive parsing only happens once so that we don't unnecessarily duplicate the work:

```
@abc.abstractmethod
def interpret(self, sents, **kwargs):
    """
    Interprets the utterance passed in as a list of parsed sentences,
    updates the internal state of the dialog, computes a confidence of the
    interpretation. May also return arguments specific to the response
    mechanism.
    """
    return sents, 0.0, kwargs
```

The `interpret` method is responsible for interpreting an incoming list of parsed sentences, updating the internal state of the `Dialog`, and computing a confidence level for the interpretation. This method will return interpreted parsed sentences that have been filtered based on whether they require a response, as well as a confidence score between 0 and 1. Later in this chapter, we'll explore a few options for calculating confidence. The `interpret` method can also accept arbitrary keyword arguments and return updated keyword arguments to influence the behavior of `respond`:

```
@abc.abstractmethod
def respond(self, sents, confidence, **kwargs):
    """
    Creates a response given the input utterances and the current state of
    the dialog, along with any arguments passed in from the listen or the
    interpret methods.
    """
    return None
```

Finally, the `respond` method accepts interpreted sentences, a confidence score, and arbitrary keyword arguments in order to produce a text-based response based on the current state of the `Dialog`. The confidence is passed to `respond` to influence the outcome; for example, if the confidence is `0.0` the method might return None or return a request for clarification. If the confidence is not strong the response might include suggested or approximate language rather than a firm answer for stronger confidences.

By subclassing the `Dialog` abstract base class, we now have a framework that enables the maintenance of conversational state in short interactions with the user. The `Dialog` object will serve as the basic building block for the rest of the conversational components we will implement throughout the rest of the chapter.

Maintaining a Conversation

A `Dialog` defines how we handle simple, brief exchanges and is an important building block for conversational agents. But how do we maintain state during a longer interaction, where the initiative may be passed back and forth between user and system multiple times and require many different types of responses?

The answer is a `Conversation`, a specialized dialog that contains multiple internal dialogs. For a chatbot, an instance of a `Conversation` is essentially the wrapped internal dialog component described by our architecture. A `Conversation` contains one or more distinct `Dialog` subclasses, each of which implements a separate internal state and handles different types of interpretations and responses. When the `Conversation` listens, it directs the input to its internal dialogs, then returns the response with the highest confidence.

In this section, we'll implement a `SimpleConversation` class that inherits the behavior of our `Dialog` class. The main role of the `SimpleConversation` class is to maintain state across a sequence of dialogs, which we'll store as an internal class attribute. Our class will also inherit from `collections.abc.Sequence` from the standard library, which will enable `SimpleConversation` to behave like a list of indexed dialogs (with the abstract method `__getitem__`) and retrieve the number of dialogs in the collection (with `__len__`):

```python
from collections.abc import Sequence


class SimpleConversation(Dialog, Sequence):
    """
    This is the most simple version of a conversation.
    """

    def __init__(self, dialogs):
        self._dialogs = dialogs

    def __getitem__(self, idx):
        return self._dialogs[idx]
```

```python
def __len__(self):
    return len(self._dialogs)
```

On Conversation.listen, we will go ahead and pass the incoming text to each of the internal Dialog.listen methods, which will in turn call the internal Dialog object's parse, interpret, and respond methods. The result is a list of (responses, confidence) tuples, and the SimpleConversation will simply return the response with the highest confidence by using the itemgetter operator to retrieve the max by the second element of the tuple. Slightly more complex conversations might include rules for tie breaking if two internal dialogs return the same confidence, but the optimal Conversation composition is one in which ties are rare:

```python
from operator import itemgetter

...

    def listen(self, text, response=True, **kwargs):
        """
        Simply return the best confidence response
        """
        responses = [
            dialog.listen(text, response, **kwargs)
            for dialog in self._dialogs
        ]

        # Responses is a list of (response, confidence) pairs
        return max(responses, key=itemgetter(1))
```

Because a SimpleConversation is a Dialog, it must implement parse, interpret, and respond. Here, we implement each of those so that they call the corresponding internal method and return the results. We also add a confidence score, which allows us to compose a conversation according to our confidence that the input has been interpreted correctly:

```python
...

    def parse(self, text):
        """
        Returns parses for all internal dialogs for debugging
        """
        return [dialog.parse(text) for dialog in self._dialogs]

    def interpret(self, sents, **kwargs):
        """
        Returns interpretations for all internal dialogs for debugging
        """
        return [dialog.interpret(sents, **kwargs) for dialog in self._dialogs]
```

```
def respond(self, sents, confidence, **kwargs):
    """
    Returns responses for all internal dialogs for debugging
    """
    return [
        dialog.respond(sents, confidence, **kwargs)
        for dialog in self._dialogs
    ]
```

The `Dialog` framework is intended to be modular, so that multiple dialog components can be used simultaneously (as in our `SimpleConversation` class) or used in a standalone fashion. Our implementation treats dialogs as wholly independent, but there are many other models such as:

Parallel/async conversations
    The first response with a positive confidence wins.

Policy-driven conversations
    Dialogs are marked as "open" and "closed."

Dynamic conversations
    Dialogs can be dynamically added and removed.

Tree structured conversations
    Dialogs have parents and children.

In the next section, we will see how we can use the `Dialog` class with some simple heuristics to build a dialog system that manages interactions with users.

Rules for Polite Conversation

In 1950, renowned computer scientist and mathematician Alan Turing first proposed what would later be known as the Turing test[2]—a machine's ability to fool a human into believing he or she was conversing with another person. The Turing test inspired a number of rule-based dialog systems over the next several decades, many of which not only passed the test, but became the first generation of conversation agents, and which continue to inform chatbot construction to this day.

Built by Joseph Weizenbaum in 1966 at MIT, ELIZA is perhaps the most well-known example. The ELIZA program used logic to match keyword- and phrase-patterns from human input and provide preprogrammed responses to move the conversation forward. PARRY, built by Kenneth Colby several years later at Stanford, responded using a combination of pattern matching and a mental model. This mental model made PARRY grow increasingly agitated and erratic to simulate a patient with para-

---

2 Alan Turing, *Computing Machinery and Intelligence*, (1950) *http://bit.ly/2GLop6D*

noid schizophrenia, and successfully fooled doctors into believing they were speaking with a real patient.

In this section, we will implement a rules-based greeting feature inspired by these early models, which uses regular expressions to match utterances. Our version will maintain state primarily to acknowledge participants entering and leaving the dialog, and respond to them with appropriate salutations and questions. This implementation of a `Dialog` is meant to highlight the importance of keeping track of the state of a conversation over time as well as to show the effectiveness of regular expression-based chatbots. We will conclude the session by showing how a test framework can be used to exercise a `Dialog` component in a variety of ways, making it more robust to the variety of user input.

Greetings and Salutations

The `Greeting` dialog implements our conversational framework by extending the `Dialog` base class. It is responsible for keeping track of participants entering and exiting a conversation as well as providing the appropriate greeting and salutation when participants enter and exit. It does this by maintaining a `participants` state, a mapping of currently active users and their names.

At the heart of the `Greeting` dialog is a dictionary, `PATTERNS`, stored as a class variable. This dictionary maps the kind of interactions (described by key) to a regular expression that defines the expected input for that interaction. In particular, our simple `Greeting` dialog is prepared for greetings, introductions, goodbyes, and roll calls. Later, we'll use these regular expressions in the `parse` method of the dialog:

```
class Greeting(Dialog):
    """
    Keeps track of the participants entering or leaving the conversation and
    responds with appropriate salutations. This is an example of a rules based
    system that keeps track of state and uses regular expressions and logic to
    handle the dialog.
    """

    PATTERNS = {
        'greeting': r'hello|hi|hey|good morning|good evening',
        'introduction': r'my name is ([a-z\-\s]+)',
        'goodbye': r'goodbye|bye|ttyl',
        'rollcall': r'roll call|who\'s here?',
    }

    def __init__(self, participants=None):
        # Participants is a map of user name to real name
        self.participants = {}

        if participants is not None:
            for participant in participants:
```

```
        self.participants[participant] = None

    # Compile regular expressions
    self._patterns = {
        key: re.compile(pattern, re.I)
        for key, pattern in self.PATTERNS.items()
    }
```

To initialize a `Greeting` we can instantiate it with or without a prior list of participants. We can think of the internal state of the dictionary as tracking a username with a real name, which we will see updated later with the introduction interpretation. To ensure fast and efficient parsing of text, we conclude initialization by compiling our regular expressions into an internal instance dictionary. Regular expression compilation in Python returns a regular expression object, saving a step when the same regular expression is used repeatedly as it will be in this dialog.

 This is a fairly minimalist implementation of the `Greeting` class, which could be extended in many ways with rules to support other speech and text patterns, as well as different languages.

Next, we will implement a `parse` method, whose purpose is to compare the incoming user-provided text to each of the compiled regular expressions to determine if it matches the known patterns for a greeting, introduction, goodbye, or attendance check:

```
def parse(self, text):
    """
    Applies all regular expressions to the text to find matches.
    """
    matches = {}
    for key, pattern in self._patterns.items():
        match = pattern.match(text)
        if match is not None:
            matches[key] = match
    return matches
```

If a match is found, `parse` returns it. This result can then be used as input for the `Greeting`-specific `interpret` method, which takes in parsed matches and determines what kind of action is called for (if any). If `interpret` receives input that matched none of the patterns, it immediately returns with a `0.0` confidence score. If any of the text was matched, `interpret` simply returns a `1.0` confidence score because there is no fuzziness to regular expression matching.

The `interpret` method is responsible for updating the internal state of the `Greeting` dialog. For example, if the input matched an introductory exchange (e.g., if the user typed "my name is `something`"), `interpret` will extract the name, add any new user to `self.participants`, and add the (new or existing) user's real name to the value corresponding to that key in the dictionary. If a greeting was detected, `interpret` will check to see if the user is known in `self.participants`, and if not, will add a keyword argument to the final return result flagging that an introduction should be requested in the `respond` method. Otherwise, if a goodbye was matched, it removes the user (if known) from the `self.participants` dictionary and from the keyword arguments:

```python
def interpret(self, sents, **kwargs):
    """
    Takes in parsed matches and determines if the message is an enter,
    exit, or name change.
    """
    # Can't do anything with no matches
    if len(sents) == 0:
        return sents, 0.0, kwargs

    # Get username from the participants
    user = kwargs.get('user', None)

    # Determine if an introduction has been made
    if 'introduction' in sents:
        # Get the name from the utterance
        name = sents['introduction'].groups()[0]
        user = user or name.lower()

        # Determine if name has changed
        if user not in self.participants or self.participants[user] != name:
            kwargs['name_changed'] = True

        # Update the participants
        self.participants[user] = name
        kwargs['user'] = user

    # Determine if a greeting has been made
    if 'greeting' in sents:
        # If we don't have a name for the user
        if not self.participants.get(user, None):
            kwargs['request_introduction'] = True

    # Determine if goodbye has been made
    if 'goodbye' in sents and user is not None:
        # Remove participant
        self.participants.pop(user)
        kwargs.pop('user', None)

    # If we've seen anything we're looking for, we're pretty confident
    return sents, 1.0, kwargs
```

Finally, our `respond` method will dictate if and how our chatbot should respond to the user. If the confidence is `0.0`, no response is provided. If the user sent a greeting or introduction, `respond` will either return a request for the new user's name or a greeting to the existing user. In the case of a goodbye, `respond` will return a generic farewell. If a user has asked about who else is in the chat, `respond` will get a list of the participants and return either all the names (if there are other participants), or just the user's name (if she/he is in there alone). If there are no users currently recorded in `self.participants`, the chatbot will respond expectantly:

```
def respond(self, sents, confidence, **kwargs):
    """
    Gives a greeting or a goodbye depending on what's appropriate.
    """
    if confidence == 0:
        return None

    name = self.participants.get(kwargs.get('user', None), None)
    name_changed = kwargs.get('name_changed', False)
    request_introduction = kwargs.get('request_introduction', False)

    if 'greeting' in sents or 'introduction' in sents:
        if request_introduction:
            return "Hello, what is your name?"
        else:
            return "Hello, {}!".format(name)

    if 'goodbye' in sents:
        return "Talk to you later!"

    if 'rollcall' in sents:
        people = list(self.participants.values())

        if len(people) > 1:
            roster = ", ".join(people[:-1])
            roster += " and {}.".format(people[-1])
            return "Currently in the conversation are " + roster

        elif len(people) == 1:
            return "It's just you and me right now, {}.".format(name)
        else:
            return "So lonely in here by myself ... wait who is that?"

    raise Exception(
        "expected response to be returned, but could not find rule"
    )
```

Note that in both the `interpret` and `respond` methods, we simply have branching logic that handles each type of matched input. As this class gets larger, it is helpful to break down these methods into smaller chunks such as `interpret_goodbye` and `respond_goodbye` to encapsulate the logic and prevent bugs. We can experiment with the `Greeting` class a bit using different inputs here:

```
if __name__ == '__main__':
    dialog = Greeting()
    # `listen` returns (response, confidence) tuples; just print the response
    print(dialog.listen("Hello!", user="jakevp321")[0])
    print(dialog.listen("my name is Jake", user="jakevp321")[0])
    print(dialog.listen("Roll call!", user="jakevp321")[0])
    print(dialog.listen("Have to go, goodbye!", user="jakevp321")[0])
```

Here are the results:

```
Hello, what is your name?
Hello, Jake!
It's just you and me right now, Jake.
```

However, it's important to note that our rule-based system is pretty rigid and breaks down quickly. For instance, let's see what happens if we leave off the user keyword argument in one of our calls to the Greeting.listen method:

```
if __name__ == '__main__':
    dialog = Greeting()
    print(dialog.listen("hey", user="jillmonger")[0])
    print(dialog.listen("my name is Jill.", user="jillmonger")[0])
    print(dialog.listen("who's here?")[0])
```

In this case, the chatbot recognizes Jill's salutation, requests an introduction, and greets the new participant. However, in the third call to listen, the chatbot doesn't have the user keyword argument and so fails to appropriately address her in the roll call response:

```
Hello, what is your name?
Hello, Jill!
It's just you and me right now, None.
```

Indeed, rules-based systems do tend to break down easily. Test-driven development, which we'll explore in the next section, can help us to anticipate and pre-empt the kinds of problems that may occur in practice with users.

Handling Miscommunication

Rigorous testing is a useful way to handle possible miscommunications and other kinds of parsing and response errors. In this section, we'll use the PyTest library to test the limits of our Greeting class, experiment with edge cases, and see where things start to break down.

To fully implement our chatbot, we would begin with a set of tests for our Dialog base class. Below we show the general framework we would use for the TestBase Classes class, testing, for instance, classes that subclass the Dialog successfully inherit the listen method.

Our first test, `test_dialog_abc`, uses the `pytest.mark.parametrize` decorator, which allows us to send many different examples into the test with little effort:

```python
import pytest


class TestBaseClasses(object):
    """
    Tests for the Dialog class
    """
    @pytest.mark.parametrize("text", [
        "Gobbledeguk", "Gibberish", "Wingdings"
    ])
    def test_dialog_abc(self, text):
        """
        Test the Dialog ABC and the listen method
        """
        class SampleDialog(Dialog):
            def parse(self, text):
                return []

            def interpret(self, sents):
                return sents, 0.0, {}

            def respond(self, sents, confidence):
                return None

        sample = SampleDialog()
        reply, confidence = sample.listen(text)
        assert confidence == 0.0
        assert reply is None
```

Next, we can implement some tests for our `Greeting` class. The first of these, `test_greeting_intro`, uses the `parametrize` decorator to test many different combinations of input strings and usernames to see if the class successfully returns a 1 for the interpretation confidence, that `respond` generates a response, and that the chatbot asks for the user's name:

```python
class TestGreetingDialog(object):
    """
    Test expected input and responses for the Greeting dialog
    """

    @pytest.mark.parametrize("text", ["Hello!", "hello", 'hey', 'hi'])
    @pytest.mark.parametrize("user", [None, "jay"], ids=["w/ user", "w/o user"])
    def test_greeting_intro(self, user, text):
        """
        Test that an initial greeting requests an introduction
        """
        g = Greeting()
        reply, confidence = g.listen(text, user=user)
        assert confidence == 1.0
```

```
        assert reply is not None
        assert reply == "Hello, what is your name?"
```

If any of these tests fail, it will serve as a signal that we should refactor our `Greeting` class so that it anticipates a broader range of possible inputs.

We should also create a `test_initial_intro` class that tests what happens when an introduction happens before a greeting. In this case, since we already know that this functionality is error-prone, we use the `pytest.mark.xfail` decorator to validate the cases that we expect are likely to fail; this will help us to remember the edge cases we want to address in future revisions:

```
    ...

    @pytest.mark.xfail(reason="a case that must be handled")
    @pytest.mark.parametrize("text", ["My name is Jake", "Hello, I'm Jake."])
    @pytest.mark.parametrize("user", [None, "jkm"], ids=["w/ user", "w/o user"])
    def test_initial_intro(self, user, text):
        """
        Test an initial introduction without greeting
        """
        g = Greeting()
        reply, confidence = g.listen(text, user=user)

        assert confidence == 1.0
        assert reply is not None
        assert reply == "Hello, Jake!"

        if user is None:
            user = 'jake'

        assert user in g.participants
        assert g.participants[user] == 'Jake'
```

Rules-based systems continue to be a very effective technique for keeping track of state within a dialog, particularly when augmented with robust edge-case exploration and test-driven development. The simple combination of regular expressions and logic to handle the exchanges (like ELIZA and PARRY, and our `Greeting` class) can be surprisingly effective. However, modern conversational agents rarely rely solely on heuristics. In the next part of the chapter, as we begin integrating linguistic features, we'll start to see why.

Entertaining Questions

One of the most common uses of chatbots is to quickly and easily answer fact-based questions such as "How long is the Nile river?" There exists a variety of fact and knowledge bases on the web such as DBPedia, Yago2, and Google Knowledge Graph; it is also very common for microknowledge bases such as FAQs to exist for specific applications. These tools provide an answer; the challenge is converting a natural language question into a database query. While statistical matching of questions to their answers is one simple mechanism for this, more robust approaches use both statistical and semantic information; for example, using a frame-based approach to create templates that can be derived into SPARQL queries or using classification techniques to identify the type of answer required (e.g., a location, an amount, etc.).

In a general chat system, however, there exists a preliminary problem—to detect when we've been asked a question, and to determine what type of question it is. An excellent first step is to consider what questions look like; we might easily employ a regular expression to look for sentences that begin with a "wh"-question ("Who," "What," "Where," "Why," "When," "How") and end in a question mark.

However, this approach is likely to lead to false positives, such as ignoring questions that start with non-"wh"-words (e.g., "Can you cook?", "Is there garlic?") or statements that "wrap" questions (e.g., "You're joining us?"). This approach may also generate false negatives, mistakenly promoting nonquestions that start with "wh"-words (e.g., "When in Rome…") or rhetorical questions that do not require a response (e.g., "Do you even lift?").

Though questions are often posed in irregular and unexpected ways, some patterns do exist. Sentences encode deep structures and relationships that go far beyond simple windowing and matching. To detect these patterns, we will need to perform some type of syntactic parsing—in other words, a mechanism that exploits context-free grammars to systematically assign syntactic structure to incoming text.

In "Extracting Keyphrases" on page 128 we saw that NLTK has a number of grammar-based parsers, but all require us to provide a grammar to specify the rules for building up parts-of-speech into phrases or chunks, which will unnecessarily limit our chatbot's flexibility. In the following sections we will instead explore pretrained *dependency parsing* and *constituency parsing* as more flexible alternatives.

Dependency Parsing

Dependency parsers are a lightweight mechanism to extract the syntactic structure of a sentence by linking phrases together with specific relationships. They do so by first identifying the head word of a phrase, then establishing links between the words that modify the head. The result is an overlapping structure of arcs that identify meaningful substructures of the sentence.

Consider the sentence "How many teaspoons are in a tablespoon?". In Figure 10-3, we see a dependency parse as visualized using SpaCy's DisplaCy module (available as of v2.0). This parse aims to tell us how the words in the sentence interact and modify each other. For instance, we can clearly see that the root of this phrase is the head verb (VERB) "are," which joins an adverbial phrase (ADV,ADJ,NOUN) "How many teaspoons" to a propositional phrase (ADP,DET,NOUN) "in a tablespoon" through the subject dependency of the head noun "teaspoons" and the prepositional dependency "in" (ADP is a cover term for prepositions).

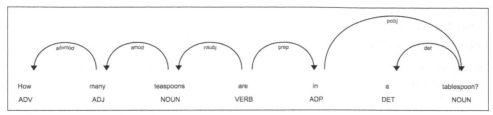

Figure 10-3. SpaCy dependency tree

 Whereas NLTK uses the Penn Treebank tagset, which we first saw in "Part-of-Speech Tagging" on page 44, SpaCy's convention is to use the Universal part-of-speech tags (e.g., "ADJ" for adjectives, "ADV" for adverbs, "PROPN" for proper nouns, "PRON" for pronouns, etc.). The Universal PoS tags are written by linguists (not programmers, like the Penn Treebank tags), which means they are generally richer, though they don't allow for things like using `tag.startswith("N")` to identify nouns.

To recreate the parse shown in Figure 10-3, we first load SpaCy's prebuilt English language parsing model. We then write a function, `plot_display_tree`, that parses incoming sentences using the prebuilt model and plots the resulting dependency parse using the `display.serve` method. If executed within a Jupyter notebook, the plot will render in the notebook; if run on the command line, the plot can be viewed in the browser at *http://localhost:5000/*:

```
import spacy
from spacy import displacy

# Required first: python -m spacy download en

spacy_nlp = spacy.load("en")

def plot_displacy_tree(sent):
    doc = spacy_nlp(sent)
    displacy.serve(doc, style='dep')
```

Dependency parsers are extremely popular for producing fast and correct grammatical analyses and when combined with part-of-speech tagging, perform much of the work required for phrase-level analysis. The relationships between words produced by dependency parsers may also be of interest to syntactic analysis. However, dependency parsing does not offer as rich and deep a view of the structure of sentences, and as such, may not always be sufficient or optimal. In our chatbot, we'll demonstrate how to leverage a more comprehensive tree representation, the constituency parse.

Constituency Parsing

Constituency parsing is a form of syntactic parsing whose goal is to break down a sentence into nested phrase structures similar to those we diagrammed when we were in grade school. The output is a tree structure that captures complex interrelationships between subphrases. Constituency parsers provide an opportunity to apply tree-traversal algorithms that easily enable computation on text, but because language is ambiguous, there is usually more than one way to construct a tree for a sentence.

We can parse our example question, "How many teaspoons in a tablespoon?", shown as a tree in Figure 10-4. Here we can see a much more complex structure of subphrases and more direct, unlabeled relationships between nodes in the tree.

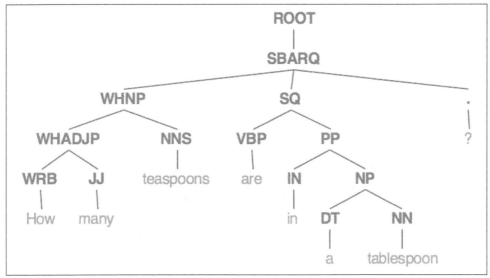

Figure 10-4. Stanford CoreNLP constituency tree

Constituency parse trees are comprised of terminal leaf nodes, the part-of-speech tag, and the word itself. The nonterminal nodes represent phrases that join the part-of-speech tags into related groupings. In this question, the root phrase is an SBARQ, a clause identified as a direct question because it is introduced by a "wh"-word. This clause is composed of a WHNP (a noun phrase with a "wh"-word) and an SQ, the main clause of the SBARQ, which itself is a verb phrase. As you can see, a lot of detail exists in this parse that gives a lot of clues about how to treat this question in its syntactic parts!

For questions and answers, the WRB, WP, and WDT tags identify words that are of interest to our particular context, and may signal a measurement-conversion question; WRB is a "wh"-adverb (e.g., a "wh"- word used as a verbal modifier, as in "When are you leaving?"); WP is a "wh"-pronoun (as in "Who won the bet?"); and WDT is a "wh"-determiner (as in "Which Springfield?").

The Stanford CoreNLP package is a comprehensive suite of natural language processing tools written in Java. It includes methods for part-of-speech tagging, syntactic parsing, named entity recognition, sentiment analysis, and more.

Setting Up the Dependencies for Stanford CoreNLP

The current version of the parser requires Java 8 (JDK1.8) or later.

Download and extract the Stanford NLP tools:

```
wget http://nlp.stanford.edu/software/stanford-ner-2015-04-20.zip
wget http://nlp.stanford.edu/software/stanford-parser-full-2015-04-20.zip
wget http://nlp.stanford.edu/software/stanford-postagger-full-2015-04-20.zip

unzip stanford-ner-2015-04-20.zip
unzip stanford-parser-full-2015-04-20.zip
unzip stanford-postagger-full-2015-04-20.zip
```

Then add these *.jars* to your Python path by opening your .bash_profile and adding the following:

```
export STANFORDTOOLSDIR=$HOME
export CLASSPATH=$STANFORDTOOLSDIR/stanford-postagger-full-2015-04-20/
    stanford-postagger.jar:$STANFORDTOOLSDIR/stanford-ner-2015-04-20/
    stanford-ner.jar:$STANFORDTOOLSDIR/stanford-parser-full-2015-04-20/
    stanford-parser.jar:$STANFORDTOOLSDIR/stanford-parser-full-2015-04-20/
    stanford-parser-3.5.2-models.jar
export STANFORD_MODELS=$STANFORDTOOLSDIR/stanford-postagger-full-2015-04-20/
    models:$STANFORDTOOLSDIR/stanford-ner-2015-04-20/classifiers
```

In a recent update to the library, NLTK made available a new module nltk.parse.stanford that enables us to use the Stanford parsers from inside NLTK (assuming you have set up the requisite *.jars* and PATH configuration) as follows:

```
from nltk.parse.stanford import StanfordParser

stanford_parser = StanfordParser(
    model_path="edu/stanford/nlp/models/lexparser/englishPCFG.ser.gz"
)
def print_stanford_tree(sent):
    """
    Use Stanford pretrained model to extract dependency tree
    for use by other methods
    Returns a list of trees
    """
    parse = stanford_parser.raw_parse(sent)
    return list(parse)
```

We can plot the Stanford constituency tree using `nltk.tree` to generate the tree shown in Figure 10-4, which allows us to visually inspect the structure of the question:

```
def plot_stanford_tree(sent):
    """
    Visually inspect the Stanford dependency tree as an image
    """
    parse = stanford_parser.raw_parse(sent)
    tree = list(parse)
    tree[0].draw()
```

As you visually explore syntax parses produced by StanfordNLP you'll notice that structures get much more complex with longer parses. Constituency parses provide a lot of information, which may simply end up being noise in some text-based applications. Both constituency and dependency parsing suffer from structural ambiguity, meaning that these parses may also produce some probability of a correct parse that can be used when computing confidence. However, the level of detail a syntax provides makes it an excellent candidate for easily identifying questions and applying frames to extract queryable information, as we'll see in the next section.

Question Detection

The pretrained models in SpaCy and CoreNLP give us a powerful way to automatically parse and annotate input sentences. We can then use the annotations to traverse the parsed sentences and look for part-of-speech tags that correspond to questions.

First, we will inspect the tag assigned to the top-level node of the ROOT (the zeroth item of the parse tree, which contains all its branches). Next, we want to inspect the tags assigned to the branch and leaf nodes, which we can do using the `tree.pos` method from `nltk.tree.Tree` module:

```
tree = print_stanford_tree("How many teaspoons are in a tablespoon?")
root = tree[0] # The root is the first item in the parsed sents tree
print(root)
print(root.pos())
```

Once parsed, we can next explore how different questions manifest using the Penn Treebank tags, which we first encountered in "Part-of-Speech Tagging" on page 44. In our example, we can see from the root that our input is an SBARQ (a direct question introduced by a "wh"-word), which in this case is a WRB (a "wh"-adverb). The sentence begins with a WHNP (a "wh"-noun phrase) that contains a WHADJP (a "wh"-adjective phrase):

```
(ROOT
  (SBARQ
    (WHNP (WHADJP (WRB How) (JJ many)) (NNS teaspoons))
    (SQ (VBP are) (PP (IN in) (NP (DT a) (NN tablespoon))))
    (. ?)))
```

```
[('How', 'WRB'), ('many', 'JJ'), ('teaspoons', 'NNS'), ('are', 'VBP'),
('in', 'IN'), ('a', 'DT'), ('tablespoon', 'NN'), ('?', '.')]
```

The major advantage of using a technique like this for question detection is the flexibility. For instance, if we change our question to "Sorry to trouble you, but how many teaspoons are in a tablespoon?", the output is different, but the WHADJP and WRB question markers are still there:

```
(ROOT
  (FRAG
    (FRAG
      (ADJP (JJ Sorry))
      (S (VP (TO to) (VP (VB trouble) (NP (PRP you))))))
    (, ,)
    (CC but)
    (SBAR
      (WHADJP (WRB how) (JJ many))
      (S
        (NP (NNS teaspoons))
        (VP (VBP are) (PP (IN in) (NP (DT a) (NN tablespoon))))))
    (. ?)))
[('Sorry', 'JJ'), ('to', 'TO'), ('trouble', 'VB'), ('you', 'PRP'), (',', ','),
('but', 'CC'), ('how', 'WRB'), ('many', 'JJ'), ('teaspoons', 'NNS'),
('are', 'VBP'), ('in', 'IN'), ('a', 'DT'), ('tablespoon', 'NN'), ('?', '.')]
```

Table 10-1 lists some of the tags we have found most useful in question detection; a complete list can be found in Bies et al.'s "Bracketing Guidelines for Treebank II Style."[3]

Table 10-1. Penn Treebank II Tags for Question Detection

Tag	Meaning	Example
SBARQ	Direct question introduced by a wh-word or a wh-phrase	"How hot is the oven?"
SBAR	Clause introduced by subordinating conjunction (e.g., indirect question)	"If you're in town, try the beignets."
SINV	Inverted declarative sentence	"Rarely have I eaten better."
SQ	Inverted yes/no question or main clause of a wh-question	"Is the gumbo spicy?"
S	Simple declarative clause	"I like jalapenos."
WHADJP	Wh-adjective phrases	The "How hot" in "How hot is the oven?"
WHADVP	Wh-adverb phrase	The "Where do" in "Where do you keep the chicory?"
WHNP	Wh-noun phrase	The "Which bakery" in "Which bakery is best?"

---

3 Ann Bies, Mark Ferguson, Karen Katz, and Robert MacIntyre, *Bracketing Guidelines for Treebank II Style: Penn Treebank Project*, (1995) *http://bit.ly/2GQKZLm*

Tag	Meaning	Example
WHPP	Wh-prepositional phrase	The "on which" in "The roux, on which this recipe depends, should not be skipped."
WRB	Wh-adverb	The "How" in "How hot is the oven?"
WDT	Wh-determiner	The "What" in "What temperature is it?"
WP$	Possessive wh-pronoun	The "Whose" in "Whose bowl is this?"
WP	Wh-pronoun	The "Who" in "Who's hungry?"

In the next section, we will see how to use these tags to detect questions most relevant to our kitchen helper bot.

From Tablespoons to Grams

The next feature we will add to our chatbot is a question-and-answer system that leverages the pretrained parsers we explored in the previous section to provide convenient kitchen measurement conversions. Consider that in everyday conversation, people frequently phrase questions about measurements as "How" questions—for example "How many teaspoons are in a tablespoon?" or "How many cups make a liter?" For our question-type identification task, we will aim to be able to interpret questions that take the form "How many X are in a Y?"

We begin by defining a class `Converter`, which inherits the behavior of our `Dialog` class. We expect to initialize a `Converter` with a knowledge base of measurement conversions, here a simple JSON file stored in `CONVERSION_PATH` and containing all of the conversions between units of measure. On initialization, these conversions are loaded using `json.load`. We also initialize a `parser` (here we use CoreNLP), as well as a `stemmer` from NLTK and an `inflect.engine` from the `inflect` library, which will enable us to handle pluralization in the `parse` and `respond` methods, respectively. Our `parse` method will use the `raw_parse` method from CoreNLP to generate constituency parses as demonstrated in the previous section:

```
import os
import json
import inflect

from nltk.stem.snowball import SnowballStemmer
from nltk.parse.stanford import StanfordParser


class Converter(Dialog):
    """
    Answers questions about converting units
    """

    def __init__(self, conversion_path=CONVERSION_PATH):
        with open(conversion_path, 'r') as f:
```

```
            self.metrics = json.load(f)

        self.inflect = inflect.engine()
        self.stemmer = SnowballStemmer('english')
        self.parser = StanfordParser(model_path=STANFORD_PATH)

    def parse(self, text):
        parse = self.parser.raw_parse(text)
        return list(parse)
```

Next, in `interpret`, we initialize a list to collect the measures we want to convert from and to, an initial confidence score of 0, and a dictionary to collect the results of our interpretation. We retrieve the root of the parsed sentence tree and use the `nltk.tree.Tree.pos` method to scan through the part-of-speech tags for ones that match the adverbial phrase question pattern (WRB). If we find any, we increment our confidence score, and begin to traverse the tree using an `nltk.util.breadth_first` search with a maximum depth of 8 (to limit recursion). For any subtrees that match the syntactic patterns in which "how many"-type questions typically arise, we identify and store any singular or plural nouns that represent the source and target measures. If we identify any numbers within the question phrase subtree, we store that in our `results` dictionary as the `quantity` for the target measure.

For demonstration purposes, we'll use a naive but straightforward mechanism for computing `confidence` here; more nuanced methods are possible and may be advisable, given your particular context. If we are successful at identifying both a source and target measure, we increment our `confidence` again and add these to our `results` dictionary. If either measure is also in our knowledge base (aka JSON lookup), we increase the `confidence` accordingly. Finally, we return a (`results`, `confidence`, `kwargs`) tuple, which the `respond` method will use to determine whether and how to respond to the user:

```
from nltk.tree import Tree
from nltk.util import breadth_first

...

    def interpret(self, sents, **kwargs):
        measures = []
        confidence = 0
        results = dict()

        # The root is the first item in the parsed sents tree
        root = sents[0]

        # Make sure there are wh-adverb phrases
        if "WRB" in [tag for word, tag in root.pos()]:
            # If so, increment confidence & traverse parse tree
            confidence += .2
            # Set the maxdepth to limit recursion
```

```
        for clause in breadth_first(root, maxdepth=8):
            #find the simple declarative clauses (+S+)
            if isinstance(clause, Tree):
                if clause.label() in ["S", "SQ", "WHNP"]:
                    for token,tag in clause.pos():
                        # Store nouns as target measures
                        if tag in ["NN", "NNS"]:
                            measures.append(token)
                        # Store numbers as target quantities
                        elif tag in ["CD"]:
                            results["quantity"] = token

    # Handle duplication for very nested trees
    measures = list(set([self.stemmer.stem(mnt) for mnt in measures]))

    # If both source and destination measures are provided...
    if len(measures) == 2:
        confidence += .4
        results["src"] = measures[0]
        results["dst"] = measures[1]

        # Check to see if they correspond to our lookup table
        if results["src"] in self.metrics.keys():
            confidence += .2
            if results["dst"] in self.metrics[results["src"]]:
                confidence += .2

    return results, confidence, kwargs
```

However, before we can implement our respond method, we need a few helper utilities. The first is convert, which converts from the units of the source measurement to those of the target measurement. The convert method takes as input string representations of the source units (src), the target units (dst), and a quantity of the source unit, which may be either a float or an int. The function returns a tuple with the (converted, source, target) units:

```
def convert(self, src, dst, quantity=1.0):
    """
    Converts from the source unit to the dest unit for the given quantity
    of the source unit.
    """
    # Stem source and dest to remove pluralization
    src, dst = tuple(map(self.stemmer.stem, (src,dst)))

    # Check that we can convert
    if dst not in self.metrics:
        raise KeyError("cannot convert to '{}' units".format(src))
    if src not in self.metrics[dst]:
        raise KeyError("cannot convert from {} to '{}'".format(src, dst))

    return self.metrics[dst][src] * float(quantity), src, dst
```

We will also add round, pluralize, and numericalize methods, which leverage utilities from the humanize library to transform numbers to more natural human-readable form:

```python
import humanize

...

    def round(self, num):
        num = round(float(num), 4)
        if num.is_integer():
            return int(num)
        return num

    def pluralize(self, noun, num):
        return self.inflect.plural_noun(noun, num)

    def numericalize(self, amt):
        if amt > 100.0 and amt < 1e6:
            return humanize.intcomma(int(amt))
        if amt >= 1e6:
            return humanize.intword(int(amt))
        elif isinstance(amt, int) or amt.is_integer():
            return humanize.apnumber(int(amt))
        else:
            return humanize.fractional(amt)
```

Finally, in the respond method, we check to see if our confidence in our interpretation is sufficiently high, and if so, we use convert to perform the actual measurement conversions, and then round, pluralize, and numericalize to ensure the final response is easy for the user to read:

```python
    def respond(self, sents, confidence, **kwargs):
        """
        Response makes use of the humanize and inflect libraries to produce
        much more human understandable results.
        """
        if confidence < .5:
            return "I'm sorry, I don't know that one."

        try:
            quantity = sents.get('quantity', 1)
            amount, source, target = self.convert(**sents)

            # Perform numeric rounding
            amount = self.round(amount)
            quantity = self.round(quantity)

            # Pluralize
            source = self.pluralize(source, quantity)
            target = self.pluralize(target, amount)
            verb = self.inflect.plural_verb("is", amount)
```

```
# Numericalize
quantity = self.numericalize(quantity)
amount = self.numericalize(amount)


return "There {} {} {} in {} {}.".format(
    verb, amount, target, quantity, source
)

except KeyError as e:
    return "I'm sorry I {}".format(str(e))
```

Now we can experiment with using the listen method on a few possible input questions to see how well our Converter class is able to handle different combinations and quantities of source and target units:

```
if __name__ == "__main__":
    dialog = Converter()
    print(dialog.listen("How many cups are in a gallon?"))
    print(dialog.listen("How many gallons are in 2 cups?"))
    print(dialog.listen("How many tablespoons are in a cup?"))
    print(dialog.listen("How many tablespoons are in 10 cups?"))
    print(dialog.listen("How many tablespoons are in a teaspoon?"))
```

The resulting output, which is in the form of (reply, confidence) tuples, shows that Converter is able to successfully produce conversions with consistently high confidence:

```
('There are 16 cups in one gallon.', 1.0)
('There are 32 cups in two gallons.', 1.0)
('There are 16 tablespoons in one cup.', 1.0)
('There are 160 tablespoons in 10 cups.', 1.0)
('There are 1/3 tablespoons in one teaspoon.', 1.0)
```

Learning to Help

While providing dynamic measurement conversions is certainly convenient, we'd like to incorporate something a bit more unique—a recipe recommender. In this section, we walk through a pipeline that will leverage a recipe corpus to perform text normalization, vectorization, and dimensionality reduction, and finally use a nearest-neighbor algorithm to provide recipe recommendations, as shown in Figure 10-5. In this case the state maintained by our Dialog variant will be an active learning model, capable of providing recommendations and incorporating user feedback to improve over time.

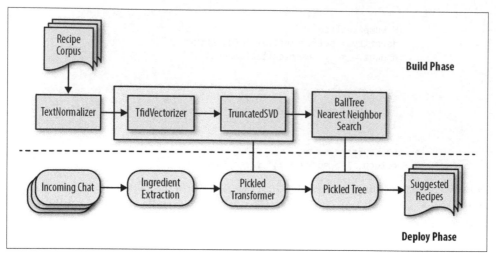

Figure 10-5. Recipe recommender schema

A Domain-Specific Corpus

To train our recommender, we'll be using a cooking corpus comprised of blog posts and articles that contain recipes for specific dishes as well as narratives and descriptions for those dishes. A similar corpus can be constructed by extracting a list of source URLs from a list of cooking blogs, crawling the websites and indexing each page on the site. Our corpus contains 60,000 HTML documents and is approximately 8 GB, stored with a flat structure:

```
food_corpus
├── 2010-12-sweet-potato-chili.html
├── 2013-09-oysters-rockefeller.html
├── 2013-07-nc-style-barbeque.html
├── 2013-11-cornbread-stuffing.html
└── 2015-04-next-level-grilled-cheese.html
```

We wrote an `HTMLCorpusReader` modeled on the one in "Corpus Readers" on page 27, adding a `titles()` method that will allow us to grab the page titles from each HTML file, which will give us a human-intelligible way to refer to each recipe:

```python
def titles(self, fileids=None, categories=None):
    """
    Parse HTML to identify titles from the head tag.
    """
    for doc in self.docs(fileids, categories):
        soup = bs4.BeautifulSoup(doc, 'lxml')
        try:
            yield soup.title.text
            soup.decompose()
        except AttributeError as e:
            continue
```

Given the size of the corpus, we leveraged a version of the `Preprocessor` introduced in Chapter 3 that uses the Python multiprocessing library to parallelize the `transform` method. In Chapter 11, we'll discuss multiprocessing and other parallelization techniques in greater depth.

Being Neighborly

The main drawback of the nearest-neighbor algorithm is the complexity of search as dimensionality increases; to find the k nearest neighbors for any given vectorized document d, we have to compute the distances from d to every other document in the corpus. Since our example corpus contains roughly 60,000 documents, this means we'll need to do 60,000 distance computations, with an operation for each dimension in our document vector. Assuming a 100,000-dimensional space, which is not unusual for text, that means 6 billion operations per recipe search!

That means we'll need to find some ways to speed up our search so our chatbot can provide recommendations quickly. First, we should perform dimensionality reduction. We are already doing some dimensionality reduction, since the `TextNormalizer` we used in Chapters 4 and 5 performs some lemmatization and other "light touch" cleaning that effectively reduces the dimensions of our data. We could further reduce the dimensionality by using the n-gram `FreqDist` class from Chapter 7 as a transformer to select only the tokens that constitute 10%–50% of the distribution.

Alternatively, we can pair our `TfidfVectorizer` with Scikit-Learn's `TruncatedSVD`, which will compress the dimensions of our vectors into fewer components (the rule of thumb for text documents is to set `n_components` to at least 200). Keep in mind that `TruncatedSVD` does not center the data before computing the Singular Value Decompositions, which may result in somewhat erratic results, depending on the distribution of the data.

We can also leverage a less computationally expensive alternative to traditional unsupervised nearest-neighbor search, such as ball tree, K-D trees, and local sensitivity hashing. A K-D tree (`sklearn.neighbors.KDTree`) is an approximation of nearest neighbor, which only computes the distances from our instance d to a subset of the full dataset. However, K-D does not perform particularly well on sparse, high-dimensional data because it uses the values of random features to partition the data (recall that with a given vectorized document, most values will be zero). Local sensitivity hashing is more performant on high-dimensional data, though the current Scikit-Learn implementation, `sklearn.neighbors.NearestNeighbors`, has been found to be inefficient and is scheduled for deprecation.

Of course, there are also approximate nearest-neighbor implementations in other libraries, such as Annoy (a C++ library with Python bindings), which is currently used by Spotify to generate dynamic song recommendations.

For our chatbot, we will use a ball tree algorithm. Like K-D trees, the ball tree algorithm partitions data points so that the nearest-neighbor search can be performed on a subset of the points (in this case, nested hyperspheres). As the dimensionality of a nearest-neighbor search space increases, ball trees have been shown to perform fairly well.[4] Conveniently, the Scikit-Learn implementation, `sklearn.neighbors.BallTree`, exposes a range of different distance metrics that can be used and compared for performance optimization.

Finally, we can accelerate our recipe recommendation search by serializing both our trained transformer (so that we can perform the same transformations on incoming text from users), and our tree, so that our chatbot can perform queries without having to rebuild the tree for every search.

First, we'll create a `BallTreeRecommender` class, which is initialized with a _k_ for the desired number of recommendations (which will default to 3), paths to a pickled fitted transformer `svd.pkl`, and fitted ball tree `tree.pkl`. If the model has already been fit, these paths will exist, and the `load` method will load them from disk for use. Otherwise, they will be fitted and saved using Scikit-Learn's `joblib` serializer in our `fit_transform` method:

```python
import pickle

from sklearn.externals import joblib
from sklearn.pipeline import Pipeline
from sklearn.neighbors import BallTree
from sklearn.decomposition import TruncatedSVD
from sklearn.feature_extraction.text import TfidfVectorizer


class BallTreeRecommender(BaseEstimator, TransformerMixin):
    """
    Given input terms, provide k recipe recommendations
    """
    def __init__(self, k=3, **kwargs):
        self.k = k
        self.trans_path = "svd.pkl"
        self.tree_path = "tree.pkl"
        self.transformer = False
```

---

4 Ting Liu, Andrew W. Moore, and Alexander Gray, _New Algorithms for Efficient High-Dimensional Nonparametric Classification_, (2006) _http://bit.ly/2GQL0io_

```
        self.tree = None
        self.load()

    def load(self):
        """
        Load a pickled transformer and tree from disk,
        if they exist.
        """
        if os.path.exists(self.trans_path):
            self.transformer = joblib.load(open(self.trans_path, 'rb'))
            self.tree = joblib.load(open(self.tree_path, 'rb'))
        else:
            self.transformer = False
            self.tree = None

    def save(self):
        """
        It takes a long time to fit, so just do it once!
        """
        joblib.dump(self.transformer, open(self.trans_path, 'wb'))
        joblib.dump(self.tree, open(self.tree_path, 'wb'))

    def fit_transform(self, documents):
        if self.transformer == False:
            self.transformer = Pipeline([
                ('norm', TextNormalizer(minimum=50, maximum=200)),
                ('transform', Pipeline([
                    ('tfidf', TfidfVectorizer()),
                    ('svd', TruncatedSVD(n_components=200))
                ])
                )
            ])
            self.lexicon = self.transformer.fit_transform(documents)
            self.tree = BallTree(self.lexicon)
            self.save()
```

Once a `sklearn.neighbors.BallTree` model has been fitted, we can use the `tree.query` method to return the distances and indices for the *k* closest documents. For our `BallTreeRecommender` class, we will add a wrapper `query` method that uses the fitted transformer to vectorize and transform incoming text and return only the indices for the closest recipes:

```
    def query(self, terms):
        """
        Given input list of ingredient terms, return k closest matching recipes.
        """
        vect_doc = self.transformer.named_steps['transform'].fit_transform(terms)
        dists, inds = self.tree.query(vect_doc, k=self.k)
        return inds[0]
```

Offering Recommendations

Assuming that we have fit our `BallTreeRecommender` on our pickled recipe corpus and saved the model artifacts, we can now implement the recipe recommendations in the context of our `Dialog` abstract base class.

Our new class `RecipeRecommender` is instantiated with a pickled corpus reader and an estimator that implements a query method, like our `BallTreeRecommender`. We use the `corpus.titles()` method referenced in "A Domain-Specific Corpus" on page 234, which will allow us to reference the stored recipes using the blog post titles as their names. If the recommender isn't already fitted, the `__init__` method will ensure that it is fit and transformed:

```
class RecipeRecommender(Dialog):
    """
    Recipe recommender dialog
    """

    def __init__(self, recipes, recommender=BallTreeRecommender(k=3)):
        self.recipes = list(corpus.titles())
        self.recommender = recommender

        # Fit the recommender model with the corpus
        self.recommender.fit_transform(list(corpus.docs()))
```

Next, the `parse` method splits the input text string into a list and performs part-of-speech tagging:

```
    def parse(self, text):
        """
        Extract ingredients from the text
        """
        return pos_tag(wordpunct_tokenize(text))
```

Our `interpret` method takes in the parsed text and determines whether it is a list of ingredients. If so, it transforms the utterance into a collection of nouns and then assigns a `confidence` score according to the percent of the input text that is nouns. Again, we are using a naive method for computing confidence here, primarily for its straightforwardness. In practice, it would be valuable to validate confidence scoring mechanisms; for instance, by having reviewers evaluate performance on an annotated test set to confirm that lower confidence scores correspond to lower quality responses:

```
    def interpret(self, sents, **kwargs):
        # If feedback detected, update the model
        if 'feedback' in kwargs:
            self.recommender.update(kwargs['feedback'])

        n_nouns = sum(1 for pos, tag in sents if pos.startswith("N"))
        confidence = n_nouns/len(sents)
```

```
            terms = [tag for pos, tag in sents if pos.startswith("N")]
            return terms, confidence, kwargs
```

Finally, the `respond` method takes in the list of nouns extracted from the `interpret` method as well as the `confidence`. If `interpret` has successfully extracted a sufficient number of nouns from the input, the `confidence` will be high enough to generate recommendations. We will retrieve these recommendations by calling the internal `recommender.query` method with the extracted nouns:

```
    def respond(self, terms, confidence, **kwargs):
        """
        Returns a recommendation if the confidence is > 0.15 otherwise None.
        """
        if confidence < 0.15:
            return None

        output = [
            "Here are some recipes related to {}".format(", ".join(terms))
        ]
        output += [
            "- {}".format(self.recipes[idx])
            for idx in self.recommender.query(terms)
        ]

        return "\n".join(output)
```

Now we can test out our new `RecipeRecommender`:

```
if __name__ == '__main__':
    corpus = HTMLPickledCorpusReader('../food_corpus_proc')
    recommender = RecipeRecommender(corpus)
    question = "What can I make with brie, tomatoes, capers, and pancetta?"
    print(recommender.listen(question))
```

And here are the results:

```
('Here are some recipes related to brie, tomatoes, capers, pancetta
- My Trip to Jamaica - Cookies and Cups
- Turkey Bolognese | Well Plated by Erin
- Cranberry Brie Bites', 0.2857142857142857)
```

As discussed in Chapter 1, machine learning models benefit from feedback, which can be used to more effectively produce results. In the context of a kitchen chatbot producing recipe recommendations, we have the perfect opportunity to create the possibility for natural language feedback. Consider implicit feedback: we know the user is interested if they respond "OK, show me the Cranberry Brie Bites recipe" and we can use this information to rank cheesy deliciousness higher in our recommendation results by modifying a new vector component specifically related to the user's preference.

Alternatively, we could initiate the conversation with the user and explicitly ask them what they thought about the recipe! Chatbots are an opportunity to get increasingly detailed user feedback that simply doesn't exist in current clickstream-based feedback mechanisms.

Conclusion

With flexible language models trained on domain-specific corpora, coupled with effective task-oriented frames, chatbots increasingly allow people to find information and receive answers not only faster than via other means, but also more intuitively. As natural language understanding and generation improve, chatting with a bot may eventually become a better experience than chatting with a human!

In this chapter we presented a framework for conversational agents centered around the abstract `Dialog` object. `Dialog` objects listen for human input, parse and interpret the input, updating an internal state, then respond if required based on the updated state. A `Conversation` is a collection of dialogs that allow us to create chatbots in a composable fashion, each dialog having their own responsibility for interpreting particular input. We presented a simple conversation that passes all input to all internal dialogs then responds with the interpretation with the highest confidence.

The `Dialog` framework allows us to easily create conversational components and add them to applications, extending them without much effort and decoupling them for easy testing. Although we couldn't get to it in this chapter, we have examples of how to implement conversations inside of a command-line chat application or a Flask-based web application in our GitHub repository for the book: *https://github.com/foxbook/atap/*.

Our kitchen helper is now capable of parsing incoming text, detecting some different types of questions, and providing measurement conversions or recipe recommendations, depending on the user's query. For next steps, we might extend our chatbot's ability to be conversational by training an n-gram language model as discussed in Chapter 7 or a connectionist model, which we'll investigate in Chapter 12 on a conversational food corpus. In the next chapter we will explore scaling techniques that enable us to build more performant language-aware data products, and see how they can be applied to accelerate the text analytics workflow from corpus ingestion and preprocessing to transformation and modeling.

## CHAPTER 11

Scaling Text Analytics with Multiprocessing and Spark

In the context of language-aware data products, text corpora are not static fixtures, but instead living datasets that constantly grow and change. Take, for instance, a question-and-answer system; in our view this is not only an application that provides answers, but one that collects questions. This means even a relatively modest corpus of questions could quickly grow into a deep asset, capable of training the application to learn better responses in the future.

Unfortunately, text processing techniques are expensive both in terms of space (memory and disk) and time (computational benchmarks). Therefore, as corpora grow, text analysis requires increasingly more computational resources. Perhaps you've even experienced how long processing takes on the corpora you're experimenting on while working through this book! The primary solution to deal with the challenges of large and growing datasets is to employ multiple computational resources (processors, disks, memory) to distribute the workload. When many resources work on different parts of computation simultaneously we say that they are operating in *parallel*.

Parallelism (parallel or distributed computation) has two primary forms. *Task parallelism* means that different, independent operations run simultaneously on the same data. *Data parallelism* implies that the same operation is being applied to many different inputs simultaneously. Both task and data parallelism are often used to accelerate computation from its sequential form (one operation at a time, one after the other) with the intent that the computation becomes faster.

It is important to remember that speed is the name of the game, and that trade-offs exist in a parallel environment. More smaller disks rather than fewer large disks means that data can be read faster off the disk, but each disk can store less and must be read separately. Computations in parallel means that the job gets done more quickly, so long as computations aren't waiting for others to complete. It takes time and effort to set up resources to perform parallel computation, and if that effort exceeds the resulting increase in speed, then parallelism is simply not worth it (see Amdahl's law[1] for more on this topic). Another consequence of speed is the requirement for approximation rather than complete computation since no single resource has a complete view of the input.

In this chapter we will discuss two different approaches to parallelism and their trade-offs. The first, multiprocessing, allows programs to use multicore machines and operating system threads and is limited by the specifications of the machine it runs on, but is far faster to set up and get going. The second, Spark, utilizes a cluster that can generally scale to any size but requires new workflows and maintenance. The goal of the chapter is to introduce these topics so that you can quickly engage them in your text analysis workflows, while also giving enough background that you can make good decisions about what technologies to employ in your particular circumstances.

Python Multiprocessing

Modern operating systems run hundreds of processes simultaneously on multicore processors. Process execution is scheduled on the CPU and allocated its own memory space. When a Python program is run, the operating system executes the code as a *process*. Processes are independent, and in order to share information between them, some external mechanism is required (such as writing to disk or a database, or using a network connection).

A single process might then spawn several *threads* of execution. A thread is the smallest unit of work for a CPU scheduler and represents a sequence of instructions that must be performed by the processor. Whereas the operating system manages processes, the program itself manages its own threads, and data inherent to a certain process can be shared among that process's threads without any outside communication.

Modern processors contain multiple cores, pipelining, and other techniques designed to optimize threaded execution. Programming languages such as C, Java, and Go can take advantage of OS threads to provide concurrency and in the multicore case, parallelism, from within a single program. Unfortunately, Python cannot take advantage of multiple cores due to the Global Interpreter Lock, or GIL, which ensures that Python bytecode is interpreted and executed in a safe manner. Therefore, whereas a Go program might achieve a CPU utilization of 200% in a dual-core computer, Python will only ever be able to use at most 100% of a single core.

---

1 Gene M. Amdahl, *Validity of the single processor approach to achieving large scale computing capabilities*, (1967) *http://bit.ly/2GQKWza*

Python provides additional mechanisms for *concurrency*, such as the `asyncio` library. Concurrency is related to parallelism, but distinct: while parallelism describes the simultaneous execution of computation, concurrency describes the composition of independent execution such that computations are scheduled to maximize the use of resources. Asynchronous programming and coroutines are beyond the scope of the book, but are a powerful mechanism for scaling text analysis particularly for I/O-bound tasks like data ingestion or database operations.

There are two primary modules for parallelism within Python: `threading` and `multiprocessing`. Both modules have a similar basic API (meaning that you can easily switch between the two if needed), but the underlying parallel architecture is fundamentally different.

The `threading` module creates Python threads. For tasks like data ingestion, which utilize system resources besides the CPU (such as disk or network), threading is a good choice to achieve concurrency. However, with `threading`, only one thread will ever execute at a time, and no parallel execution will occur.

To achieve parallelism in Python, the `multiprocessing` library is required. The multiprocessing module creates additional child processes with the same code as the parent process by either *forking* the parent on Unix systems (the OS snapshots the currently running program into a new process) or by *spawning* on Windows (a new Python interpreter is run with the shared code). Each process runs its own Python interpreter and has its own GIL, each of which can utilize 100% of a CPU. Therefore, if you have a quad-core processor and run four multiprocesses, it is possible to take advantage of 400% of your CPU.

The multiprocessing architecture in Figure 11-1 shows the typical structure of a parallel Python program. It consists of a parent (or main) program and multiple child processes (usually one per core, though more is possible). The parent program schedules work (provides input) for the children and consumes results (gathers output). Data is passed to and from children and the parent using the `pickle` module. When the parent process terminates, the child processes generally also terminate, though they can also become orphaned and continue running on their own.

In Figure 11-1, two different vectorization tasks are run in parallel and the `main` process waits for them all to complete before moving on to a fitting task (e.g., two models on each of the different vectorization methods) that also runs in parallel. *Forking* causes multiple child processes to be instantiated, whereas *joining* causes child processes to be ended, and control is passed back to the primary process. For instance, during the first vectorize task, there are three processes: the main process and the child processes A and B. When vectorization is complete, the child processes end and are joined back into the main processes. The parallel job in Figure 11-1 has six parallel tasks, each completely independent except that the fit tasks must start after the vectorization is complete.

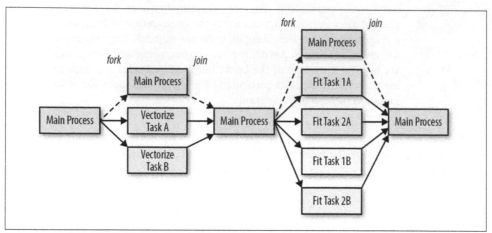

Figure 11-1. Task parallelism architecture

In the next section, we will explore how to achieve this type of task parallelism using the multiprocessing library.

Running Tasks in Parallel

In order to illustrate how multiprocessing can help us perform machine learning on text, let's consider an example where we would like to fit multiple models, cross-validate them, and save them to disk. We will begin by writing three functions to generate a naive Bayes model, a logistic regression, and a multilayer perceptron. Each function in turn creates three different models, defined by Pipelines, that extract text from a corpus located at a specified path. Each task also determines a location to write the model to, and reports results using the logging module (more on this in a bit):

```
from transformers import TextNormalizer, identity

from sklearn.pipeline import Pipeline
from sklearn.naive_bayes import MultinomialNB
from sklearn.linear_model import LogisticRegression
from sklearn.feature_extraction.text import TfidfVectorizer
from sklearn.neural_network import MLPClassifier


def fit_naive_bayes(path, saveto=None, cv=12):

    model = Pipeline([
        ('norm', TextNormalizer()),
        ('tfidf', TfidfVectorizer(tokenizer=identity, lowercase=False)),
```

```
            ('clf', MultinomialNB())
    ])

    if saveto is None:
        saveto = "naive_bayes_{}.pkl".format(time.time())

    scores, delta = train_model(path, model, saveto, cv)
    logger.info((
        "naive bayes training took {:0.2f} seconds "
        "with an average score of {:0.3f}"
    ).format(delta, scores.mean()))


def fit_logistic_regression(path, saveto=None, cv=12):
    model = Pipeline([
        ('norm', TextNormalizer()),
        ('tfidf', TfidfVectorizer(tokenizer=identity, lowercase=False)),
        ('clf', LogisticRegression())
    ])

    if saveto is None:
        saveto = "logistic_regression_{}.pkl".format(time.time())

    scores, delta = train_model(path, model, saveto, cv)
    logger.info((
        "logistic regression training took {:0.2f} seconds "
        "with an average score of {:0.3f}"
    ).format(delta, scores.mean()))


def fit_multilayer_perceptron(path, saveto=None, cv=12):
    model = Pipeline([
        ('norm', TextNormalizer()),
        ('tfidf', TfidfVectorizer(tokenizer=identity, lowercase=False)),
        ('clf', MLPClassifier(hidden_layer_sizes=(10,10), early_stopping=True))
    ])

    if saveto is None:
        saveto = "multilayer_perceptron_{}.pkl".format(time.time())

    scores, delta = train_model(path, model, saveto, cv)
    logger.info((
        "multilayer perceptron training took {:0.2f} seconds "
        "with an average score of {:0.3f}"
    ).format(delta, scores.mean()))
```

For simplicity, the pipelines for `fit_naive_bayes`, `fit_logis
tic_regression`, and `fit_multilayer_perceptron` share the first
two steps, using the text normalizer and vectorizer as discussed in
Chapter 4; however, you can imagine that different feature extraction methods might be better for different models.

While each of our functions can be modified and customized individually, each must also share common code. This shared functionality is defined in the `train_model()` function, which creates a `PickledCorpusReader` from the specified path. The `train_model()` function uses this reader to create instances and labels, compute scores using the `cross_val_score` utility from Scikit-Learn, fit the model, write it to disk using `joblib` (a specialized `pickle` module used by Scikit-Learn), and return the scores:

```python
from reader import PickledCorpusReader

from sklearn.externals import joblib
from sklearn.model_selection import cross_val_score


@timeit
def train_model(path, model, saveto=None, cv=12):
    # Load the corpus data and labels for classification
    corpus = PickledCorpusReader(path)
    X = documents(corpus)
    y = labels(corpus)

    # Compute cross validation scores
    scores = cross_val_score(model, X, y, cv=cv)

    # Fit the model on entire dataset
    model.fit(X, y)

    # Write to disk if specified
    if saveto:
        joblib.dump(model, saveto)

    # Return scores as well as training time via decorator
    return scores
```

 Note that our `train_model` function constructs the corpus reader itself (rather than being passed a reader object). When considering multiprocessing, all arguments to functions as well as return objects must be serializable using the `pickle` module. If we imagine that the `CorpusReader` is only created in the child processes, there is no need to pickle it and send it back and forth. Complex objects can be difficult to pickle, so while it is possible to pass a `CorpusReader` to the function, it is sometimes more efficient and simpler to pass only simple data such as strings.

The `documents()` and `labels()` are helper functions that read the data from the corpus reader into a list in memory as follows:

```python
def documents(corpus):
    return [
        list(corpus.docs(fileids=fileid))
        for fileid in corpus.fileids()
    ]


def labels(corpus):
    return [
        corpus.categories(fileids=fileid)[0]
        for fileid in corpus.fileids()
    ]
```

We can keep track of the time of execution using a `@timeit` wrapper, a simple debugging decorator that we will use to compare performance times:

```python
import time
from functools import wraps

def timeit(func):
    @wraps(func)
    def wrapper(*args, **kwargs):
        start = time.time()
        result = func(*args, **kwargs)
        return result, time.time() - start
    return wrapper
```

Python's `logging` module is generally used to coordinate complex logging across multiple threads and modules. The `logging` configuration is at the top of the module, outside of any function, so it is executed when the code is imported. In the configuration, we can specify the `%(processName)s` directive, which allows us to determine which process is writing the log message. The logger is set to the module's name so that different modules' log statements can also be disambiguated:

```python
import logging

# Logging configuration
logging.basicConfig(
    level=logging.INFO,
    format="%(processName)-10s %(asctime)s %(message)s",
    datefmt="%Y-%m-%d %H:%M:%S"
)
logger = logging.getLogger(__name__)
logger.setLevel(logging.INFO)
```

 Logging is not multiprocess-safe for writing to a single file (though it is thread-safe). Generally speaking, writing to stdout or stderr should be fine, but more complex solutions exist to manage multiprocess logging in an application context. As a result, it is a good practice to start with logging (instead of print statements) to prepare for production environment.

At long last, we're ready to actually execute our code in parallel, with a run_parallel function. This function takes a path to the corpus as an argument, the argument that is shared by all tasks. The task list is defined, then for each function in the task list, we create an mp.Process object whose name is the name of the task, target is the callable, and args and kwargs are specified as a tuple and a dictionary, respectively. To keep track of the processes we append them to a procs list before starting the process.

At this point, if we did nothing, our main process would exit as the run_parallel function is complete, which could cause our child processes to exit prematurely or to be orphaned (i.e., never terminate). To prevent this, we loop through each of our procs and join them, rejoining each to the main process. This will cause the main function to block (wait) until the processes' join method is called. By looping through each proc, we ensure that we don't continue until all processes have completed, at which point we can log how much total time the process took:

```python
def run_parallel(path):
    tasks = [
        fit_naive_bayes, fit_logistic_regression, fit_multilayer_perceptron,
    ]

    logger.info("beginning parallel tasks")
    start = time.time()

    procs = []
    for task in tasks:
        proc = mp.Process(name=task.__name__, target=task, args=(path,))
        procs.append(proc)
        proc.start()

    for proc in procs:
        proc.join()

    delta = time.time() - start
    logger.info("total parallel fit time: {:0.2f} seconds".format(delta))


if __name__ == '__main__':
    run_parallel("corpus/")
```

Running these three tasks in parallel requires a little extra thought and a bit more work to ensure that everything is set up correctly. So what do we get out of it? In Table 11-1, we show a comparison of task and total time averaged over ten runs.

Table 11-1. Sequential versus parallel fit times (average over 10 runs)

Task	Sequential	Parallel
Fit Naive Bayes	86.93 seconds	94.18 seconds
Fit Logistic Regression	91.84 seconds	100.56 seconds
Fit Multilayer Perceptron	95.16 seconds	103.40 seconds
Fit Total	273.94 seconds	103.47 seconds

We can see that each individual task takes slightly longer when running in parallel; potentially, this extra time represents the minimal amount of overhead required to set up and manage multiprocessing. This slight increase in time is more than made up for in the total run time—roughly the length of the longest fit task and 2.6x times faster than running each task sequentially. When running a significant number of modeling tasks, multiprocessing clearly makes a difference!

While this use of `multiprocessing.Process` demonstrates a number of essential concepts, far more common is the use of a process pool, which we will discuss in the next section.

 It is important to keep in mind how much data is being loaded into memory, especially in a multiprocessing context. On a single machine, each process has to share memory. On a 16 GB machine, loading a 4 GB corpus in four task processes will completely consume the available memory and will slow down the overall execution. It is common to stagger task parallel execution to avoid such issues, starting longer-running tasks first, then starting up faster tasks. This can be done with delays using sleep or process pools as we'll see in the next section.

Process Pools and Queues

In the previous section we looked at how to use the `multiprocessing.Process` object to run individual tasks in parallel. The `Process` object makes it easy to define individual functions to run independently, closing the function when it is complete. More advanced usage might employ subclasses of the `Process` object, each of which must implement a `run()` method that defines their behavior.

In larger architectures this allows easier management of individual processes and their arguments (e.g., naming them independently or managing database connections or other per-process attributes) and is generally used for *task parallel* execution. With task parallelism, each task has independent input and output (or the output of one task may be the input to another task). In contrast, *data parallelism* requires the same task to be *mapped* to multiple inputs. Because the input is independent, each task can be applied in parallel. For *data parallelism*, the `multiprocessing` library provides simpler abstractions in the form of `Pools` and `Queues`, which we'll explore in this section.

 A common combination of both data and task parallelism is to have two data parallel tasks; the first *maps* an operation to many data inputs and the second *reduces* the map operation to a set of aggregations. This style of parallel computing has been made very popular by Hadoop and Spark, which we will discuss in the next section.

Larger workflows can be described as a directed acyclic graph (DAG), where a series of parallel steps is executed with synchronization points in between. A synchronization point ensures that all parts of the processing have completed or caught up before execution continues. Data is also generally exchanged at synchronization points, sent out to parallel tasks from the main task, or retrieved by the main task.

Data parallel execution is still appropriate for the Python multiprocessing library, however, some additional considerations are required. The first is how many processes to use and how. For simple operations, it is inefficient to run a process for each input and then tear the process down (or worse, run one process per input, which would swamp your operating system). Instead, a fixed number of processes is instantiated in a `multiprocessing.Pool`, each of which read input, apply the operation, then send output until the input data is exhausted.

This leads to the second consideration: How do you safely send and receive data from a process, ensuring no duplication or corruption? For this, you need to use a `multiprocessing.Queue`, a data structure that is both thread- and multiprocessing-safe because operations are synchronized with locks to ensure that only one process or thread has access to the queue at a time. A process can safely `put(item)` an item on the queue and another process can safely `get()` an item from the queue in a first-in, first-out (FIFO) fashion.

A common architecture for this type of processing is shown in Figure 11-2. The `Pool` forks n processes, each of which gets to work reading an input queue and sending their data to an output queue. The main process continues by *enqueuing* input data into the input queue. Generally once it's done enqueuing the input data, the main process also enqueues n *semaphores*, flags that tell the processes in the process pool that there is no more data and they can terminate. The main process then can join the pool waiting for all processes to complete, or begin work immediately fetching data from the output queue for final processing.

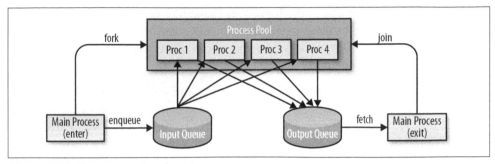

Figure 11-2. Process pool and queues

If this all sounds like a lot of work to set up each data structure and maintain the code for enqueuing and processing, don't worry, the multiprocessing library provides simple methods on the Pool object to perform this work. The methods, apply, map, imap, and starmap each take a function and arguments and send them to the pool for processing, blocking until returning a result. These methods also have an _async counterpart—for example, apply_async does not block but instead returns an Asyn chronousResult object that is filled in when the task is done, or can call callbacks on success or error when completed. We'll see how to use apply_async in the next section.

Parallel Corpus Preprocessing

Adapting a corpus reader to use multiprocessing can be fairly straightforward when you consider that each document can be independently processed for most tasks, particularly for things like frequency analysis, vectorization, and estimation. In these cases, all multiprocessing requires is a function whose argument is a path on disk, and the fileids read from the corpus can be mapped to a process pool.

Probably the most common and time-consuming task applied to a corpus, however, is preprocessing the corpus from raw text into a computable format. Preprocessing, discussed in Chapter 3, takes a document and converts it into a standard data structure: a list of paragraphs that are lists of sentences, which in turn are lists of (token, part of speech) tuples. The final result of preprocessing is usually saving the document as a pickle, which is both usually more compact than the original document as well as easily loaded into Python for further processing.

In Chapter 3, we created a Preprocessor class that wrapped a CorpusReader object so that a method called process was applied to each document path in the corpus. The main entry point to run the preprocessor was a transform method that kicked off transforming documents from the corpus and saving them into a target directory.

Here we will extend that class, which gives us the ability to use `apply_async` with a callback that saves state. In this case we create a `self.results` list to store the results as they come back from the `process()` method, but it is easy to adapt `on_result()` to update a process or do logging.

Next, we modify the `transform` method to count the cores available on the local machine using `mp.cpu_count()`. We then create the process pool, enqueuing the tasks by iterating over all the `fileids` and applying them to the pool (which is where the callback functionality comes into play to modify the state). Finally we close the pool (with `pool.close()`), meaning that no additional tasks can be applied and the child processes will join when done, and we wait for them to complete (with `pool.join()`):

```
class ParallelPreprocessor(Preprocessor):

    def on_result(self, result):
        self.results.append(result)

    def transform(self, tasks=None):
        [...]

        # Reset the results
        self.results = []

        # Create a multiprocessing pool
        tasks = tasks or mp.cpu_count()
        pool  = mp.Pool(processes=tasks)

        # Enqueue tasks on the multiprocessing pool and join
        for fileid in self.fileids():
            pool.apply_async(
                self.process, (fileid,), callback=self.on_result
            )

        # Close the pool and join
        pool.close()
        pool.join()

        return self.results
```

 The results of multiprocessing are significant. Anecdotally, on a subset of the Baleen corpus, which consisted of about 1.5 million documents, serial processing took approximately 30 hours—a rate of about 13 documents per second. Using a combination of task and data parallelism with 16 workers, the preprocessing task was reduced to under 2 hours.

Although this introduction to threads and multiprocessing was brief and high-level hopefully it gives you a sense of the challenges and opportunities provided by parallelism. Many text analysis tasks can be sped up and scaled linearly simply by using the `multiprocessing` module and applying already existing code. By running multiprocessing code on a modern laptop or by using a large compute-optimized cloud instance, it is relatively simple to take advantage of multiprocessing without the overhead of setting up a cluster. Compared to cluster computations, programs written with multiprocessing are also easier to reason about and manage.

Cluster Computing with Spark

Multiprocessing is a simple and effective way to take advantage of today's multicore commercial hardware; however, as processing jobs get larger, there is a physical and economic limit to the number of cores available on a single machine. At some point buying a machine with twice the number of cores becomes more expensive than buying two machines to get the same number of processors. This simple motivation has ushered in a new wave of particularly accessible cluster computing methodologies.

Cluster computing concerns the coordination of many individual machines connected together by a network in a consistent and fault-tolerant manner—for example, if a single machine fails (which becomes more likely when there are many machines), the entire cluster does not fail. Unlike the multiprocessing context, there is no single operating system scheduling access to resources and data. Instead, a framework is required to manage *distributed data storage*, the storage and replication of data across many nodes, and *distributed computation*, the coordination of computation tasks across networked computers.

 While beyond the scope of this book, distributed data storage is a necessary preliminary step before any cluster computation can take place if you want the cluster computation to happen reliably. Generally, cluster filesystems like HDFS or S3 and databases like Cassandra and HBase are used to manage data on disk.

In the rest of the chapter, we will explore the use of Apache Spark as a distributed computation framework for text analysis tasks. Our treatment serves only as a brief introduction and does not go into the depth required of such a large topic. We leave installation of Spark and PySpark to the reader, though detailed information can be found in the Spark documentation.[2] For a more comprehensive introduction, we recommend *Data Analytics with Hadoop* (O'Reilly).[3]

---

2 The Apache Software Foundation, *Apache Spark: Lightning-fast cluster computing*, (2018) *http://bit.ly/2GKR6k1*

3 Benjamin Bengfort and Jenny Kim, *Data Analytics with Hadoop: An Introduction for Data Scientists*, (2016) *https://oreil.ly/2JHfi8V*

Anatomy of a Spark Job

Spark is an execution engine for distributed programs whose primary advantage is support for in-memory computing. Because Spark applications can be written quickly in Java, Scala, Python, and R it has become synonymous with Big Data science. Several libraries built on top of Spark such as Spark SQL and DataFrames, MLlib, and GraphX mean that data scientists used to local computing in notebooks with these tools feel comfortable very quickly in the cluster context. Spark has allowed applications to be developed upon datasets previously inaccessible to machine learning due to their scope or size; a category that many text corpora fall into. In fact, cluster computing frameworks were originally developed to handle text data scraped from the web.

Spark can run in two modes: client mode and cluster mode. In cluster mode, a job is submitted to the cluster, which then computes independently. In client mode, a local client connects to the cluster in an interactive fashion; jobs are sent to the cluster and the client waits until the job is complete and data is returned. This makes it possible to interact with the cluster using PySpark, an interactive interpreter similar to the Python shell, or in a Juypter notebook. For dynamic analysis, client mode is perfect for quickly getting answers to questions on smaller datasets and corpora. For more routine or longer running jobs, cluster mode is ideal.

In this section we will briefly explore how to compose Python programs using Spark's version 2.x API. The code can be run locally in PySpark or with the `spark-submit` command.

With PySpark:

```
$ pyspark
Python 3.6.3 (v3.6.3:2c5fed86e0, Oct  3 2017, 00:32:08)
[GCC 4.2.1 (Apple Inc. build 5666) (dot 3)] on darwin
Type "help", "copyright", "credits" or "license" for more information.
Welcome to
      ____              __
     / __/__  ___ _____/ /__
    _\ \/ _ \/ _ `/ __/  '_/
   /__ / .__/\_,_/_/ /_/\_\   version 2.3.0
      /_/

Using Python version 3.6.3 (v3.6.3:2c5fed86e0, Oct  3 2017 00:32:08)
SparkSession available as 'spark'.
>>> import hello
```

With `spark-submit`:

```
$ spark-submit hello.py
```

In practice we would use a series of flags and arguments in the above `spark-submit` command to let Spark know, for example, the URL for the cluster (with `--master`), the entry point for the application (with --class), the location for the driver to execute in the deployment environment (with --deploy-mode), etc.

A connection to the cluster, called the SparkContext, is required. Generally, the SparkContext is stored in a global variable, sc, and if you launch PySpark in either a notebook or a terminal, the variable will immediately be available to you. If you run Spark locally, the SparkContext is essentially what gives you access to the Spark execution environment, whether that's a cluster or a single machine. To create a stand-alone Python job, creating the SparkContext is the first step, and a general template for Spark jobs is as follows:

```python
from pyspark import SparkConf, SparkContext

APP_NAME = "My Spark Application"


def main(sc):
    # Define RDDs and apply operations and actions to them.


if __name__ == "__main__":
    # Configure Spark
    conf = SparkConf().setAppName(APP_NAME)
    sc   = SparkContext(conf=conf)

    # Execute Main functionality
    main(sc)
```

Now that we have a basic template for running Spark jobs, the next step is to load data from disk in a way that Spark can use, as we will explore in the next section.

Distributing the Corpus

Spark jobs are often described as *directed acyclic graphs* (DAGs), or as acyclic data flows. This refers to a style of programming that envisions data loaded into one or more partitions, and subsequently transformed, merged, or split until some final state is reached. As such, Spark jobs begin with *resilient distributed datasets* (RDDs), collections of data partitioned across multiple machines, which allows safe operations to be applied in a distributed manner.

The simplest way to create RDDs is to organize data similarly to how we organized our corpus on disk—directories with document labels, and each document as its own file on disk. For example, to load the hobbies corpus introduced in "Loading Yellowbrick Datasets" on page 165, we use sc.wholeTextFiles to return an RDD of (file name, content) pairs. The argument to this method is a path that can contain wildcards and point to a directory of files, a single file, or compressed files. In this case, the syntax `"hobbies/*/*.txt"` looks for any file with a *.txt* extension under any directory in the *hobbies* directory:

```
corpus = sc.wholeTextFiles("hobbies/*/*.txt")
print(corpus.take(1))
```

The `take(1)` action prints the first element in the corpus RDD, allowing you to visualize that the `corpus` is a collection of tuples of strings. With the hobbies corpus, the first element shows as follows:

```
[('file:/hobbies/books/56d62a53c1808113ffb87f1f.txt',
"\r\n\r\nFrom \n\n to \n\n, Oscar voters can't get enough of book
adaptations. Nowhere is this trend more obvious than in the Best
Actor and Best Actress categories.\n\n\r\n\r\nYes, movies have
been based on books and true stories since the silent film era,
but this year represents a notable spike...")]
```

Saving data to disk and parsing it can be applied to a variety of formats including other text formats like JSON, CSV, and XML or binary formats like Avro, Parquet, Pickle, Protocol Buffers, etc., which can be more space-efficient. Regardless, once preprocessing has been applied (either with Spark or as described in "Parallel Corpus Preprocessing" on page 251), data can be stored as Python objects using the `RDD.saveAsPickleFile` method (similar to how we stored pickle files for our preprocessed corpus) and then loaded using `sc.pickleFile`.

Efficient Storage with JSON

Storing many small files on a cluster can be complex because of data transfer issues and namespace management, not to mention the space savings that compressing larger files can bring. As a result, it is generally better to store data in fewer, larger files rather than in many, smaller files.

One common storage method for concatenating data into larger files is called JSON lines (also known as JSONL) where each line of the file is a serialized JSON object rather than the entire file. JSON lines can be loaded and parsed into an RDD as follows:

```
import json

corpus = sc.wholeTextFiles("corpus/*.jsonl")
corpus = corpus.flatMap(
    lambda d: [
        json.loads(line)
        for line in d[1].split("\n")
        if line
    ]
)
```

In this case, we map a function that returns an array of JSON objects, parsed from each line in the document. By using `flatMap`, the list of lists is flattened into a single list; therefore the RDD is a collection of Python dictionaries, each parsed from a line in every file in the dataset.

Now that we've loaded our hobbies corpus into RDDs, the next step is to apply transformations and actions to them, which we will discuss more in the next section.

RDD Operations

There are two primary types of operations in a Spark program: *transformations* and *actions*. Transformations are operations that manipulate data, creating a new RDD from an existing one. Transformations do not immediately cause execution to occur on the cluster, instead they are described as a series of steps applied to one or more RDDs. Actions, on the other hand, do cause execution to occur on the cluster, causing a result to be returned to the driver program (in client mode) or data to be written to disk or evaluated in some other fashion (in cluster mode).

Transformations are evaluated lazily, meaning they are applied only when an action requires a computed result, which allows Spark to optimize how RDDs are created and stored in memory. For users, this can cause gotchas; at times exceptions occur and it is not obvious which operation caused them; other times an action causes a very long running procedure to be sent to the cluster. Our rule of thumb is to develop in client mode on a sample of the total dataset, then create applications that are submitted in cluster mode.

The three most common transformations—`map`, `filter`, and `flatMap`—each accept a function as their primary argument. This function is applied to each element in the RDD and each returned value is used to create the new RDD.

For instance, we can use the Python `operator` module to extract the hobbies subcategory for each document. We create a `parse_label` function that can extract the category name from the document's filepath. As in the example we looked at before, the `data` RDD of (`filename`, `content`) key-value pairs is created by loading whole text files from the specified corpus path. We can then create the `labels` RDD by mapping `itemgetter(0)`, an operation that selects only filenames from each element of the `data` RDD, then mapping the `parse_label` function to each:

```
import os
from operator import itemgetter

def parse_label(path):
    # Returns the name of the directory containing the file
```

```
    return os.path.basename(os.path.dirname(path))

data = sc.wholeTextFiles("hobbies/*/*.txt")
labels = data.map(itemgetter(0)).map(parse_label)
```

Note that at this point, nothing is executed across the cluster because we've only defined transformations, not actions. Let's say we want to get the count of the documents in each of the subcategories.

While our `labels` RDD is currently a collection of strings, many Spark operations (e.g., `groupByKey` and `reduceByKey`) work only on key-value pairs. We can create a new RDD called `label_counts`, which is first transformed by mapping each label into a key-value pair, where the key is the label name, and the value is a 1. We can then `reduceByKey` with the `add` operator, which will sum all the 1s by key, giving us the total count of documents per category. We then use the `collect` action to execute the transformations across the cluster, loading the data, creating the `labels` and `label_count` RDD, and returning a list of (`label`, `count`), tuples, which can be printed in the client program:

```
from operator import add

label_count = labels.map(lambda l: (l, 1)).reduceByKey(add)
for label, count in label_count.collect():
    print("{}: {}".format(label, count))
```

The result is as follows:

```
books: 72
cinema: 100
gaming: 128
sports: 118
cooking: 30
```

 Other actions include `reduce` (which aggregates elements of the collection), `count` (which returns the number of elements in the collection), and `take` and `first` (which return the first item or the first *n* items from the collection, respectively). These actions are useful in interactive mode and debugging, but take care when working with big RDDs—it can be easy to try to load a large dataset into the memory of a machine that can't store it! More common with big datasets is to use `takeSample`, which performs a random uniform sample with or without replacement on the collection, or to simply save the resulting dataset back to disk to be operated on later.

As we've discussed in previous sections, Spark applications are defined by data flow operations. We first load data into one or more RDDs, apply transformations to those

RDDs, join and merge them, then apply actions and save the resulting data to disk or aggregate data and bring it back to a driver program. This is a powerful abstraction that allows us to think about data as a collection rather than as a distributed computation, enabling cluster computing without requiring much effort on the analyst's part. More complex usage of Spark involves creating DataFrames and Graphs, a little of which we'll see in the next section.

NLP with Spark

Natural language processing is a special interest of the distributed systems community. This is not only because some of the largest datasets are text (in fact, Hadoop was designed specifically to parse HTML documents for search engines), but also because cutting-edge, language-aware applications require especially large corpora to be effective. As a result, Spark's machine learning library, MLLib,[4] boasts many tools for intelligent feature extraction and vectorization of text similar to the ones discussed in Chapter 4, including utilities for frequency, one-hot, TF–IDF, and word2vec encoding.

Machine learning with Spark starts with a collection of data similar to an RDD, the SparkSQL DataFrame. Spark DataFrames are conceptually equivalent to relational database tables or their Pandas counterparts, coordinating data by row and column as a table. However, they add rich optimizations that take advantage of the SparkSQL execution engine, and are quickly becoming the standard for distributed data science.

If we wanted to use SparkMLLib on our hobbies corpus, we would first transform the corpus RDD using a `SparkSession` (exposed as the global variable `spark` in PySpark) to create a `DataFrame` from the collection of tuples, identifying each column by name:

```
# Load data from disk
corpus = sc.wholeTextFiles("hobbies/*/*.txt")

# Parse the label from the text path
corpus = corpus.map(lambda d: (parse_label(d[0]), d[1]))

# Create the dataframe with two columns
df = spark.createDataFrame(corpus, ["category", "text"])
```

The `SparkSession` is the entry point to SparkSQL and the Spark 2.x API. To use this in a `spark-submit` application, you must first build it, similar to how we constructed the the `SparkContext` in the previous section. Adapt the Spark program template by adding the following lines of code:

---

4 The Apache Software Foundation, *MLlib: Apache Spark's scalable machine learning library*, (2018) *http://bit.ly/ 2GJQP0Y*

```
from pyspark.sql import SparkSession
from pyspark import SparkConf, SparkContext

APP_NAME = "My Spark Text Analysis"


def main(sc, spark):
    # Define DataFrames and apply ML estimators and transformers


if __name__ == "__main__":
    # Configure Spark
    conf = SparkConf().setAppName(APP_NAME)
    sc   = SparkContext(conf=conf)

    # Build SparkSQL Session
    spark = SparkSession(sc)

    # Execute Main functionality
    main(sc, spark)
```

With our corpus structured as a Spark `DataFrame`, we can now get to the business of fitting models and transforming datasets. Luckily, Spark's API is very similar to the Scikit-Learn API, so transitioning from Scikit-Learn or using Scikit-Learn and Spark in conjunction is not difficult.

From Scikit-Learn to MLLib

Spark's MLLib has been rapidly growing and includes estimators for classification, regression, clustering, collaborative filtering, and pattern mining. Many of these implementations are inspired by Scikit-Learn estimators, and for Scikit-Learn users, MLLib's API and available models will be instantly recognizable.

However, it is important to remember that Spark's core purpose is to perform computations on extremely large datasets in a cluster. It does so using optimizations in distributed computation. This means that easily parallelized algorithms are likely to be available in MLLib, while others that are not easily constructed in a parallel fashion, may not. For example, Random Forest involves randomly splitting the dataset and fitting decision trees on subsets of the data that can easily be partitioned across machines. Stochastic gradient descent, on the other hand, is very difficult to parallelize because it updates after each iteration. Spark chooses strategies to optimize cluster computing, not necessarily the underlying model. For Scikit-Learn users, this may manifest in less accurate models (due to Spark's approximations) or fewer hyperparameter options. Other models (e.g., k-nearest neighbor) may simply be unavailable because they cannot be effectively distributed.

Like Scikit-Learn, the Spark ML API centers around the concept of a `Pipeline`. `Pipe lines` allow a sequence of algorithms to be constructed together so as to represent a single model that can learn from data and produce estimations in return.

In Spark, unlike Scikit-Learn, fitting an estimator or pipeline returns a completely new model object instead of simply modifying the internal state of the estimator. The reason for this is that RDDs are immutable.

Spark's `Pipeline` object is composed of *stages*, and each of these stages must be either a `Transformer` or an `Estimator`. Transformers convert one `DataFrame` into another by reading a column from the input `DataFrame`, mapping it to a `transform()` method, and appending a new column to the `Dataframe`. This means that all transformers generally need to specify the input and output column names, which must be unique.

Estimators implement a `fit()` method, which learns from data and then returns a new *model*. Models are themselves transformers, so estimators also define input and output columns on the `DataFrame`. When a *predictive model* calls `transform()`, the estimations or predictions are stored in the output column. This is slightly different from the Scikit-Learn API, which has a `predict()` method, but the `transform()` method is more appropriate in a distributed context since it is being applied to a potentially very large dataset.

Pipeline stages must be unique to ensure compile-time checking and an acyclic graph, which is the graph of transformations and actions in the underlying spark execution. This means that `input Col` and `outputCol` parameters must be unique in each stage and that an instance cannot be used twice as different stages.

Because model storage and reuse is critical to the machine learning workflow, Spark can also export and import models on demand. Many `Transformer` and `Pipeline` objects have a `save()` method to export the model to disk and an associated `load()` method to load the saved model.

Finally, Spark's MLLib contains one additional concept: the `Parameter`. `Parameters` are distributed data structures (objects) with self-contained documentation. Such a data structure is required for machine learning because these variables must be *broadcast* to all executors in the cluster in a safe manner. Broadcast variables are read-only data that is pickled and available as a global in each executor in the cluster.

Some parameters may even be updated during the `fit` process, requiring *accumulation*. Accumulators are distributed data structures that can have associative and commutative operations applied to them in a parallel-safe manner. Therefore, many parameters must be retrieved or set using special `Transformer` methods, the most generic of which are `getParam(param)`, `getOrDefault(param)`, and `setParams()`. It is possible to view a parameter and its associated values with the `explainParam()` method, a useful and routinely used utility in PySpark and Jupyter notebooks.

Now that we have a basic understanding of the Spark MLLib API, we can explore some examples in detail in the next section.

Feature extraction

The first step to natural language processing with Spark is extracting features from text, tokenizing and vectorizing utterances and documents. Spark provides a rich toolset of feature extraction methodologies for text including indexing, stopwords removal, and *n*-gram features. Spark also provides vectorization utilities for frequency, one-hot, TF–IDF, and Word2Vec encoding. All of these utilities expect input as a list of tokens, so the first step is generally to apply tokenization.

In the following snippet, we initialize a Spark `RegexTokenizer` transformer with several parameters. The `inputCol` and `outputCol` parameters specify how transformers will work on the given DataFrame; the regular expression, `"\\w+"`, specifies how to chunk text; and `gaps=False` ensures this pattern will match words instead of matching the space between words. When the corpus DataFrame (here we assume the corpus has already been loaded) is transformed, it will contain a new column, "tokens," whose data type is an array of strings, the data type required for most other feature extraction:

```
from pyspark.ml.feature import RegexTokenizer

# Create the RegexTokenizer
tokens = RegexTokenizer(
    inputCol="text", outputCol="tokens",
    pattern="\\w+", gaps=False, toLowercase=True)

# Transform the corpus
corpus = tokens.transform(corpus)
```

This tokenizer will remove all punctuation and split hyphenated words. A more complex pattern such as `"\\w+|\$[\\d\.]+|\\S+"` will split punctuation but not remove it and even capture money expressions such as `"$8.31"`.

 Occasionally Spark models will have defaults for `inputCol` and `out putCol`, such as `"features"` or `"predictions"`, which can lead to errors or incorrect workflows; generally it is best to specify these parameters specifically on each transformer and model.

Because converting documents to feature vectors involves multiple steps that need to be coordinated together, vectorization is composed as a `Pipeline`. Creating local variables for each transformer and then putting them together into a `Pipeline` is very common but can make Spark scripts verbose and prone to user error. One solution to this is to define a function that can be imported into your script that returns a `Pipeline` of standard vectorization for your corpus.

The `make_vectorizer` function creates a `Pipeline` with a `Tokenizer` and a `HashingTF` vectorizer to map tokens to their term frequencies using the *hashing trick*, which computes the Murmur3 hash of the token and uses that as the numeric feature. This function can also add stopwords removal and TF–IDF transformers to the `Pipeline` on demand. In order to ensure that the DataFrame is being transformed with unique columns, each transformer assigns a unique output column name and uses `stages[-1].getOutputCol()` to determine the input column name from the stage before:

```python
def make_vectorizer(stopwords=True, tfidf=True, n_features=5000):
    # Creates a vectorization pipeline that starts with tokenization
    stages = [
        Tokenizer(inputCol="text", outputCol="tokens"),
    ]

    # Append stopwords to the pipeline if requested
    if stopwords:
        stages.append(
            StopWordsRemover(
                caseSensitive=False, outputCol="filtered_tokens",
                inputCol=stages[-1].getOutputCol(),
            ),
        )

    # Create the Hashing term frequency vectorizer
    stages.append(
        HashingTF(
            numFeatures=n_features,
            inputCol=stages[-1].getOutputCol(),
            outputCol="frequency"
        )
    )

    # Append the IDF vectorizer if requested
    if tfidf:
        stages.append(
            IDF(inputCol=stages[-1].getOutputCol(), outputCol="tfidf")
        )

    # Return the completed pipeline
    return Pipeline(stages=stages)
```

Because of the `HashingTF` and `IDF` models, this vectorizer needs to be fit on input data; `make_vectorizer().fit(corpus)` ensures that `vectors` will be a model that is able to perform transformations on the data:

```
vectors = make_vectorizer().fit(corpus)
corpus = vectors.transform(corpus)
corpus[['label', 'tokens', 'tfidf']].show(5)
```

The first five rows of the result are as follows:

```
+-----+--------------------+--------------------+
|label|              tokens|               tfidf|
+-----+--------------------+--------------------+
|books|[, name, :, ian, ...|(5000,[15,24,40,4...|
|books|[, written, by, k...|(5000,[8,177,282,...|
|books|[, last, night,as...|(5000,[3,9,13,27,...|
|books|[, a, sophisticat...|(5000,[26,119,154...|
|books|[, pools, are, so...|(5000,[384,569,60...|
+-----+--------------------+--------------------+
only showing top 5 rows
```

Once the corpus is transformed it will contain six columns, the two original columns, and the four columns representing each step in the transformation process; we can select three for inspection and debugging using the DataFrame API.

Now that our features have been extracted, we can begin to create models and engage the model selection triple, first with clustering and then with classification.

Text clustering with MLLib

At the time of this writing, Spark implements four clustering techniques that are well suited to topic modeling: *k*-means and bisecting *k*-means, Latent Dirichlet Allocation (LDA), and Gaussian mixture models (GMM). In this section, we will demonstrate a clustering pipeline that first uses `Word2Vec` to transform the bag-of-words into a fixed-length vector, and then `BisectingKMeans` to generate clusters of similar documents.

Bisecting *k*-means is a top-down approach to hierarchical clustering that uses *k*-means to recursively bisect clusters (e.g., *k*-means is applied to each cluster in the hierarchy with k=2). After the cluster is bisected, the split with the highest overall similarity is reserved, while the remaining data continues to be bisected until the desired number of clusters is reached. This method converges quickly and because it employs several iterations of k=2 it is generally faster than *k*-means with a larger *k*, but it will create very different clusters than the base *k*-means algorithm alone.

In the code snippet, we create an initial `Pipeline` that defines our input and output columns as well as the parameters for our transformers, such as the fixed size of the word vectors and the *k* for *k*-means. When we call `fit` on our data, our Pipeline will produce a model, which can then in turn be used to transform the corpus:

```
from tabulate import tabulate
from pyspark.ml import Pipeline
from pyspark.ml.clustering import BisectingKMeans
from pyspark.ml.feature import Word2Vec, Tokenizer

# Create the vector/cluster pipeline
pipeline = Pipeline(stages=[
    Tokenizer(inputCol="text", outputCol="tokens"),
    Word2Vec(vectorSize=7, minCount=0, inputCol="tokens", outputCol="vecs"),
    BisectingKMeans(k=10, featuresCol="vecs", maxIter=10),
])

# Fit the model
model = pipeline.fit(corpus)
corpus = model.transform(corpus)
```

To evaluate the success of our cluster, we must first retrieve the `BisectingKMeans` and `Word2Vec` objects and store them in local variables: `bkm` by accessing the last stage of the *model* (not the Pipeline) and `wvec` the penultimate stage. We use the `computeCost` method to compute the sum of square distances to the assigned center of each document (here, again, we assume corpus documents have already been loaded). The smaller the cost, the tighter and more defined the clusters we have. We can also compute the size in number of documents each cluster is composed of:

```
# Retrieve stages
bkm = model.stages[-1]
wvec = model.stages[-2]

# Evaluate clustering
cost = bkm.computeCost(corpus)
sizes = bkm.summary.clusterSizes
```

To get a text representation of each center, we first must loop through every cluster index (`ci`) and cluster centroid (`c`) by enumerating the cluster centers. For each center we can find the seven closest synonyms, the word vectors that are closest to the center, then construct a table that displays the center index, the size of the cluster, and the associated synonyms. We can then pretty-print the table with the `tabulate` library:

```
# Get the text representation of each cluster
table = [["Cluster", "Size", "Terms"]]
for ci, c in enumerate(bkm.clusterCenters()):
    ct = wvec.findSynonyms(c, 7)
    size = sizes[ci]
    terms = " ".join([row.word for row in ct.take(7)])
    table.append([ci, size, terms])

# Print the results
print(tabulate(table))
print("Sum of square distance to center: {:0.3f}".format(cost))
```

With the following results:

```
Cluster  Size  Terms
-------  ----  -------------------------------------------------------------
      0    81  the"soros caption,"bye markus henkes clarity. presentation,elon
      1     3  novak hiatt  veered monopolists,then,would clarity. cilantro.
      2     2  publics. shipmatrix. shiri flickr groupon,meanwhile,has sleek!
      3     2  barrymore 8,2016 tips? muck glorifies tags between,earning
      4   265  getting sander countervailing officers,ohio,then voter. dykstra
      5   550  back peyton's condescending embryos racist,any voter. nebraska
      6   248  maxx,and davan think'i smile,i 2014,psychologists thriving.
      7   431  ethnography akhtar problem,and studies,taken monica,california.
      8   453  instilled wife! pnas,the ideology,with prowess,pride
      9   503  products,whereas attacking grouper sets,facebook flushing,
Sum of square distance to center: 39.750
```

We can see that some of our clusters appear to be very large and diffuse, so our next steps would be to perform evaluations as discussed in Chapters 6 and 8 to modify k until a suitable model is achieved.

Text classification with MLLib

Spark's classification library currently includes models for logistic regression, decision trees, random forest, gradient boosting, multilayer perceptrons, and SVMs. These models are well suited for text analysis and commonly used for text classification. Classification will work similarly to clustering, but with the added steps of having to index labels for each document, as well as applying an evaluation step that computes the accuracy of the model. Because the evaluation should be made on test data that the model was not trained on, we need to split our corpus into train and test splits.

After the vectorization step, we'll encode the document labels using StringIndexer, which will convert our DataFrame column of strings into a column of indices in [0, len(column)], ordered by frequency (e.g., the most common label will receive index 0). We can then split the DataFrame into random splits, the training data composed of 80% of the dataset and the test data composed of 20%:

```
from pyspark.ml.feature import StringIndexer

# Create the vectorizer
vector = make_vectorizer().fit(corpus)

# Index the labels of the classification
labelIndex = StringIndexer(inputCol="label", outputCol="indexedLabel")
labelIndex = labelIndex.fit(corpus)

# Split the data into training and test sets
training, test = corpus.randomSplit([0.8, 0.2])
```

In the preceding snippet, both the `vector` and `labelIndex` transformers were fit on all of the data before the split to ensure that all indices and terms are encoded. This may or may not be the right strategy for real models depending on your expectations of real data.

We can now create a `Pipeline` to construct a label and document encoding process preliminary to a `LogisticRegression` model:

```
from pyspark.ml.classification import LogisticRegression

model = Pipeline(stages=[
    vector, labelIndex, clf
]).fit(training)

# Make predictions
predictions = model.transform(test)
predictions.select("prediction", "indexedLabel", "tfidf").show(5)
```

If we wanted to evaluate the model, we would next use Spark's classification evaluation utilities. For example:

```
from pyspark.ml.evaluation import MulticlassClassificationEvaluator

evaluator = MulticlassClassificationEvaluator(
    labelCol="indexedLabel",
    predictionCol="prediction",
    metricName="f1"
)

score = evaluator.evaluate(predictions)
print("F1 Score: {:0.3f}".format(score))
```

Spark has other utilities for cross-validation and model selection, though these utilities are aware of the fact that models are trained on large datasets. Generally speaking, splitting large corpora and training models multiple times to get an aggregate score takes a long time on the corpus, so cacheing and active training are important parts of the modeling process to minimize duplicated workload. Understanding the trade-offs when using a distributed approach to machine learning brings us to our next topic—employing local computations across the global dataset.

Local fit, global evaluation

If you have been running the Spark code snippets locally using PySpark or `spark-submit` you may have noticed that Spark doesn't seem blazingly fast as advertised; indeed it was probably slower than the equivalent modeling with Scikit-Learn on your local machine. Spark has a large overhead, creating processes that monitor jobs and perform a lot of communication between processes to synchronize them and ensure fault tolerance; the speed becomes clear when datasets are much larger than those that can be stored on a single computer.

One way to deal with this is to perform the data preprocessing and vectorization in parallel on the cluster, take a sample of the data, fit it locally, and then evaluate it globally across the entire dataset. Although this reduces the advantage of training models on large datasets, it is often the only way to produce narrow or specialized models on a cluster. This technique can be used to produce different models for different parts of the dataset or to rapidly iterate in the testing process.

First, we vectorize our corpus, then take a sample. By ensuring the vectorization occurs on the cluster, we can be assured that the Scikit-Learn model we employ will not be dependent on terms or other states that may be excluded by the sampling process. The sample is conducted without replacement (the first `False` argument) and gathers 10% of the data (the `0.1` argument). Be careful when choosing a size of the data to sample; you could easily bring in too much data into memory even with only 10% of the corpus! The `collect()` action executes the sampling code, then brings the dataset into memory on the local machine as a list. We can then construct X and y from the returned data and fit our model:

```
# Vectorize the corpus on the cluster
vector = make_vectorizer().fit(corpus)
corpus = vector.transform(corpus)

# Get the sample from the dataset
sample = corpus.sample(False, 0.1).collect()
X = [row['tfidf'] for row in sample]
y = [row['label'] for row in sample]

# Train a Scikit-Learn Model
clf = AdaBoostClassifier()
clf.fit(X, y)
```

To evaluate our model we will `broadcast` it to the cluster, and to compute accuracy, we will use one `accumulator` to compute the number of predictions and another to compute the incorrect ones:

```
# Broadcast the Scikit-Learn Model to the cluster
clf = sc.broadcast(clf)

# Create accumulators for correct vs incorrect
correct = sc.accumulator(0)
incorrect = sc.accumulator(1)
```

To use these variables in parallel execution we need a way to reference them into the DataFrame operations. In Spark, we do this by sending a *closure*. One common strategy to do this is to define a function that returns a closure on demand. We can define an accuracy closure that applies the `predict` method of the classifier to the data, then increments the correct or incorrect accumulators by comparing the predicted answer

---

with the actual label. To create this closure we define the `make_accuracy_closure` function as follows:

```python
def make_accuracy_closure(model, correct, incorrect):
    # model should be a broadcast variable
    # correct and incorrect should be accumulators
    def inner(rows):
        X = []
        y = []

        for row in rows:
            X.append(row['tfidf'])
            y.append(row['label'])

        yp = model.value.predict(X)
        for yi, ypi in zip(y, yp):
            if yi == ypi:
                correct.add(1)
            else:
                incorrect.add(1)
    return inner
```

We can then use `foreachPartition` action on the corpus DataFrame to have each executor send their portion of the DataFrame into the accuracy closure, which updates our accumulators. Once complete we can compute the accuracy of the model against the global dataset:

```python
# Create the accuracy closure
accuracy = make_accuracy_closure(clf, incorrect, correct)

# Compute the number incorrect and correct
corpus.foreachPartition(accuracy)

accuracy = float(correct.value) / float(correct.value + incorrect.value)
print("Global accuracy of model was {}".format(accuracy))
```

The strategy of fitting locally and evaluating globally actually allows developers to easily construct and evaluate multiple models in parallel and can improve the speed of the Spark workflow, particularly during the investigation and experiment phases. Multiple models can be more easily cross-validated on medium-sized datasets, and models with partial distributed implementations (or no implementation at all) can be more fully investigated.

This is a generalization of the "last mile computing" strategy that is typical with big data systems. Spark allows you to access huge amounts of data in a timely fashion, but to make use of that data, cluster operations are generally about filtering, aggregating, or summarizing data into context, bringing it into a form that can fit into the memory of a local machine (using cloud computing resources, this can be dozens or even hundreds of gigabytes). This is one of the reasons that the interactive model of Spark execution is so favored by data scientists; it easily allows a combination of local and cluster computing as demonstrated in this section.

Conclusion

One of the best things about conducting text analysis in the information age is how easy it is to create virtuous cycles of applications that use text analysis and then generate more text data from human responses. This means that machine learning corpora quickly grow beyond what is practical to compute on in a single process or even a single machine. As the amount of time to conduct an analysis increases, the productivity of iterative or experimental workflows decreases—some method of scaling must be employed to maintain momentum.

The multiprocessing module is the first step to scaling analytics. In this case, code already employed for analysis simply has to be adapted or included in a multiprocessing context. The multiprocessing library takes advantage of multicore processors and the large amounts of memory available on modern machines to execute code simultaneously. Data is still stored locally, but with a beefy enough machine, huge amounts of work can be shortened to manageable chunks.

When the size of the data grows large enough to no longer fit on a single machine, cluster computing methodologies must be used. Spark provides an execution framework that allows for interactive computing between a local computer running PySpark in a Jupyter notebook and the cluster that runs many executors that operate on a partition of the data. This interactivity combines the best of both worlds of sequential and parallel computing algorithms. While working with Spark does require a change in the code and programming context and may even necessitate the choice of other machine learning libraries, the advantage is that large datasets that would otherwise be unavailable to text analytics techniques can become a rich fabric for novel applications.

The key to working with distributed computation is making sure the trade-offs are well understood. Understanding whether an operation is compute or I/O bound can save many headaches diagnosing why jobs are taking longer than they should or using way too many resources (and help us balance task and data parallelism). Moreover, parallel execution takes additional overhead, which must be worth the cost; understanding this helps us make decisions that enhance experimental development without getting in the way. Finally, recognizing how algorithms are approximated in a distributed context is important to building meaningful models and interpreting the results.

Spark is the first in a wave of modern technologies that are allowing us to handle more and more data to create meaningful models. In the next chapter we will explore distributed techniques for training so-called deep models—neural networks with multiple hidden layers.

## CHAPTER 12

Deep Learning and Beyond

In this book, we have made an effort to emphasize techniques and tools that are sufficiently robust to support *practical* applications. At times this has meant skimming over promising though less mature libraries and those intended primarily for individual research. Instead, we have favored tools that scale easily from ad hoc analyses on a single machine to large clusters managing interactions for many hundreds of thousands of users. In the last chapter, we explored several such tools, from the Python multiprocessing library to the powerhouse Spark, which enable us to run many models in parallel, and do so rapidly enough to engage large-scale production applications. In this chapter we will discuss an equally significant advancement, neural networks, which are quickly becoming the new state of the art in natural language processing.

Ironically, neural networks are in some sense one of the most "old school" technologies covered in this book, with computational roots dating back to work done nearly 70 years ago. For most of this history, neural networks could not have been considered a practical machine learning method. However, this has changed rapidly over the last two decades thanks to three main advances: first, the dramatic increases in compute power made possible with GPUs and distributed computing in the early 2000s; then, the optimizations in learning rates over the last decade, which we'll discuss later in the chapter; and finally, with the open source Python libraries like PyTorch, TensorFlow, and Keras that have been made available in the last few years.

A full discussion of these advances is well beyond the scope of this book, but here we will provide a brief overview of neural networks as they relate to the machine learning model families explored in Chapters 5 through 9. We will work through a case study of a sentiment classification problem particularly well-suited to the neural network model family, and finally, discuss present and future trajectories in this area.

Applied Neural Networks

As application developers, we tend to be cautiously optimistic about the kinds of bleeding-edge technologies that sound good on paper but can lead to headaches when it comes to operationalization. For this reason, we feel compelled to begin this chapter with a justification of why we've chosen to end this book with a chapter on neural networks.

The current trade-offs between traditional models and neural networks concern two factors: model complexity and speed. Because neural networks tend to take longer to train, they can impede rapid iteration through the workflow discussed in Chapter 5. Neural networks are also typically more complex than traditional models, meaning that their hyperparameters are more difficult to tune and modeling errors are more challenging to diagnose.

However, neural networks are not only increasingly practical, they also promise non-trivial performance gains over traditional models. This is because unlike traditional models, which face performance plateaus even as more data become available, neural models continue to improve.

Neural Language Models

In Chapter 7, we introduced the notion that a language model could be learned from a sufficiently large and domain-specific corpus using a probabilistic model. This is known as a *symbolic* model of language. In this chapter we consider a different approach: the neural or *connectionist* language model.

The connectionist model of language argues that the units of language interact with each other in meaningful ways that are not necessarily encoded by sequential context. For instance, the contextual relationship of words may be sequential, but may also be separated by other phrases, as we see in Figure 12-1. In the first example, a successful symbolic model would assign high probabilities to "heard," "listened to," and "purchased." However, in the second example, it would be difficult for our model to predict the next word, which depends on knowledge that "Yankee Hotel Foxtrot," mentioned in the earlier part of the sentence, is an album.

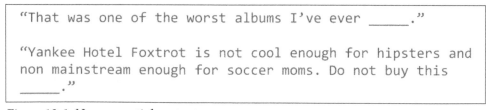

Figure 12-1. Nonsequential context

Since many interactions are not directly interpretable, some intermediary representation must be used to describe the connections, and connectionist models tend to use artificial neural networks (ANNs) or Bayesian networks to learn the underlying relationships.

Traditional *symbolic* models require significant engineering effort to manage *n*-gram smoothing and backoff, and can suffer from the requisite RAM needed to hold so many *n*-grams in memory. Connectionist models, on the other hand, approach the problem by scaling model complexity. In fact, the primary benefit of a neural model approach is to avoid lengthy feature engineering because neural models create infinitely smoothed functions from large arbitrary inputs.

In the next few sections, we will discuss some of the types of neural networks, unpack their components, and demonstrate how a connectionist model might be implemented in an applied context—in this case, to perform sentiment analysis.

Artificial Neural Networks

Neural networks comprise a very broad and variegated family of models, but are more or less all evolved from the perceptron, a linear classification machine developed in the late 1950s by Frank Rosenblatt at Cornell and modeled on the learning behavior of the human brain.

At the core of the neural network model family are several components, as shown in Figure 12-2—an *input layer*, a vectorized first representation of the data, a *hidden layer* consisting of *neurons* and *synapses*, and an *output layer* containing the predicted values. Within the hidden layer, synapses are responsible for transmitting signals between the neurons, which rely on a nonlinear *activation function* to buffer those incoming signals. The synapses apply weights to incoming values, and the activation function determines if the weighted inputs are sufficiently high to activate the neuron and pass the values on to the next layer of the network.

In a *feedforward network*, signals travel from the input to the output layer in a single direction. In more complex architectures like *recurrent* and *recursive* networks, signal buffering can combine or recur between the nodes within a layer.

There are many variations on activation functions, but generally it makes sense to use a nonlinear one, which allows the neural network to model more complex decision spaces. Sigmoidal functions are very common, though they can make gradient descent slow when the slope is almost zero. For this reason, rectified linear units or "ReLUs," which output the sum of the weighted inputs (or zero if that sum is negative), have become increasingly popular.

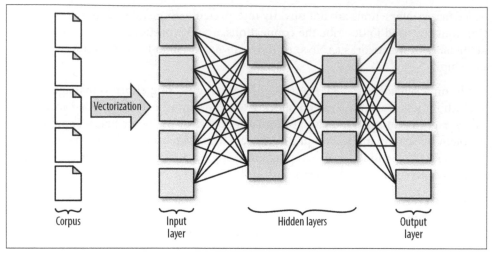

Figure 12-2. Neural model components

Backpropagation is the process by which error, computed at the final layer of the network, is communicated back through the layers to incrementally adjust the synapse weights and improve accuracy in the next training iteration. After each iteration, the model calculates the gradient of the loss function to determine the direction in which to adjust the weights.

Training a multilayer perceptron

Multilayer perceptrons are one of the simplest forms of feedforward artificial neural networks. In this section, we will train a multilayer perceptron using the Scikit-Learn library.

Our input data is a series of 18,000 reviews of albums from the website Pitchfork.com[1]; each review contains the text of the review, in which the music reviewer discusses the relative merits of the album and the band, as well as a floating-point numeric score between 0 and 10. An excerpt[2] can be seen in Figure 12-3.

We would like to predict the relative positivity or negativity of a review given the text. Scikit-Learn's neural net module, `sklearn.neural_network`, enables us to train a multilayer perceptron to perform classification or regression using the now familiar `fit` and `predict` methods. We'll attempt both a regression to predict the actual numeric score of an album and a classification to predict if the album is "terrible," "okay," "good," or "amazing."

---

1 Condé Nast, *Pitchfork: The Most Trusted Voice In Music*, (2018) *http://bit.ly/2GNLO7F*

2 Larry Fitzmaurice, *Review of Coldplay's Ghost Stories*, (2014) *http://bit.ly/2GQL1ms*

> "*Ghost Stories* is unmistakably Coldplay's "breakup album,"
> a subdued work that finds Chris Martin and his band
> crisply moping through mid-tempo soundscapes and fuzzy
> electronic touches that have the visceral impact of a down
> comforter tumbling down a flight of stairs... Rating: 4.4"
>
> - Larry Fitzmaurice
> May 20, 2014

Figure 12-3. Sample Pitchfork review

First, we create a function, `documents`, to retrieve the pickled, part-of-speech tagged documents from our corpus reader object, a `continuous` function to get the original numeric ratings of each album, and a `categorical` function that uses NumPy's `digitize` method to bin the ratings into our four categories:

```python
import numpy as np

def documents(corpus):
    return list(corpus.reviews())

def continuous(corpus):
    return list(corpus.scores())

def make_categorical(corpus):
    """
    terrible : 0.0 < y <= 3.0
    okay     : 3.0 < y <= 5.0
    great    : 5.0 < y <= 7.0
    amazing  : 7.0 < y <= 10.1
    """
    return np.digitize(continuous(corpus), [0.0, 3.0, 5.0, 7.0, 10.1])
```

Next, we add a `train_model` function, which will take as input a path to the pickled corpus, a Scikit-Learn estimator, and keyword arguments for whether the labels are continuous, an optional path for storing the fitted model, and the number of folds to use in cross-validation.

Our function instantiates a corpus reader, calls the `documents` function as well as either `continuous` or `make_categorical` to get the input values X and the target values y. We then calculate the cross-validated scores, fit and store the model using the `joblib` utility from Scikit-Learn, and return the scores:

```
from sklearn.externals import joblib
from sklearn.model_selection import cross_val_score

def train_model(path, model, continuous=True, saveto=None, cv=12):
    """
    Trains model from corpus at specified path; constructing cross-validation
    scores using the cv parameter, then fitting the model on the full data.
    Returns the scores.
    """
    # Load the corpus data and labels for classification
    corpus = PickledReviewsReader(path)
    X = documents(corpus)
    if continuous:
        y = continuous(corpus)
        scoring = 'r2_score'
    else:
        y = make_categorical(corpus)
        scoring = 'f1_score'

    # Compute cross-validation scores
    scores = cross_val_score(model, X, y, cv=cv, scoring=scoring)

    # Write to disk if specified
    if saveto:
        joblib.dump(model, saveto)

    # Fit the model on entire dataset
    model.fit(X, y)

    # Return scores
    return scores
```

 As with other Scikit-Learn estimators, MLPRegressor and MLP Classifier expect NumPy arrays of floating-point values, and while arrays can be dense or sparse, it's best to scale input vectors using one-hot encoding or a standardized frequency encoding.

To create our models for training, we will build two pipelines to streamline the text normalization, vectorization, and modeling steps:

```
if __name__ == '__main__':
    from transformer import TextNormalizer
    from reader import PickledReviewsReader

    from sklearn.pipeline import Pipeline
    from sklearn.neural_network import MLPRegressor, MLPClassifier
    from sklearn.feature_extraction.text import TfidfVectorizer

    # Path to postpreprocessed, part-of-speech tagged review corpus
    cpath = '../review_corpus_proc'
```

```
regressor = Pipeline([
    ('norm', TextNormalizer()),
    ('tfidf', TfidfVectorizer()),
    ('ann', MLPRegressor(hidden_layer_sizes=[500,150], verbose=True))
])
regression_scores = train_model(cpath, regressor, continuous=True)

classifier = Pipeline([
    ('norm', TextNormalizer()),
    ('tfidf', TfidfVectorizer()),
    ('ann', MLPClassifier(hidden_layer_sizes=[500,150], verbose=True))
])
classifer_scores = train_model(cpath, classifier, continuous=False)
```

 Similar to choosing k for k-means clustering, selecting the best number and size of hidden layers in an initial neural network prototype is more art than science. The more layers and more nodes per layer, the more complex our model will be, and more complex models require more training data. A good rule of thumb is to start with a simple model (our initial layer should not contain more nodes than we have instances, and should consist of no more than two layers), and iteratively add complexity while using k-fold cross-validation to detect overfit.

Scikit-Learn provides many features for tuning neural networks and can be customized. For example, by default, both `MLPRegressor` and `MLPClassifier` use the ReLU activation function, which can be specified with the `activation` param, and stochastic gradient descent to minimize the cost function, which can be specified with the `solver` param:

```
Mean score for MLPRegressor: 0.27290534221341
Mean score for MLPClassifier: 0.7115215174722
```

The `MLPRegressor` is fairly weak, showing a very low goodness of fit to the data as described by the R^2 score. Regression benefits from reducing the number of dimensions particularly with respect to the number of instances. We can reason about this through the lens of the curse of dimensionality; the Pitchfork reviews are on average about 1,000 words in length, and each word adds another dimension to our decision space. Since our corpus consists of only about 18,000 reviews total, our `MLPRegressor` simply doesn't have enough instances to predict scores to the degree of float-point numeric precision.

However, we can see that the `MLPClassifier` has much better results, and is probably worth additional tuning. To improve our `MLPClassifier`'s performance, we can experiment with adding and removing complexity. We can add complexity by adding more layers and neurons to `hidden_layer_sizes`. We can also increase the `max_iter` param to increase the number of training epochs and give our model more time to learn from backpropagation.

We can also decrease the complexity of the model by removing layers, decreasing the number of neurons, or adding a regularization term to the loss function using the `alpha` param, which, similar to a `sklearn.linear_model.RidgeRegression`, will artificially shrink the parameters to help prevent overfitting.

Using the Scikit-Learn API to construct neural models is very convenient for simple models. However, as we will see in the next section, libraries like TensorFlow provide much more in the way of flexibility and tuning of the model architecture, as well as speed, leveraging GPUs to scale for higher performance on larger datasets.

Deep Learning Architectures

Frequently grouped together by the term *deep learning*, models such as recurrent neural networks (RNNs), long short-term memory networks (LSTMs), recursive neural tensor networks (RNTNs), convolutional neural networks (CNNs or ConvNets), and generative adversarial networks (GANs) have become increasingly popular in recent years.

While people generally define deep neural networks as neural networks with multiple hidden layers, the term "deep learning" is really not meaningfully distinct from modern ANNs. However, different architectures do implement unique functionalities within the layers that enable them to model very complex data.

Convolutional neural networks (CNNs), for instance, combine multilayer perceptrons with a convolutional layer that iteratively builds a map to extract important features, as well as a pooling stage that reduces the dimensionality of the features but preserves their most informative components. CNNs are highly effective for modeling image data and performing tasks like classification and summarization.

For modeling sequential language data, variations on recurrent neural nets (RNNs) like long short-term memory (LSTM) networks have been shown to be particularly effective. The architecture of an RNN allows the model to maintain the order of words in the sequence and to keep track of long-term dependencies. LSTMs, for example, implement gated cells that allow for functions like "memory" and "forgetting." Variants of this model are very popular for machine translation and natural language generation tasks.

TensorFlow: A framework for deep learning

TensorFlow is a distributed computation engine that exposes a framework for deep learning. Developed by Google for the purpose of parallelizing models across not only GPUs but also networks of many machines, it was made open source in November 2015 and has since become one of the most popular publicly available deep learning libraries.

TensorFlow presumes the user has fairly substantial familiarity with neural network architectures, and is geared toward building data flow graphs with a significant degree of customization. In the TensorFlow workflow, we begin by specifying each layer and all hyperparameters, then compile those steps into a static graph, and then run a session to begin the training. While this makes deep learning models easier to control and optimize as their complexity increases, it also makes rapid prototyping much more challenging.

In essence, deep learning models are just chains of functions, which means that many deep learning libraries tend to have a functional or verbose, declarative style. As such, an ecosystem of other libraries, including Keras, TF-slim, TFLearn, and SkFlow, have quickly evolved to provide a more abstract, object-oriented interface for deep learning. In the next section, we will demonstrate how to use TensorFlow through the Keras API.

Keras: An API for deep learning

While it is often grouped together with deep learning frameworks like TensorFlow, Caffe, Theano, and PyTorch, Keras exposes a general API spec for deep learning. The original Keras interface was written for a Theano backend, but following TensorFlow's open sourcing and dramatic popularity, the Keras API quickly became the default for many TensorFlow users, and was pulled into the TensorFlow core in early 2017.

In Keras, everything is an object, which makes it a particularly convenient tool for prototyping. In order to roughly recreate the multilayer perceptron classifier we used in the previous section, we can create a `build_network` function that instantiates a `Sequential` Keras model, adds two `Dense` (meaning *fully connected*) hidden layers, the first with 500 nodes and the second with 150, and both of which employ rectified linear units for the `activation` parameter. Note that in our first hidden layer, we are required to pass in a tuple, `input_shape` for the shape of the input layer.

In the output layer we must specify a function to condense the dimensions of the previous layer into the same space as the number of classes in our classification problem. In this case we use *softmax*, a popular choice for natural language processing because it represents a categorical distribution that aligns with the tokens of our corpus. The `build_network` function then calls the `compile` method, specifying the desired `loss` and `optimizer` functions for gradient descent, and finally returns the compiled network:

```
from keras.layers import Dense
from keras.models import Sequential

N_FEATURES = 5000
N_CLASSES = 4

def build_network():
    """
    Create a function that returns a compiled neural network
    """
    nn = Sequential()
    nn.add(Dense(500, activation='relu', input_shape=(N_FEATURES,)))
    nn.add(Dense(150, activation='relu'))
    nn.add(Dense(N_CLASSES, activation='softmax'))
    nn.compile(
        loss='categorical_crossentropy',
        optimizer='adam',
        metrics=['accuracy']
    )
    return nn
```

The `keras.wrappers.scikit_learn` module exposes `KerasClassifier` and `Keras Regressor`, two wrappers that implement the Scikit-Learn interface. This means that we can incorporate `Sequential` Keras models as part of a Scikit-Learn `Pipeline` or `Gridsearch`.

To use the `KerasClassifier` in our workflow, we begin our pipeline as in the previous section, with a `TextNormalizer` (as described in "Creating a custom text normalization transformer" on page 72) and a Scikit-Learn `TfidfVectorizer`. We use the vectorizer's `max_features` parameter to pass in the `N_FEATURES` global variable, which will ensure our vectors have the same dimensionality as our compiled neural network's `input_shape`.

For those of us spoiled by Scikit-Learn estimators, which are flush with sensible default hyperparameters, building deep learning models can be a bit frustrating at first. Keras and TensorFlow assume very little about the size and shape of your incoming data, and will not intuit the hyperparameters of the decision space. Nevertheless, learning to construct TensorFlow models via the Keras API enables us not only to build custom models, but also to train them in a fraction of the time of a `sklearn.neural_network` model.

Finally, we add the `KerasClassifier` to the pipeline, passing in the network's build function, desired number of epochs, and an optional batch size. Note that we must pass `build_network` in as a function, not as an instance of the compiled network:

```
if __name__ == '__main__':
    from sklearn.pipeline import Pipeline
    from transformer import TextNormalizer
    from keras.wrappers.scikit_learn import KerasClassifier
    from sklearn.feature_extraction.text import TfidfVectorizer

    pipeline = Pipeline([
        ('norm', TextNormalizer()),
        ('vect', TfidfVectorizer(max_features=N_FEATURES)),
        ('nn', KerasClassifier(build_fn=build_network,
                               epochs=200,
                               batch_size=128))
    ])
```

We can now run and evaluate our pipeline using a slightly modified version of our train_model function. Just as in the previous section, this function will instantiate a corpus reader, call documents and make_categorical get the input and target values X and y, compute cross-validated scores, fit and store the model, and return the scores.

Unfortunately, at the time of this writing, pipeline persistence for a Scikit-Learn wrapped Keras model is somewhat challenging, since the neural network component must be saved using the Keras-specific save method as a hierarchical data format (*.h5*) file. As a workaround, we use Pipeline indexing to store first the trained neural network and then the remainder of the fitted pipeline using joblib:

```
def train_model(path, model, saveto=None, cv=12):
    """
    Trains model from corpus at specified path and fits on full data.
    If a saveto dictionary is specified, writes Keras and Sklearn
    pipeline components to disk separately. Returns the scores.
    """
    corpus = PickledReviewsReader(path)
    X = documents(corpus)
    y = make_categorical(corpus)

    scores = cross_val_score(model, X, y, cv=cv, scoring='accuracy', n_jobs=-1)
    model.fit(X, y)

    if saveto:
        model.steps[-1][1].model.save(saveto['keras_model'])
        model.steps.pop(-1)
        joblib.dump(model, saveto['sklearn_pipe'])

    return scores
```

Now, back in our if-main statement, we provide the path to the corpus and the dictionary of paths where our serialized model will be stored:

```
cpath = '../review_corpus_proc'
mpath = {
    'keras_model'   : 'keras_nn.h5',
    'sklearn_pipe'  : 'pipeline.pkl'
}
scores = train_model(cpath, pipeline, saveto=mpath, cv=12)
```

With 5,000 input features to our neural network, our preliminary Keras classifier performed fairly well; on average, our model is able to predict whether a Pitchfork review considered an album "terrible," "okay," "great," or "amazing":

```
Mean score for KerasClassifier: 0.70533893018807
```

While the mean score of our Scikit-Learn classifier was slightly higher, using Keras, the training took only two hours on a MacBook Pro with all available cores, or roughly one-sixth the training time of the Scikit-Learn `MLPClassifier`. As a result, we can see that tuning the Keras model (e.g., adding more hidden layers and nodes, adjusting the activation or cost functions, randomly "dropping out," or setting a fraction of inputs to zero to avoid overfitting, etc.) will allow for more rapid improvements to our model.

However, one of the main challenges for our model is the small size of the dataset; neural networks generally outperform other machine learning model families, but only beyond some threshold of available training data (for more discussion on this, see Andrew Ng's "Why Is Deep Learning Taking Off?"[3]). In the next section of this chapter, we will explore a much larger dataset, as well as experimenting with using the kinds of syntactic features we saw in Chapters 7 and 10 to improve the signal-to-noise ratio.

Sentiment Analysis

So far we have been treating our reviews as pure bags of words, which is not uncommon for neural networks. Activation functions typically require input to be in the discrete range of [0,1] or [-1,1], which makes one-hot encoding a convenient vectorization method.

However, the bag-of-words model is problematic for more nuanced text analytics tasks because it captures the broad, most important elements of text rather than the microsignals that describe meaningful adjustments or modifications. Language generation, which we explored briefly in Chapters 7 and 10, is an application for which bag-of-words models are frequently insufficient for capturing the intricacies of human speech patterns. Another such case is sentiment analysis, where the relative positivity or negativity of a statement is a function of a complex interplay between

---

3 Andrew Ng, *Why is Deep Learning Taking Off?*, (2017) *http://bit.ly/2JJ93kU*

---

positively and negatively associated modifiers and nonlexical factors like sarcasm, hyperbole, and symbolism.

In Chapter 1 we briefly introduced sentiment analysis to describe the importance of contextual features. Whereas a language feature like gender is often encoded in the structure of language, sentiment is often much too complex to be encoded at the token level. Take, for example, this sample text from a set of Amazon customer reviews of patio, lawn, and garden equipment:

> I used to use a really primitive manual edger that I inherited from my father. Blistered hands and time wasted, I decided there had to be a better way and this is surely it. Edging is one of those necessary evils if you want a great looking house. I don't edge every time I mow. Usually I do it every other time. The first time out after a long winter, edging usually takes a little longer. After that, edging is a snap because you are basically in maintenance mode. I also use this around my landscaping and flower beds with equally great results. The blade on the Edge Hog is easily replaceable and the tell tale sign to replace it is when the edge starts to look a little rough and the machine seems slower.
>
> —Amazon reviewer

If we predict the rating using a count of the "positive" and "negative" review words as with the gendered words in Chapter 1, what score would you expect to see? In spite of many of the negative-seeming words (e.g., "primitive," "blistered," "wasted," "rough," "slower"), this text corresponds to a 5-star review—the highest possible rating!

Even if we were to take a single sentence from the review (e.g., "Edging is one of those necessary evils if you want a great-looking house.") we can see how positive and negative phrases modify each other, with the effect of sometimes inverting or magnifying the sentiment. The parse tree in Figure 12-4 illustrates how these syntactic chunks combine to influence the overall sentiment of the review.

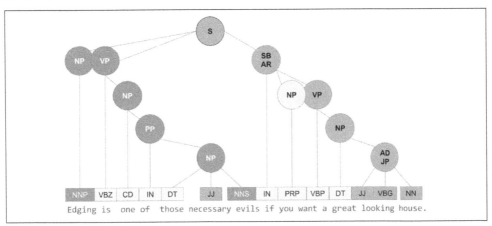

Figure 12-4. Syntax analysis

Deep Structure Analysis

A syntactic chunking approach to sentiment analysis was proposed by Richard Socher (2013).[4] Socher et al. propose that sentiment classification using a phrase tree-bank (i.e., a corpus that has been syntactically annotated) allows for a more nuanced prediction of the overall sentiment of the utterance. They demonstrated how classifying sentiment phrase-by-phrase rather than on the entire utterance level ultimately results in significant improvements in accuracy, particularly because it enables complex modeling of the effects of negation at various levels of the parse tree, as we saw in Figure 12-4.

Socher also introduced a novel approach to neural network modeling, the *recursive neural tensor network*. Unlike standard feedforward and recurrent models, *recursive networks* anticipate hierarchical data and a training process that amounts to the traversal of a tree. These models employ embeddings, like those introduced in Chapter 4, to represent words or "leaves" of the tree, along with a compositionality function that determines how the vectorized leaves should be recursively combined to represent the phrases.

Like the `KerasClassifier` we built earlier in this chapter, recursive neural networks use activation functions in the hidden layers to model nonlinearly, as well as a compression function to reduce the dimensionality of the final layer to match the number of classes (usually two in the case of sentiment analysis), such as *softmax*.

 It's important to note that the efficacy of Socher's model is also due in large part to the massive training set. Socher's team constructed the training data by extracting every syntactically possible phrase from thousands of rottentomatoes.com movie reviews, which were then manually scored by Amazon Mechanical Turk workers via a labeling interface. The results, original Matlab code, and a number of visualizations of sentiment parse trees are available via the Stanford Sentiment Treebank.[5]

In the next section, we'll implement a sentiment classifier that borrows some of the ideas from Socher's work, leveraging the structure of language as a tool for boosting signal.

---

4 Richard Socher, Alex Perelygin, Jean Y. Wu, Jason Chuang, Christopher D. Manning, Andrew Y. Ng, and Christopher Potts, *Recursive Deep Models for Semantic Compositionality Over a Sentiment Treebank*, (2013) *http://bit.ly/2GQL2Xy*

5 Jean Wu, Richard Socher, Rukmani Ravisundaram, and Tayyab Tariq, *Stanford Sentiment Treebank*, (2013) *https://stanford.io/2GQL3uA*

Predicting sentiment with a bag-of-keyphrases

In the previous section, we used Keras to train a simple multilayer perceptron to fairly successfully predict how a Pitchfork music critic would score an album, based on the words contained in their review. In this section, we'll attempt to build a more complex model with a larger corpus and a "bag-of-keyphrases" approach.

For our new corpus, we will use a subset of the Amazon product reviews corpus compiled by Julian McAuley of the University of California at San Diego.[6] The full dataset contains over one million reviews of movies and television, each of which is comprised of the text of the review and its score. The scores are categorical, ranging from the lowest rating of 1 to the highest rating of 5.

The premise of our model is that most of the semantic information in our text will be contained in small syntactic substructures within the sentences. Instead of using a bag-of-words approach, we will implement a lightweight method to leverage the syntactic structure of our review text by adding a new `KeyphraseExtractor` class, which will modify the keyphrase extraction technique from Chapter 7 to transform our review corpus documents in a vector representation of the document keyphrases.

In particular, we will use a regular expression to define a grammar that uses the part-of-speech tags to identify adverbial phrases ("without care") and adjective phrases ("terribly helpful"). We can then chunk our text into keyphrases using the NLTK `RegexpParser`. We will be using a neural network model that requires us to know in advance the total number of features (in other words, the lexicon) and the length of each document, so we'll add these parameters to our `__init__` function.

 Setting hyperparameters for the maximum vocabulary and document length cutoff will depend on the data and require iterative feature engineering. We might begin by computing the total number of unique keywords and setting our `nfeatures` parameter to be less than that number. For document length, we might count the number of keywords in each document in our corpus and take the mean.

---

6 Julian McAuley, *Amazon product data*, (2016) *http://bit.ly/2GQL2H2*

```
class KeyphraseExtractor(BaseEstimator, TransformerMixin):
    """
    Extract adverbial and adjective phrases, and transform
    documents into lists of these keyphrases, with a total
    keyphrase lexicon limited by the nfeatures parameter
    and a document length limited/padded to doclen
    """
    def __init__(self, nfeatures=100000, doclen=60):
        self.grammar = r'KT: {(<RB.> <JJ.*>|<VB.*>|<RB.*>)|(<JJ> <NN.*>)}'
        self.chunker = RegexpParser(self.grammar)
        self.nfeatures = nfeatures
        self.doclen = doclen
```

To further reduce complexity, we'll add a `normalize` method that removes punctuation from each tokenized, tagged sentence and lowercases the words, and a `extract_candidate_phrases` that uses our grammar to extract keyphrases from each sentence:

```
    ...
    def normalize(self, sent):
        is_punct = lambda word: all(unicat(c).startswith('P') for c in word)
        sent = filter(lambda t: not is_punct(t[0]), sent)
        sent = map(lambda t: (t[0].lower(), t[1]), sent)
        return list(sent)

    def extract_candidate_phrases(self, sents):
        """
        For a document, parse sentences using our chunker created by
        our grammar, converting the parse tree into a tagged sequence.
        Extract phrases, rejoin with a space, and yield the document
        represented as a list of its keyphrases.
        """
        for sent in sents:
            sent = self.normalize(sent)
            if not sent: continue
            chunks = tree2conlltags(self.chunker.parse(sent))
            phrases = [
                " ".join(word for word, pos, chunk in group).lower()
                for key, group in groupby(
                    chunks, lambda term: term[-1] != 'O'
                ) if key
            ]
            for phrase in phrases:
                yield phrase
```

To pass the size of the input layer to our neural network, we use a `get_lexicon` method to extract the keyphrases from each review and build a lexicon with the desired number of features. Finally, a `clip` method will ensure each document includes only keyphrases from the lexicon:

```
    ...
    def get_lexicon(self, keydocs):
        """
        Build a lexicon of size nfeatures
        """
        keyphrases = [keyphrase for doc in keydocs for keyphrase in doc]
        fdist = FreqDist(keyphrases)
        counts = fdist.most_common(self.nfeatures)
        lexicon = [phrase for phrase, count in counts]
        return {phrase: idx+1 for idx, phrase in enumerate(lexicon)}

    def clip(self, keydoc, lexicon):
        """
        Remove keyphrases from documents that aren't in the lexicon
        """
        return [lexicon[keyphrase] for keyphrase in keydoc
                if keyphrase in lexicon.keys()]
```

While our `fit` method is a no-op, simply returning `self`, the `transform` method will do the heavy lifting of extracting the keyphrases, building the lexicons, clipping the documents, and then padding each using Keras' `sequence.pad_sequences` function so that they're all of the same desired length:

```
from keras.preprocessing import sequence

    ...
    def fit(self, documents, y=None):
        return self

    def transform(self, documents):
        docs = [list(self.extract_candidate_phrases(doc)) for doc in documents]
        lexicon = self.get_lexicon(docs)
        clipped = [list(self.clip(doc, lexicon)) for doc in docs]
        return sequence.pad_sequences(clipped, maxlen=self.doclen)
```

Now we will write a function to build our neural network; in this case we'll be building a long short-term memory (LSTM) network.

Our LSTM will begin with an `Embedding` layer that will build a vector embedding from our keyphrase documents, specifying three parameters: the total number of features (e.g., the total size of our keyphrase lexicon), the desired dimensionality of the embeddings, and the `input_length` of each keyphrase document. Our 200-node LSTM layer is nested between two `Dropout` layers, which will randomly set a fraction of the input units to 0 during each training cycle to help prevent overfitting. Our final layer specifies the number of expected targets for our sentiment classification:

```
N_FEATURES = 100000
N_CLASSES = 2
DOC_LEN = 60
```

```
def build_lstm():
    lstm = Sequential()
    lstm.add(Embedding(N_FEATURES, 128, input_length=DOC_LEN))
    lstm.add(Dropout(0.4))
    lstm.add(LSTM(units=200, recurrent_dropout=0.2, dropout=0.2))
    lstm.add(Dropout(0.2))
    lstm.add(Dense(N_CLASSES, activation='sigmoid'))
    lstm.compile(
        loss='categorical_crossentropy',
        optimizer='adam',
        metrics=['accuracy']
    )
    return lstm
```

We will be training our sentiment model as a binary classification problem (as Socher did in his implementation), so we will add a `binarize` function to bin our labels into two categories for use in our `train_model` function. The two classes will roughly correspond to "liked it" or "hated it":

```
def binarize(corpus):
    """
    hated it : 0.0 < y <= 3.0
    liked it : 3.0 < y <= 5.1
    """
    return np.digitize(continuous(corpus), [0.0, 3.0, 5.1])

def train_model(path, model, cv=12, **kwargs):
    corpus = PickledAmazonReviewsReader(path)
    X = documents(corpus)
    y = binarize(corpus)
    scores = cross_val_score(model, X, y, cv=cv, scoring='accuracy')
    model.fit(X, y)

    ...

    return scores
```

Finally, we'll specify our `Pipeline` input and components, and call our `train_model` function to get our cross-validated scores:

```
if __name__ == '__main__':
    am_path = '../am_reviews_proc'
    pipeline = Pipeline([
        ('keyphrases', KeyphraseExtractor()),
        ('lstm', KerasClassifier(build_fn=build_nn,
                                 epochs=20,
                                 batch_size=128))
    ])

    scores = train_model(am_path, pipeline, cv=12)
Mean score: 0.8252357452734355
```

The preliminary results of our model are surprisingly effective, suggesting that keyphrase extraction is a useful way to reduce dimensionality for text data without totally discarding the semantic information encoded in syntactic structures.

The Future Is (Almost) Here

It is an exciting time for text analysis, not only because of the many new industrial applications for machine learning on text, but also thanks to the burgeoning technologies available to support these applications. The hardware advances made over the last few decades, and the corresponding open source implementations made available in the last few years, have moved neural networks from the space of academic research to the realm of practical application. Applied text analyses therefore need to be prepared to integrate new hardware as well as academic research into existing code bases to stay current and relevant. Just as language changes, so too must language processing.

Some of the biggest challenges in natural language processing—machine translation, summarization, paraphrasing, question-and-answer, and dialog—are currently being addressed with neural networks. Increasingly, research efforts in deep learning models for language data endeavor to move from language processing to understanding.

While current commercial applications are very recognizable, they are still relatively few. Technologies such as Alexa's speech recognition, Google Translate app's machine translation, and Facebook's image captioning for visually impaired users are increasingly connecting text, sound, and images in innovative ways. Many of the features that emerge in the next few years will involve algorithmic improvements and hybrid models that, for instance, can combine image classification with natural language generation, or speech recognition with machine translation.

However, we will also begin to see more smaller-scale text analytics developed to subtly improve the user experience of everyday applications—text autocompletion, conversational agents, improved product recommendations, etc. Such applications will rely not (or not exclusively) on massive datasets, but on custom, domain-specific corpora geared to specific use cases.

While there are currently few companies with sufficient data, staff, and high-performance compute power to make applied neural networks practical and cost-effective, this too is changing. However, for the majority of data scientists and applications developers, the future of applied text analysis will be less about algorithmic innovation and more about spotting interesting problems in the wild and applying robust and scalable tools and techniques to build small, but high-value features that differentiate our applications from those of previous generations.

Glossary

agglomerative

Agglomerative clustering is a type of hierarchical clustering that produces clusters starting with single instances that are iteratively aggregated by similarity until all belong to a single group.

application programming interface (API)

An application programming interface formally defines how software components communicate. A data API might provide users with a systematic way to read or fetch information from the internet. The Scikit-Learn API exposes generalized access to machine learning algorithms implemented via class inheritance.

bag-of-words (BOW)/continuous bag-of-words (CBOW)

Bag-of-words is a method of encoding text, such that every document from the corpus is transformed into a vector whose length is equal to the vocabulary of the corpus. The primary insight of a bag-of-words representation is that meaning and similarity are encoded in vocabulary.

baleen

Baleen is an open source automated ingestion service for blogs to construct a corpus for natural language processing research.

betweenness centrality

Given a node N in a graph G, the betweenness centrality indicates how connected G is as a result of N. Betweenness centrality is computed as the ratio of the shortest paths in G that include N to the total number of shortest paths in G.

bias

Bias is one of two sources of error in supervised learning problems, computed as the difference between an estimator's predicted value and the true value. High bias indicates that the estimator's predictions deviate from the correct answers by a significant amount.

canonicalization

Canonicalization is one of three primary tasks involved in entity resolution, which entails converting data with more than one possible representation into a standard form.

centrality

In a network graph, centrality is a measure of the relative importance of a node. Important nodes are connected directly or indirectly to the most nodes and thus have higher centrality.

chatbot

A chatbot is a program that participates in turn-taking conversations and whose aim is to interpret input text or speech and to output appropriate, useful responses.

classification

Classification is a type of supervised machine learning that attempts to learn patterns between instances composed of independent variables and their relationship to a given categorical target variable. A classifier can be trained to minimize error between predicted and actual categories in the training data, and once fit, can be deployed to assign categorical labels to new instances based on the patterns detected during training.

classification report/classification heatmap

The classification report shows a representation of the main classification metrics (precision, recall, and F1 score) on a per-class basis.

closeness centrality

Closeness centrality computes the average path distance from a node N in a graph G to all other nodes, normalized by the size of the graph. Closeness centrality describes how fast information originating at N will spread throughout G.

clustering

Unsupervised learning or clustering is a way of discovering hidden structure in unlabeled data. Clustering algorithms aim to discover latent patterns in unlabeled data using features to organize instances into meaningfully dissimilar groups.

confusion matrix

A confusion matrix is one method for evaluating the accuracy of a classifier. After the classifier has been fit, a confusion matrix is a report of how individual test values for each of the predicted classes compare to their actual classes.

connectionist language model

A connectionist model of language argues that units of language interact with each other in meaningful ways that are not necessarily encoded by sequential context, but can be learned with a neural network approach.

corpus/corpora

A corpus is a collection of related documents or utterances that contain natural language.

corpus reader

A corpus reader is a programmatic interface to read, seek, stream, and filter documents, and furthermore to expose data wrangling techniques like encoding and preprocessing for code that requires access to data within a corpus.

cross-validation/*k*-fold cross-validation

Cross-validation, or *k*-fold cross-validation, is the process of independently fitting a supervised learning model on k slices (training and test splits) of a dataset, which allows us to compare models and estimate in advance which will be most performant with unseen data. Cross-validation helps to balance the bias/variance trade-off.

data product

Data products are software applications that derive value from data and in turn generate new data.

deduplication

Deduplication is one of three primary tasks involved in entity resolution that entails eliminating duplicate (exact or virtual) copies of repeated data.

deep learning

Deep learning broadly describes the large family of neural network architectures that contain multiple, interacting hidden layers.

degree

The degree of a node N of a graph G is the number of edges of G that touch N.

degree centrality

Degree centrality measures the neighborhood size (degree) of each node in a graph G and normalizes by the total number of nodes in G.

dialog system

In the context of a chatbot, a dialog system is an internal component that interprets input, maintains internal state, and produces responses.

diameter

The diameter of a graph G is the number of nodes traversed in the shortest path between the two most distant nodes of G.

discourse

Discourse is written or formally spoken communication and is generally more structured than informal written or spoken communication.

distributed representation

A distributed representation is a method of encoding text along a continuous scale. This means that the resulting document vector is not a simple mapping from token position to token score, but instead a feature space embedded to represent word similarity.

divisive

Divisive clustering is a type of hierarchical clustering that produces clusters by gradually dividing data, beginning with a cluster containing all instances and finishing with clusters containing single instances.

doc2vec

Doc2vec (an extension of word2vec) is an unsupervised algorithm that learns fixed-length feature representations from variable length documents.

document

In the context of text analytics, a document is a single instance of discourse. Corpora are comprised of many documents.

dropout

In the context of neural network, a dropout layer is designed to help prevent overfitting by randomly setting a fraction of the input units to 0 during each training cycle.

edge/link

An edge E between nodes N and V in a graph G represents a connection between N and V.

eigenvector centrality

Eigenvector centrality measures the centrality of a node N in a graph G by the degree of the nodes to which N is connected. Even if N has a small number of neighbors, if those neighbors have a very high degree, N may outrank some of its neighbors in eigenvector centrality. Eigenvector centrality is the basis of several variants such as Katz centrality and PageRank.

elbow curve

The elbow method visualizes multiple k-means clustering models with different values for k. Model selection is based on whether or not there is an "elbow" in the curve. If the curve looks like an arm with a clear change in angle from one part of the curve to another, an inflection point is the optimal value for k.

entity

An entity is a unique thing (e.g., person, organization, product) with a set of attributes that describe it (e.g., name, address, shape, title, price, etc.). An entity may have multiple references across data sources, such as a person with two different email addresses, a company with two different phone numbers, or a product listed on two different websites.

entity resolution (ER)

Entity resolution is the task of disambiguating records that correspond to real-world entities across and within datasets.

entropy

Entropy measures the uncertainty or surprisal of a language model's probability distribution.

estimator

In the context of the Scikit-Learn API, an estimator is any object that can learn from data. For instance, an estimator can be a machine learning model form, a vectorizer, or a transformer.

F1 score

The F1 score is a weighted harmonic mean of precision. Recall that the best score is 1.0 and the worst is 0.0. Generally speaking, F1 scores are lower than accuracy measures as they embed precision and recall into their computation. As a rule of thumb, the weighted average of F1 should be used to compare classifier models, not global accuracy.

feature

In machine learning, data is represented as a numeric feature space, where each property of the vector representation is a feature.

feature extraction

In the context of text analytics pipelines, feature extraction is the process of transforming documents into vector representations such that machine learning methods can be applied.

feature union

A feature union allows multiple data transformations to be performed independently and then concatenated into a composite vector.

frequency distribution

A frequency distribution displays the relative frequency of outcomes (e.g., tokens, keyphrases, entities) in a given sample.

generalizable

A generalizable model balances bias and variance to make meaningful predictions on unseen data.

grammar

A grammar is a set of rules that specify the components of well-structured sentences in a language.

graph

A network graph is a data structure made of nodes connected by edges and can be used to model complex relationships, including textual and intertextual relationships.

graph analytics

A graph analytics approach to text analysis leverages the structure of graphs and the computational measures of graph theory to understand relationships between entities or other textual elements.

hapaxes/hapax legomena

A hapax is a term that only appears once in a corpus.

hidden layer

In a neural network, a hidden layer consists of neurons and synapses that connect the input layer to the output layer. Synapses transmit signals between neurons, whose activation functions buffer incoming signals, thereby training the model.

hierarchical clustering

Hierarchical clustering is a type of unsupervised learning that produces clusters with a predetermined ordering in a tree-structure so that a variable number of clusters exist at each level. Hierarchical models can be either agglomerative (bottom up) or divisive (top down).

hyperparameter

In machine learning, hyperparameters are the parameters that define how the model operates; they are not directly learned during fit but are defined on instantiation. Examples include the alpha (penalty) for regularization, the kernel function in a support vector machine, the number of leaves or depth of a decision tree, the number of neighbors used in a nearest neighbor classifier, and the number of clusters in a k-means clustering.

ingestion

In the context of data science, ingestion is the process by which we collect and store data.

instance

In machine learning, instances are the points on which algorithms operate. In the context of text analytics, an instance is an entire document or complete utterance.

language model

A language model attempts to take as input an incomplete phrase and infer the following words that most likely complete the utterance.

latent Dirichlet allocation (LDA)

Latent Dirichlet Allocation is a topic discovery technique, in which topics are represented as the probability that each of a given set of terms will occur. Documents can in turn be represented in terms of a mixture of these topics.

latent semantic analysis (LSA)

Latent Semantic Analysis is a vector-based approach that can be used as a topic modeling technique that finds groups of documents with the same words and produces a sparse term-document matrix.

lexicon

In the context of text analysis, a lexicon is a set of all of the unique vocabulary words from a corpus. Lexical resources often include mappings from this set to other utilities such as word senses, synonym sets, or phonetic representations.

long tail

A long tail, or Zipfian distribution, displays a large number of occurrences far from the central part of the frequency distribution.

machine learning

Machine learning describes a broad set of methods for extracting meaningful patterns from existing data and applying those patterns to make decisions or predictions on future data.

model selection triple

The model selection triple describes a general machine learning workflow that involves repeated iteration through feature engineering, model selection, and hyperparameter tuning to arrive at the most accurate, generalizable model.

morphology

Morphology is the form of things, such as individual words or tokens. Morphological analysis describes the process of understanding how words are constructed and how word forms influence their part-of-speech.

multiprocessing

Multiprocessing refers to the use of more than one central processing unit (CPU) at a time, and to the ability of a system to support or allocate tasks between more than one processor at a time.

n-gram

An n-gram is an ordered sequence of either characters or words of length N.

natural language processing

Natural language processing refers to a suite of computational techniques for mapping between formal and natural languages.

natural language understanding

Natural language understanding is a subtopic within natural language processing that refers to the computational techniques used to approximate the interpretation of natural language.

neighborhood (graphs)

In the context of a network graph G and a given node N, the neighborhood of N is the subgraph F of G that contains all of the nodes adjacent (i.e., connected via an edge) to N.

network

A network is a data structure made of nodes connected by edges and can be used to model complex relationships, including textual and intertextual relationships. *See also "graph."*

neural network

Neural networks refer to a family of models that are defined by an input layer (a vectorized representation of input data), a hidden layer that consists of neurons and synapses, and an output layer with the predicted values. Within the hidden layer, synapses transmit signals between neurons, which rely on an activation function to buffer incoming signals. The synapses apply weights to incoming values, and the activation function determines if the weighted inputs are sufficiently high to activate the neuron and pass the values on to the next layer of the network.

node/vertex

In the context of a graph data structure, a node is the fundamental unit of data. Nodes are connected by edges to form networks.

one-hot encoding

One-hot encoding is a boolean vector encoding method that marks a particular vector index with a value of true if the token exists in the document and false if it does not.

ontology

An ontology is a data structure that encodes meaning by specifying the properties and relationships of concepts and categories in a particular domain of discourse.

order

In the context of a network graph G, the order of G is defined as the number of nodes in G.

overfitting

In the context of supervised learning, overfitting a model means that the model has memorized the training data and is completely accurate on data it has seen before, but varies widely on unseen data.

paragraph vector

A paragraph vector is an unsupervised algorithm that learns fixed-length feature representations from variable-length documents, which enables us to extend word2vec to document-length instances.

parallelism

Parallelism refers to multiprocessing computation and includes task parallelism (where different, independent operations run simultaneously on the same data) and data parallelism (where the same operation is being applied to many different inputs simultaneously).

parsing

In the context of text analytics, parsing is the process of breaking utterances down into composite pieces (e.g., documents into paragraphs, paragraphs into sentences, sentences into tokens), then building them into syntactic or semantic structures that can be computed upon.

part-of-speech

Parts-of-speech are the classes assigned to parsed text that indicate how tokens are functioning in the context of a sentence. Example parts-of-speech include nouns, verbs, adjectives, and adverbs.

partitive clustering

In the context of text analytics, partitive clustering methods partition documents into groups that are represented by a central vector (the centroid) or described by a density of documents per cluster. Centroids represent an aggregated value (e.g., mean or median) of all member documents and are a convenient way to describe documents in that cluster.

perplexity

Perplexity is a measure of how predictable the text is by evaluating the entropy (the level of uncertainty or surprisal) of the language model's probability distribution.

pipeline

In the context of text analytics, a model pipeline is a method for chaining together a series of transformers that combine (for instance) normalization, vectorization, and feature analysis into a single, well-defined mechanism.

precision

Precision is the ability of a classifier *not* to label an instance positive that is actually negative. For each class, it is defined as the ratio of true positives to the sum of true and false positives. Said another way, "For all instances classified as positive, what percent was correct?"

principal component analysis (PCA)

Principal Component Analysis is a method for transforming features into a new coordinate system that captures as much of the variability in the data as possible. PCA is often used as a dimensionality reduction technique for dense data.

property graph

In the context of a network graph, a property graph embeds information into the graph by allowing for labels and weights to be stored as additional information on graph nodes and edges.

recall

Recall is the ability of a classifier to find all positive instances. For each class, it is defined as the ratio of true positives to the sum of true positives and false negatives. Said another way, "For all instances that were actually positive, what percent was classified correctly?"

record linkage

Record linkage is one of three primary tasks involved in entity resolution, which entails identifying records that reference the same entity across different sources.

regression

Regression is a supervised learning technique that attempts to learn patterns between instances composed of independent variables and their relationship to a continuous target variable. A regressor can be trained to minimize error between predicted and actual values in the training data, and once fit, can be deployed to assign predicted target values to new instances based on the patterns detected during training.

rss

RSS is a category of web-based feeds that publish updates to online content in a standardized, computer-readable format.

scraping

Scraping refers to the process (whether automated, semiautomated, or manual) of gathering and copying information from the web to a data store.

segmentation

In the context of text analytics, segmentation refers to the process of breaking paragraphs down into sentences to arrive at more granular units of discourse.

semantics

Semantics refer to the meaning of language (e.g., the meaning of a document or sentence).

sentence boundaries

Sentence boundaries such as capitalized words and certain punctuation marks indicate the beginning and ending of sentences. Most automated parsing and part-of-speech tagging tools rely on the existence of sentence boundaries.

sentiment analysis

Sentiment analysis refers to the process of computationally identifying and categorizing emotional polarity expressed in an utterance—e.g., to determine the relative negativity or positivity of the writer or speaker's feelings.

shortest path

Given a network graph G that contains nodes N and V, the shortest path between N and V is the one that contains the fewest edges.

silhouette score

A silhouette score is a method for quantifying the density and separation of clusters produced by a centroidal clustering model. The score is calculated by averaging the silhouette coefficient (density) for each sample, computed as the difference between the average intracluster distance and the mean nearest-cluster distance for each sample, normalized by the maximum value.

singular value decomposition (SVD)

Singular Value Decomposition is a matrix factorization technique that transforms an original feature space into three matrices, including a diagonal matrix of singular values that describe a subspace. Singular Value Decomposition is a popular dimensionality reduction technique for sparse data and is used in Latent Semantic Analysis (LSA).

size (graphs)

In a graph G, the size of G is defined as the number of edges it contains.

steering

Steering is the process of guiding the machine learning process—e.g., by visually evaluating a series of different classification report heat maps to determine which fitted model is most performant, or inspecting the trade-off between bias and variance along different values of a certain hyperparameter.

stopwords

Stopwords are words that are manually excluded from a text model, often because they occur very frequently in all documents in a corpus.

symbolic language model

Symbolic language models treat text as discrete sequences of tokens with probabilities of occurrence.

synset

The synset for a word W is a collection of cognitive synonyms that express distinct concepts related to W.

syntax

Syntax describes the sentence formation rules defined by grammar.

t-distributed stochastic neighbor embedding (t-SNE)

T-distributed stochastic neighbor embedding is a nonlinear dimensionality reduction method. t-SNE can be used to cluster similar documents by decomposing high-dimensional document vectors into two dimensions using probability distributions from both the original dimensionality and the decomposed dimensionality.

term frequency-inverse document frequency (TF–IDF)

Term frequency–inverse document frequency is an encoding method that normalizes the frequency of tokens in a document with respect to the rest of the corpus. TF–IDF measures the relevance of a token to a document by the scaled frequency of the appearance of the term in the document, normalized by the inverse of the scaled frequency of the term in the entire corpus.

token

Tokens are the atomic unit of data in text analysis. They are strings of encoded bytes that represent semantic information, but do not contain any other information (such as a word sense).

tokenization

Tokenization is the process of breaking down sentences by isolating tokens.

topic modeling

Topic modeling is an unsupervised machine learning technique for abstracting topics from collections of documents. *See also "clustering."*

training and test splits

In supervised machine learning, data is divided into training and test splits on which models can be fit independently in order to compare (cross-validate) models and estimate in advance which will be most performant with unseen data. Dividing data into train and test splits is generally used to ensure that the model does not become overfit and is generalizable with respect to data the model was not trained on.

transformer

A transformer is a special type of estimator that creates a new dataset from an old one based on rules that it has learned from the fitting process.

transitivity

In a network graph, transitivity is a measure of the likelihood that two nodes with a common connection are neighbors.

traversal

In the context of a graph, traversal is the process of traveling between nodes along edges.

underfitting

Underfitting a model generally describes the scenario where a fitted model makes the same predictions every time (i.e., has low variance), but deviates from the correct answer by a significant amount (i.e., has high bias). Underfitting is symptomatic of not having enough data points, or not training a complex enough model.

unsupervised learning

Unsupervised learning or clustering is a way of discovering hidden structures in unlabeled data. Clustering algorithms aim to discover latent patterns in unlabeled data using features to organize instances into meaningfully dissimilar groups.

utterance

Utterances are short, self-contained chains of spoken or written speech. In speech analysis, utterances are usually bound by clear pauses. In text analysis, utterances are typically bound by punctuation meant to convey pauses.

variance

Variance is one of two sources of error in supervised learning problems, computed as the average of the squared distances from each point to the mean. Low variance is an indication of an underfit model, which generally makes the same predictions every time regardless of the features. High variance is an indication of overfit, when the estimator has memorized the training data and may generalize poorly on unseen data.

vectorize/vectorization

Vectorization is the process of transforming non-numeric data (e.g., text, images, etc.) into vector representations on which machine learning methods can be applied.

visualizer

A visualizer is a visual diagnostic tool that extends estimators to allow human steering of the feature analysis, model selection, and hyperparameter tuning processes (i.e., the model selection triple).

word sense

Word sense refers to the intended meaning of a particular word, given a context and assuming that many words have multiple connotations, interpretations, and usages.

word2vec

The word2vec algorithm implements a word embedding model that produces distributed representations of text, such that words are embedded in space along with similar words based on their context.

WORM storage

Write-once read-many (or WORM) storage refers to the practice of persisting a version of the original data that is not modified during the extraction, transformation, or modeling phases.

Index

A

accumulators, 261, 268
acyclic data flows, 255
agglomerative clustering, 108-111, 293
application programming interface (API),
    defined, 293

B

backoff, 145-147
backpropagation, 276
bag-of-keyphrases, 287-291
bag-of-words (BOW), 13
    defined, 55, 293
    text vectorization with, 56
Baleen ingestion engine, 21
    defined, 293
    disk structure, 25-27
ball tree algorithm, 236
BaseEstimator interface (Scikit-Learn API), 68
betweenness centrality, 193-195, 197, 293
bias, defined, 293
bias–variance trade-off, 86
bisecting k-means clustering, 264
blocking
    defined, 202
    fuzzy, 202-205
    with structure, 202

C

canonicalization, 201, 293
centrality, 193-197, 293
chatbots, 4, 207-240
    defined, 209, 293
    dialogs, 210-213

Greeting, 216-220
handling miscommunication, 220-222
maintaining a conversation, 213-215
question detection, 227-229
recipe recommender system, 233-240
rules, 215-222
classification
    defined, 294
classification error, diagnosing, 173-176
    classification report heatmaps, 174-175
    confusion matrix, 175-176
classification heatmap, 174-175, 294
classification report, 92, 174-175, 294
classifier models, 84
closeness centrality, 195, 197, 294
closure, 268
cluster computing, with Spark, 253-270
clustering
    agglomerative, 108-111
    and model selection, 170-172
    by document similarity, 99-111
    defined, 294
    distance metrics, 99-102
    efficient storage with JSON, 256
    for text similarity, 97-111
    hierarchical, 107-111
    partitive, 102-107
    text clustering with MLLib, 264-266
    unsupervised learning on text, 97-99
    visualizing, 170-172
clustering coefficient, 199
co-occurrence plots, 157-159
collocation, 136
concurrency, parallelism vs., 243

conditional frequencies, 141-143
confidence score, 211
confusion matrix
    defined, 294
    for classification error information, 175-176
connectionist language model, 274, 294
constituency parsing, 225
context-aware text analysis, 125-149
    grammar-based feature extraction, 126-132
    n-gram language models, 139-149
context-free grammars, 126
contextual features of language, 13-14
continuous bag-of-words (CBOW), 66, 293
conversation
    fundamentals, 208-215
    maintaining, 213-215
    polite, 215-222
convolutional neural networks (CNNs), 280
corpus (corpora)
    about, 19
    annotated, 20
    defined, 294
    disk structure, 24-27
    domain-specific, 20
    unannotated, 20
corpus monitoring, 33
corpus preprocessing and wrangling, 37-53
    breaking down documents, 38
    deconstructing documents into paragraphs,
        20, 39-42
    intermediate corpus analytics, 45-47
    intermediate preprocessing and storage,
        48-51
    parallel preprocessing, 251-253
    part-of-speech tagging, 44
    pickle method, 49
    reading the processed corpus, 51
    segmentation, 42
    tokenization, 43
    transformation, 47-52
corpus readers, 27-35
    annotated, 29
    defined, 27, 294
    n-gram-aware, 133-135
    reading a corpus from a database, 34
    reading an HTML corpus, 31-34
    reading the processed corpus, 51
    streaming data access with NLTK, 28-31
corpus transformation, 47-52

intermediate preprocessing and storage,
    48-51
    pickle method, 49
    reading the processed corpus, 51
cosine distance, 101
cross-validation
    defined, 294
    streaming access to k splits, 88
    text classification, 86-89
custom corpora, building, 19-36
    about corpora, 19
    Baleen ingestion engine, 21
    corpus readers, 27-35
    data management, 22-27
    domain-specific corpora, 20

D

data management
    Baleen disk structure, 25-27
    corpus disk structure, 24-27
    for building custom corpora, 22-27
data parallelism, 241, 249
data products
    defined, 4, 294
    language-aware, 4-8
    model selection triple workflow, 7
    pipeline for, 5-8
data science, 2-3
data, language as, 8-16
database, reading a corpus from, 34
deduplication, 294
deep learning
    architectural frameworks, 280-284
    defined, 294
    Keras API, 281-284
    TensorFlow framework, 280
deep structure analysis, 286-291
degree, 187, 294
degree centrality, 193-195, 294
dendrogram plot, 107
dependency parsers, 223-224
dialog, 210-213
dialog system, 209, 295
diameter (graph), 187, 295
directed acyclic graphs (DAGs), 250
    pipelines as, 74
    Spark jobs as, 255
discourse, defined, 295
disk structure

Baleen, 25-27
corpus, 24-27
dispersion plots, 159-162
distance metrics, 99-102
distributed computation, 253
distributed data storage, 253
distributed representation
    defined, 295
    text vectorization with, 65-68
    with Gensim, 66
divisive clustering, 107, 295
doc2vec algorithm, 66, 295
documents
    breaking down, 38
    clustering by similarity, 99-111
    deconstructing into paragraphs, 20, 39-42
    defined, 295
    identifying/extracting core content, 38
domain-specific corpora, 20
dropout layer, 289, 295

E

edge, defined, 185, 295
edit distance, 101
eigenvector centrality, 195, 295
elbow curves, 179, 295
entities
    defined, 295
    extraction, 131
entity pairs, finding, 190
entity resolution (ER), 200-205
    blocking with structure, 202
    defined, 201, 295
    fuzzy blocking, 202-205
    on a graph, 201
entropy, 9, 295
estimator, 69, 295
Euclidean distance, 99

F

F1 score, 93-94, 296
feature analysis
    defined, 19
feature extraction, 296
    (see also text vectorization)
    and feature unions, 77-79
    for NLP, 262-264
    grammar-based, 126-132
    n-gram-based, 132-139

feature space visualization, 152-170
    guided feature engineering, 162-170
    visual feature analysis, 152-162
feature unions, 77-79, 296
features
    defined, 55, 296
    identifying most informative, 165-170
    linguistic, 10-13
feedforward network, 275
forking, 243
frequency distribution, 296
frequency vectors, 57-59
    Gensim and, 59
    in Scikit-Learn, 58
    with NLTK, 58
frequency, in n-gram modeling, 140-143
fuzzy blocking, 202-205

G

generalizable model, 86, 296
Gensim
    about, xiii
    distributed representation implementation,
        66
    frequency vector encoding, 59
    LDA in, 114-117
    LSA with, 120
    one-hot encoding with, 61
    TF–IDF text vectorization with, 64
GensimVectorizer transformer, 70
grammar, defined, 296
grammar-based feature extraction, 126-132
    context-free grammars, 126
    entity extraction, 131
    keyphrase extraction, 128
    n-gram feature extraction, 132-139
    syntactic parsers, 127
graph analysis of text, 183-205
    analyzing graph structure, 186
    creating a graph-based thesaurus, 185
    creating a social graph, 189-192
    defined, 296
    entity resolution, 200-205
    extracting graphs from text, 189-200
    graph computation/analysis, 185
    insights from social graph, 192-200
    visual analysis of graphs, 187
    workflow, 189
graph, defined, 296

Graph-tool, 184
GraphExtractor class, 191
GridSearch, 76
guided feature engineering, 162-170
    most informative features, 165-170
    part-of-speech tagging, 162-165

H

hairball effect, 197
hapax/hapax legomena, 73, 296
heatmaps, 174-175
hidden layer, 275, 279, 296
hierarchical clustering, 107-111
    and agglomerative clustering, 108-111
    defined, 296
HTML corpora
    and Baleen disk structure, 25-27
    corpus monitoring, 33
    reading, 31-34
hyperparameters
    defined, 296
    optimization with GridSearch, 76
    visual steering, 177-179

I

ingestion
    Baleen ingestion engine, 21
    defined, 296
    RSS and, 21
instances, defined, 55, 297

J

Jaccard distance, 101
joining, 243
JSON, storage with, 256

K

k splits, streaming access to, 88
k-fold cross-validation, 88, 294
k-means clustering, 103-107
    about, 103-105
    handling uneven geometries, 106
    optimizing, 105
Keras API, 281-284
keyphrases, extracting, 128
kitchen measurement conversion system,
    229-233
Kneser–Ney smoothing, 147-147

L

language
    computational models, 8
    connectionist models, 274, 294
    contextual features, 13-14
    features, 10-13
    neural models, 274-284
language model, defined, 297
language-aware data products, 4-8
    model selection triple workflow, 7
    pipeline for, 5-8
latent Dirichlet allocation (LDA), 111-118
    defined, 297
    Gensim implementation, 114-117
    in Scikit-Learn, 112-114
    LSA vs., 119
    visualizing topics, 117
latent semantic analysis (LSA), 119-121
    defined, 297
    with Gensim, 120
    with Scikit-Learn, 119
lemmatization, 72
lexical units, 20
lexicon, 297
linguistic features, 10-13
link, 295
logging, 247
long short-term memory (LSTM) networks,
    280, 289
long tail distribution
    defined, 297
    frequency-based encoding and, 59

M

machine learning
    defined, 297
    goal of, xii
Mahalanobis distance, 100
Manhattan distance, 99
MapReduce, 250
Minkowski distance, 100
MLLib
    NLP and, 260-262
    text classification with, 266-267
    text clustering with, 264-266
model diagnostics
    class visualization, 172
    cluster visualization, 170-173
    diagnosing classification error, 173-176

text visualization, 170-176
model operationalization, 94
model selection triple workflow, 7, 297
morphology, 16, 297
multilayer perceptron, 276-280
multiprocessing
    defined, 297
    parallel corpus preprocessing, 251-253
    process pools and queues, 249-251
    Python, 242-253
    running tasks in parallel, 244-249

N

n gram, defined, 297
n-gram analysis, 14
n-gram feature extraction, 132-139
    choosing the right n-gram window, 135
    n-gram-aware corpus reader, 133-135
    significant collocations, 136
n-gram language models, 139-149
    backoff and smoothing, 145-149
    frequency/conditional frequency, 140-143
    language generation, 147
    maximum likelihood estimation, 143-145
n-gram viewer, 153
Naive Bayes, 84
natural language
    and computation, 1-17
    computational challenges of, x-xii
    data science paradigm, 2-3
    language as data, 8-16
    language-aware data products, 4-8
    tokens vs. words, x
natural language processing (NLP)
    defined, 297
    feature extraction for, 262-264
    Spark MLLib and, 260-262
    Spark operations, 259-270
    speeding up, 267-270
    text classification with MLLib, 266-267
    text clustering with MLLib, 264-266
natural language tool kit (NLTK)
    about, xiii
    frequency vectors with, 58
    one-hot encoding with, 60
    streaming data access with, 28-31
    TF-IDF text vectorization with, 63
natural language understanding, 297
neighborhood (graphs), 187, 297

network visualization, 154-157
network, defined, 297
NetworkX, xiii, 184
neural language models, 274-284
neural networks, 273-291
    components, 275-280
    deep learning architectures, 280-284
    defined, 298
    neural language models, 274-284
    sentiment analysis, 284-291
    training a multilayer perceptron, 276-280
nodes, 185, 298
non-negative matrix factorization (NNMF), 121

O

one-hot encoding
    defined, 298
    text vectorization with, 59-62
    with Gensim, 61
    with NLTK, 60
    with Scikit-Learn, 60
ontology, 15, 298
operationalization of text classification model, 94
order, 187, 298
overfitting, 86, 298

P

paragraph vector
    defined, 298
    doc2vec and, 66
paragraphs, deconstructing documents into, 20, 39-42
parallelism, 298
    (see also scaling text analytics)
    corpus preprocessing, 251-253
    primary forms of, 241
parameters, defined, 261
parsing, defined, 298
part-of-speech tagging, 44, 162-165, 298
partitive clustering, 102-107
    defined, 298
    k-means clustering, 103-107
perceptron, multilayer, 276-280
perplexity, 9, 145, 298
pickle
    corpus transformation with, 49
    model operationalization with, 94

pipelines, 74-79
    and feature unions, 77-79
    basics, 75
    defined, 298
    GridSearch extension, 76
precision, defined, 93, 299
principal component analysis (PCA), 74, 299
process pools, 249-251
property graph model, 191, 299

Q

questions, chatbots and, 222-233
    constituency parsing, 225
    dependency parsing, 223-224
    question detection, 227-229
queues, 249-251

R

recall, 93, 299
recipe recommender chatbot system, 233-240
    adding speed to, 235-237
    domain-specific corpus for, 234
    implementing recipe recommendations,
        238-240
record linkage, 299
recurrent neural nets (RNNs), 280
recursive neural tensor network, 286
regression, 299
relational database management systems, 23
resilient distributed datasets (RDDs), 255-257
RSS
    defined, 299
    text ingestion via, 21

S

scale-free networks, 198
scaling text analytics, 241-271
    cluster computing with Spark, 253-270
    Python multiprocessing, 242-253
Scikit-Learn
    about, xiii
    frequency vectors in, 58
    LDA with, 112-114
    LSA with, 119
    NNMF with, 122
    one-hot encoding with, 60
    Pipeline object, 74-79
    TF–IDF text vectorization with, 64

Scikit-Learn API, 68-74, 70-74
    BaseEstimator interface, 68
    creating a custom Gensim vectorization
        transformer, 70
    creating a custom text normalization trans-
        former, 72-74
    extending TransformerMixin, 70-74
scraping, defined, 299
segmentation, 42, 299
semantic analysis, 15
semantics, 15, 299
semi-structured data, 8
sentence boundaries, defined, 299
sentences, 20, 42
sentiment analysis, 13
    bag-of-keyphrases approach to, 287-291
    deep structure analysis, 286-291
    defined, 83, 299
    neural networks and, 284-291
separability, 86
Shannon–Weaver model, 208
shortest path, defined, 299
significant collocations, 136
silhouette coefficient, 178, 299
silhouette score, 299
singular value decomposition (SVD)
    defined, 300
    LSA and, 119
size (graphs), 187, 300
small world phenomenon, 200
smoothing, 145-147
social graphs
    centrality, 193-197
    creating, 189-192
    finding entity pairs, 190
    implementing graph extraction, 191
    insights from, 192-200
    property graph model, 191
    structural analysis, 197-200
spaCy, xiii
Spark
    about, 254
    client mode vs. cluster mode, 254
    cluster computing with, 253-270
    distributing corpus, 255-259
    feature extraction for NLP, 262-264
    MLLib, 260-262
    NLP with, 259-270
    RDD operations, 257-259

speeding up NLP with, 267-270
text classification with MLLib, 266-267
text clustering with MLLib, 264-266
spawning, 243
speech data, 5
(see also chatbots)
Sqlite database, reading a corpus from, 34
steering, 177-179, 300
(see also visual steering)
stemming, 72
stopwords
defined, 300
TF-IDF and, 65
structural analysis, 197-200
structured data, 8
supervised learning, classification as, 82
support, in classification model evaluation, 93
symbolic language model, 300
synsets, 185, 300
syntactic analysis, 15
syntactic parsers, 127
syntax, 15, 300

T

t-distributed stochastic neighbor embedding (t-SNE)
cluster visualization with, 170-172
defined, 300
tagging, part-of-speech, 44, 162-165
task parallelism, 241
TensorFlow, 280
term frequency-inverse document frequency (TF-IDF)
computing, 63
defined, 300
Gensim text vectorization, 64
NLTK text vectorization, 63
Scikit-Learn text vectorization, 64
text vectorization, 62-65
text analysis
tools for, xii
text classification, 81-96
about, 82-85
building a text classification application, 85-95
building an application for, 85-95
classifier models, 84
cross-validation, 86-89
identifying classification problems, 82-84

model construction, 89-91
model evaluation, 91-94
model operationalization, 94
visualizing classes, 172
with MLLib, 266-267
text meaning representations (TMRs), 183
text normalization transformer, 72-74
text vectorization, 55-68
distributed representation, 65-68
frequency vectors, 57-59
one-hot encoding, 59-62
TF-IDF, 62-65
with BOW, 56
text visualization, 151-180
feature space visualization, 152-170
model diagnostics, 170-176
visual steering, 177-179
TF-IDF distance, 101
thematic meaning representations (TMRs), 15
thesaurus, graph-based, 185
thread, 242
tokenization, 43, 300
tokens
defined, 300
language models and, 9
part-of-speech tagging, 44
words vs., x
topic modeling, 111-123
defined, 300
latent semantic analysis (LSA), 119-121
non-negative matrix factorization (NNMF), 121
with latent Dirichlet allocation (LDA), 111-118
training and test splits, 300
transformations
creating a custom Gensim vectorization transformer, 70
creating a custom text normalization transformer, 72-74
defined, 257
pipelines and, 74-79
Scikit-Learn API, 68-74
transformer, defined, 70, 300
transitivity, 199, 301
traversal, defined, 301
tweets, 24

U

underfitting, 86, 301
unstructured data, language as, 8
unsupervised learning
  defined, 301
  for exploratory text analysis, 97-99
utterance
  defined, 301
  semantics and, 15

V

variance
  bias-variance trade-off, 86
  defined, 301
vectorization, 301
  (see also text vectorization)
visual feature analysis, 152-162
  co-occurrence plots, 157-159
  n-gram viewer, 153
  network visualization, 154-157
  text x-rays and dispersion plots, 159-162
visual steering, 177-179
  elbow curves, 179
  silhouette scores, 178
visualization
  defined, 151

network, 154-157
of class, 172
of cluster, 170-172
of feature space, 152-170
visualizer, defined, 301

W

word sense, 13, 301
word2vec algorithm, 66, 301
words, tokens vs., x
write-once, read-may (WORM) storage, 23, 301

Y

Yellowbrick, 165-169
  about, xiii
  FreqDistVisualizer, 166
  loading datasets, 165
  PosTagVisualizer, 163
  TSNEVisualizer, 171

Z

Zipfian (long tail) distribution
  defined, 297
  frequency-based encoding and, 59

About the Authors

Benjamin Bengfort is a data scientist who lives inside the Beltway but ignores politics (the normal business of DC) favoring technology instead. He is currently working to finish his PhD at the University of Maryland where he studies machine learning and distributed computing. His lab does have robots (though this field of study is not one he favors) and, much to his chagrin, they seem to constantly arm said robots with knives and tools; presumably to pursue culinary accolades. Having seen a robot attempt to slice a tomato, Benjamin prefers his own adventures in the kitchen where he specializes in fusion French and Guyanese cuisine as well as BBQ of all types. A professional programmer by trade, a Data Scientist by vocation, Benjamin's writing pursues a diverse range of subjects from Natural Language Processing, to Data Science with Python to analytics with Hadoop and Spark.

Dr. Rebecca Bilbro is a data scientist, Python programmer, teacher, speaker, and author in Washington, DC. She specializes in visual diagnostics for machine learning, from feature analysis to model selection and hyperparameter tuning, and has conducted research on natural language processing, semantic network extraction, entity resolution, and high dimensional information. An active contributor to the open source software community, Rebecca enjoys collaborating with other developers on inclusive, high-impact projects like Yellowbrick—a pure Python package that aims to take predictive modeling out of the black box. In her spare time, she can often be found either out-of-doors riding bicycles with her family or inside practicing the ukulele. Rebecca earned her doctorate from the University of Illinois, Urbana-Champaign, where her research centered on communication and visualization practices in engineering.

Tony Ojeda is a data scientist, author, and entrepreneur with expertise in business process optimization and over a decade of experience creating and implementing innovative data products and solutions. He is the founder of District Data Labs, a data science consulting and corporate training firm, research lab, and open source collaborative where people from diverse backgrounds come together to work on interesting projects, push themselves beyond their current capabilities, and help each other become more successful data scientists. He also cofounded Data Community DC, a professional organization that supports and promotes data scientists and the work they do. In his spare time, he enjoys swimming, running, practicing martial arts, as well as discovering delicious restaurants to patronize and fascinating TV shows to watch. Tony has a Masters in Finance from Florida International University and an MBA with concentrations in Strategy and Entrepreneurship from DePaul University in Chicago.

Colophon

The animal on the cover of *Applied Text Analysis with Python* is the kit fox (*Vulpes macrotis*), a small mammal native to the American Southwest and northern Mexico. It is the smallest species of fox in North America, with a weight ranging from 3.5 to 6 pounds and height ranging from 17.9 to 21.1 inches. Notably, kit foxes have disproportionately large ears, which give them excellent hearing and allow them to regulate their body temperature. They have a gray fur coat, often with red and orange coloring.

Kit foxes live in dry, desert regions and are nocturnal, hunting their prey at night. They eat smaller mammals like mice, rabbits, and voles, along with insects, lizards, and birds. Kit foxes are socially monogamous, mating annually between December and February. Litters are born in March and April and usually contain 1 to 7 pups. Both parents assist in rearing the young, who become independent and leave the communal den after 5 to 6 months.

Although kit foxes are not currently listed as endangered, there are no reliable estimates of their population. There are indications that their population is declining in areas where agriculture has spread into previously uninhabited regions. They also face intense competition for prey with other predators, such as coyotes, bobcats, and golden eagles.

Many of the animals on O'Reilly covers are endangered; all of them are important to the world. To learn more about how you can help, go to *animals.oreilly.com*.

The cover image is from *Lydekker's Royal Natural History*. The cover fonts are URW Typewriter and Guardian Sans. The text font is Adobe Minion Pro; the heading font is Adobe Myriad Condensed; and the code font is Dalton Maag's Ubuntu Mono.

Learn from experts.
Find the answers you need.

Sign up for a **10-day free trial** to get **unlimited access** to all of the content on Safari, including Learning Paths, interactive tutorials, and curated playlists that draw from thousands of ebooks and training videos on a wide range of topics, including data, design, DevOps, management, business—and much more.

Start your free trial at:

oreilly.com/safari

(No credit card required.)

9 781491 963043